A Feast of Fishes

A Feast of Fishes

by
Elizabeth H. Bray
Anne T. Buttrick
Mary H. Thomsen

and
THE NEW ENGLAND AQUARIUM COUNCIL

Illustrations by Judith Dufour Love

THE GLOBE PEQUOT PRESS
CHESTER, CONNECTICUT

Published Summer 1988 by The Globe Pequot Press
© 1988 by The New England Aquarium Council

Library of Congress Cataloging-in-Publication Data

A Feast of fishes.

  Includes index.
  1. Cookery (Fish) 2. Cookery (Shellfish)
I. New England Aquarium Council.
TX747.F39 1988   641.6′92   88-757
ISBN 0-87106-662-9

Book design by K. A. Lynch
Typography by TRG, North Branford, Connecticut.

Manufactured in the United States of America
First Edition / First Printing

John H. Prescott
Executive Director, New England Aquarium

Michael Filisky
Acting Curator of Education

Leslie Kaufman
Curator of Exhibit Research and Development

Lois Mann
Supervisor of Council Programs

The New England Aquarium is a private, non-profit aquatic museum dedicated to making known the world of water through education, research, conservation, and exhibition. Attendance at the museum surpassed 1.1 million last year; and for five of the past seven years, it has had the highest attendance of all museums in New England. It is the first of the "modern" aquariums in the country and has recently become a major center for the rescue and rehabilitation of stranded aquatic animals. Staff members of the Aquarium understand and appreciate the value of fish as a natural food resource, and many of them have contributed to this book.

Contents

Preface

The New England Aquarium was founded to foster an appreciation of the diversity, importance, and beauty of aquatic life through education, research, conservation, and exhibition. For many children and adults, our giant ocean tank, tidepool, and other galleries have been an inspiration for a lifetime of appreciation for the world of water.

We believe that A *Feast of Fishes* is another link to that world. Just as the exhibits and programs reflect our concern with conservation and education, so, too, does this book. Because seafood is one of our most nutritional food sources, the Aquar-

ium hopes to encourage cooks to enjoy as wide a variety of fishes as possible, including many that are underutilized and/or raised through aquaculture. By making wise choices, we can help reduce the harvest of those species whose numbers are dwindling.

For every fish, there is a taste and texture, a new world to be enjoyed and shared with friends and family. We hope our cookbook will challenge your curiosity and expand your tastes and knowledge. And we hope you will enjoy many feasts of fishes in the future.

John H. Prescott
Executive Director
New England Aquarium

Introduction

A *Feast of Fishes* presents a veritable banquet of seafood taken from the richly abundant, incredibly varied life in the water. The recipes, too, run the gamut of shellfish and fishes*, some familiar to cooks and some not so familiar. Our cookbook is meant to be your companion in enjoyment of this variety—from mako shark to the traditional halibut. The book contains 61 different species, which makes it easy to try fish you may have never prepared. Here is your chance to discover new delicacies along with the time-tested favorites.

You will find the fishes grouped with their families and listed in order of their places in evolution. Fishes in a family have many similarities and are often good substitutes for one another in recipes. Try something new; it is an eating adventure and also a way to help preserve species. We can learn from the tapir, a land animal known for teaching its young to eat only foods that are plentiful. From generation to generation, tapirs consume different but abundant foods.

This book also includes information about, and recipes for, farm-raised fishes. Be an alert consumer. If a species is threatened or endangered, ask your fishmonger not to carry it unless it is a "cultured" fish. If you're not sure what species are threatened, check with your local department of fisheries.

In writing this book, we are sharing with you our fascination for the world of water. Fishes are not only beautiful and instructive creatures, they are also extraordinarily nutritious, naturally low in calories, and, because there is little waste, a good value. Seafood is easy to prepare and lends itself to so many wonderful dishes; we hope you will enjoy it often. Let this book be a springboard to learn about fishes as they become a more important part of our cuisine. Taste with enjoyment the difference among species as you would among wines.

---

*"Fish" or "fishes"? "Fish" refers to a particular kind or species, whether one or many. The bass in the pond is (or are) fish, whether one or sixty. If there are both trout and bass in the pond, they are "fishes."

Chapter 1

Buying, Storing, and Cooking Fish

How to Buy,

Description	What to Look For	What to Avoid
Fin Fish		
Whole Fish a whole gutted fish **Whole Dressed or Pan-Dressed Fish** a whole gutted fish, scaled, with or without head and/or tail	• clear and slightly protruding eyes • red to bright pink gills • shiny, bright skin • firm flesh, elastic to touch • clean body cavity • fresh marine aroma	• dull or sunken eyes • brown or graying • dry or off color skin • soft flesh • bloody body cavity • strong unpleasant fishy smell or ammonia odor
Fish Steak a cross-section slice of a pan-dressed fish **Fish Fillet** a boneless side of flesh cut from the pan-dressed fish, with or without skin **Fish Chunk** a small portion, usually boneless, cut from a thick steak	• flesh should be firm to the touch • flesh should have a moist appearance • flesh should have a natural sheen • fresh marine aroma	• soft flesh • gaping between segments of flesh • dry or off-color flesh • strong unpleasant fishy smell or ammonia odor
Shellfish: Mollusks		
Squid, Fresh or Frozen	• whole fresh or fresh-frozen squid should be cream colored with gray to brown spots • clear eyes • cleaned squid meat should be white and firm	• off color • strong odor • dull eyes • soft flesh
Octopus, Fresh or Frozen	• firm flesh • pleasant marine aroma	
Shucked Scallops shucked, uncooked. In U.S. only the scallop muscle is eaten. In other countries the whole scallop is consumed.	• firm texture • white to creamy orange color • sweet marine aroma	• soft texture • dark color • strong or sour fishy odor
Live Clams, Mussels, & Oysters live mollusk in shell	• tightly closed shells or shells that close when tapped * exception: soft-shelled or steamer clams cannot shut their shells completely	• open shells that do not respond to tapping • limp necks in steamer clams • cracked shells

Store, and Freeze Seafood

How to Store	How to Freeze
• rinse fish and pat dry before using • to store, wrap in waxed freezer-type paper and store in coldest part of refrigerator • cook within 24–48 hours	• small fish may be frozen whole or pan-dressed • high-fat fish should be rubbed with lemon juice or an ascorbic acid solution • low-fat fish should be rinsed in a saltwater solution • wrap fish in freezer paper or plastic and freeze at once
• rinse and pat dry • wrap in waxed paper or plastic and store in coldest part of refrigerator • cook within 24 hours	• do not refreeze seafood that has been thawed • wrap rinsed fresh squid or octopus in plastic for freezing
• refrigerate in store container until ready to cook • cook within 24 hours	• place in plastic freezer container and seal tightly • do not refreeze if scallops were previously frozen
• store in unsealed container in coldest part of refrigerator • live mollusks must have oxygen • use within 24 hours	• do not freeze live mollusks

3

Description	What to Look For	What to Avoid

Shellfish: Mollusks

Description	What to Look For	What to Avoid
Live Clams, Mussels, & Oysters, cont'd live mollusk in shell	• necks should retract or move when touched • whole shells, free from cracks	
Shucked Clams, Mussels, & Oysters uncooked meats removed from live mollusk cooked, fresh or frozen	• meats should be plump and covered with clear liquid from clam, mussel, or oyster • meats should be free from shell bits • fresh meats should be clean • frozen meats should be purchased while still frozen	• dry or off color • bits of shell • unpleasant or strong fishy odor
Live Periwinkles, Whelks, & Conchs	• operculum tightly shut • fresh marine scent	• gaping operculum • strong odor
Cooked Periwinkles, Whelks, & Conchs In general only the muscular foot is eaten.	• clean, sweet smelling meats • know the source of these mollusks	

Shellfish: Crustaceans

Description	What to Look For	What to Avoid
Live Crabs, Crayfish, & Lobster live crustaceans	• lively animal, legs and antennae moving • shells should be hard * exception: soft-shelled crabs	• limp crab, crayfish, or lobster • soft-shelled crabs will appear weak but should be alive
Cooked Crabs, Crayfish, & Lobster cooked whole crustacean in the shell	• should be freshly cooked or freshly cooked and frozen • sweet aroma	• soft shell • strong odor
cooked: picked meats, meats removed from the shell	• firm meat with some reddish tint on edges. Some crabmeat will have brownish edges • free from shell bits • sweet aroma	• soft meats • off color • shell particles • strong odor
Shrimp, Fresh or Fresh Frozen Most shrimp sold in the U.S. is headless and has been frozen. It is sold with shell or "shelled and deveined." (cleaned)	• firm shells • purchase in frozen state or inquire about length of thawing • clean scent • firm flesh, when shelled and deveined	• soft shells • soft flesh • strong odor
Shrimp, Cooked cooked with or without shell	• firm meat • moist appearance • pleasant salty aroma	• soft meat • dry, off color • strong odor

How to Store	How to Freeze
• store in covered plastic container • uncooked: use within 24 hours • cooked: use within 24–48 hours	• should be frozen as soon as shucked or cooked and frozen • freeze in plastic containers
• store in unsealed container in coldest part of refrigerator • live mollusks must have oxygen • use within 24 hours • cooked meats should be stored in plastic container	• do not freeze live mollusks • freeze cooked meats in plastic container
• store in large paper bag with holes punched in it (live crustaceans need oxygen to live) • store on ice or in refrigerator	• do not freeze live crustaceans
• store in plastic bag in refrigerator • use within 24 hours	• freeze in plastic bag or container
• store in plastic container in refrigerator • use within 24 hours or freeze	• freeze in plastic bag or container
• store in plastic bag • use within 12 hours if thawed • use within 24 hours if fresh	• do not refreeze thawed shrimp • freeze fresh shrimp in plastic bags
• store in plastic bag • use within 24–48 hours	• do not refreeze thawed cooked shrimp • freeze cooked shrimp in plastic container

Buying and Storing Seafood

Freshness is the most important quality to look for when purchasing and preparing seafood. With today's improved transportation and refrigeration, fresh fish should be readily available in all markets. When they are in season, local fish (whether from salt or fresh water) are the most abundant, generally the freshest, and usually the best value. Farmed seafood, a rapidly expanding industry, offers the advantage of year-round availability and better prices. Salmon and oysters are two excellent examples of successful aquaculture.

Use the five senses to help select the best seafood. LOOK at the fish; its flesh should be moist and have a natural sheen. SMELL the fish; it should have no unpleasant odor, it should have a clean marine aroma, like fresh seawater. When seafood is freshly caught and prepared, its flesh has a clean marine aroma that is really quite subtle; if it has been improperly stored or is too old it will have a strong "fishy" odor. The classic "fishy" smell with a hint of ammonia is actually produced by bacteria growing in the improperly stored seafood and is a good indicator of a spoiled product. TOUCH the fish; its flesh should be firm and elastic. TASTE the fish, if at all possible; it should not taste strong or heavily "fishy." And perhaps most important, LISTEN to the fishmonger's advice; he should know his fish and be happy to share his knowledge.

Pay careful attention to the conditions at the market. Whole fish should be kept on well-drained ice and never permitted to lie in accumulating liquid. Live shell fish should be kept on ice or in a chilled "lobster pool." Cut fish, such as fillets or steaks, and shucked or cooked shellfish, on the other hand, should be protected by paper or plastic from any direct contact with the ice. Fresh seafood should not be sealed in plastic wrap, which can foster the growth of bacteria. Look for a market where fish is properly displayed and don't be afraid to ask to smell the seafood. The reputable fishmonger will be proud of his high-quality products and will recognize you as a discerning customer.

If the purchased seafood has to be transported some distance before it can be refrigerated, you should request a small bag of ice to keep it chilled in transit. Taking a small cooler with an ice pack to the market in hot weather is a good method of keeping the seafood chilled in transit. Always remember that refrigeration is the most important requisite in maintaining freshness in seafood.

Although the ideal for seafood is out-of-the-water-and-into-the-pan, this is not always possible. Freshly frozen fish is better than "stale" fresh fish, and most fish freezes well. Live shellfish may be kept an additional 24 hours in the refrigerator after purchase, but cooked seafood should be consumed immediately or frozen for future use.

How Much Seafood to Purchase and Serve

Everyone has different appetites and capacities for food, so no hard and fast rules can really be set down about quantities of fish to buy for each person. However, it is always safer to err on the more generous side and have leftovers than to skimp on portions.

SEAFOOD	PER PERSON
Fish, whole	3/4 to 1 pound
Fish, dressed	1/2 to 3/4 pound
Fish fillets	1/4 to 1/3 pound
Fish steaks	1/3 to 1/2 pound
Clams in shell	6 to 12 clams
Clams, shucked/minced	1/4 to 1/2 pint
Oysters in shell	6 to 12 oysters

SEAFOOD	PER PERSON
Oysters, shucked	1/4 to 1/2 pint
Mussels in shell	12 to 18 mussels
Scallops, shucked	1/4 to 1/3 pound
Lobster, whole/live	1 to 2 depending on size
Lobster meat	1/4 to 1/3 pound
Crab, whole/live	1 to 4 depending on size
Crabmeat	1/4 to 1/3 pound
Shrimp, headless, raw with shell	1/3 to 1/2 pound
Shrimp, peeled, deveined, raw	1/3 to 1/2 pound
Shrimp, peeled, deveined, cooked	1/4 to 1/3 pound
Surimi (imitation crabmeat)	1/4 to 1/3 pound

Cooking Methods

Today a wide choice of fish and shellfish is available throughout the country. Imported species as well as well as those that are caught locally can be found from coast to coast. As you become familiar with a greater variety of fishes, you may wish to try a few new recipes and new cooking methods.

Timing is probably the most important element in successful preparation of fish. A method of estimating accurate cooking time was developed by the Canadian Department of Fisheries and popularized by the late James Beard. In this book we will refer to it as the "Canadian Guideline" for the sake of brevity. Use this guideline in cooking fish, as it practically guarantees perfect results.

To utilize the Canadian Guideline, *measure the fish at its thickest point and allow* 10 *minutes of cooking time for each inch of thickness*—no matter what cooking method is being employed. For example, if a bluefish is 2 inches thick, at its thickest point, it will require 20 minutes of cooking; 4 inches thick, 40 minutes of cooking. If you are cooking fish that is still frozen, double the amount of time. Just to make certain it is thoroughly cooked, however, insert the tip of a sharp knife to check for color and ease of flaking. When it is done, fish flakes easily, and its meat becomes opaque, losing its translucent quality. Always take care not to overcook fish. Overcooking results in tough, dry flesh.

Fish cookery may be divided into three basic categories:

1. **Dry Heat**—Baking, broiling, and grilling. Using high heat, fish will cook quickly, retaining maximum flavor and moisture. Fish with relatively high fat content (such as bluefish, salmon, or mackerel) are particularly good when cooked by one of these methods. Leaner fish should be basted or wrapped in a protective coating to help retain juices if they are cooked by dry heat.

2. **Moist Heat**—Steaming, poaching, braising, soups, and stews. These methods require a liquid and, as a consequence, cook fish at lower temperatures than dry heat. Moist heat is suitable for fish and shellfish. Often the cooking liquid is used in a sauce or in the finished product.

3. **Oil or Fat**—Sautéing or pan-frying, stir-frying, and deep-frying. The high temperature of the cooking oil or fat helps to seal in the flavor of the fish. Both fish and shellfish may be cooked by in this manner.

A *note about microwaving*: Fish may be cooked in a microwave oven, but remember that microwaving is very fast and may overcook the fish. Because there is such variety in microwave ovens, we suggest that you follow the manufacturers' guidelines for your oven.

Dry Heat: Baking

Baking is an excellent and quick way to prepare fish. Preheat the oven to 400 to 450 degrees. The use of a very hot oven seals in the natural juices and flavor of the fish. Determine the necessary cooking time by measuring the thickness of the fish using the Canadian Guideline.

Rub a baking pan with a small amount of butter or oil to prevent the fish from sticking to the pan. Lemon slices or celery leaves under the fish also will prevent sticking and will add flavor. Place the fish, either whole or portioned, in the pan and cook until done. This simple preparation may be varied by the addition of a favorite herb, a few drops of wine, or a dash of lemon juice. For a slightly richer taste try basting the fish with melted butter.

For fish with little internal fat, try one of several good ways to keep fish moist during baking:

1. Wrap fish in parchment paper, in foil, or in some leafy greens.
2. Coat fish with crumbs or cover with a sauce or julienned vegetables.
3. Leave the head and tail on the fish during baking, as this helps to retain moisture.
4. Marinate and/or baste fish while it is cooking.
5. Stuff the fish (measure the thickness after it has been stuffed to calculate the correct cooking time, using the Canadian Guideline).

Dry Heat: Broiling

Broiling must be done with care, as it is easy to overcook the fish with such intense heat. Steaks, fillets, and chunks of fish on skewers

9

are well suited to broiling. The fish should be about an inch thick, as thinner portions tend to cook too fast and thicker ones char on the exterior while remaining under-done inside. Folding the thin end of a fillet under itself will give a more uniform thickness.

Preheat the broiler to 550 de-grees. Determine the cooking time using the Canadian Guideline. Oil a broiling pan or rack to prevent the fish from sticking. Rub the exposed side of the fish with a small amount of melted butter or oil and place it on the broiling pan or rack. Broil the fish approximately 3 inches from the broiler element. Basting the fish during cooking will add fla-vor as well as moisture. A simple baste can be made with lemon juice, soy sauce, and melted butter or a butter substitute.

Dry Heat: Grilling

Grilling over an open fire is one of the oldest and easiest methods of fish cookery. It is also the one with the most variables. The fish may be skewered or placed on a metal grill directly over the heat, whether it is gas, electricity, char-coal, or wood. Different kinds of wood, such as mesquite and apple, or charcoal, burn with different de-grees of intensity and impart differ-ent flavors to the fish. Some grills allow the cooking surface to be raised or lowered so that the dis-tance from the heat source is an-other variable. Other grills have covers that hold the heat in during the cooking process.

Steaks and thick fillets with skin may be placed directly on the grill;

chunks of fish and thinner fillets cook more successfully when they are threaded on skewers. If whole fish are to be grilled, a wire basket for this purpose facilitates matters. It is important to preheat the grill and, if using charcoal or wood, to have the coals glowing hot but not flaming. Marinating and/or basting the fish during cooking helps to re-tain moisture. Fresh herbs may be thrown on glowing embers to add yet another taste. Use the Cana-dian Guideline to determine the correct length of cooking time.

Moist Heat: Steaming

Steaming is a simple and quick method of preparing low-calorie yet flavorful fish dishes. A basic steamer consists of a deep pot with a tight-fitting lid and a metal or bamboo rack. The rack *must* keep the fish *above* the boiling liquid, and there must be enough space around it for the steam to circulate.

Small whole fish, steaks, and fil-lets are well suited to steaming. Use the Canadian Guideline for correct timing. (Shellfish may be steamed too, but refer to individual recipes.) The addition of wine or herbs to the liquid will make the steam aro-matic and lend a delicate flavor to the fish. Bring the liquid to a boil, place the fish on the rack above the liquid, and cover the pot tightly. The steam from the boiling liquid will envelope the fish, cooking it with intense moist heat.

To serve the fish, remove the rack from the cooking pot, taking care not to burn yourself on the es-caping steam.

Moist Heat: Poaching

When poaching fish or shellfish, it is very important to have the cooking liquid *simmering, not boiling*. Poaching is particularly suitable for whole fish and is the best method if the fish is to be served cooled. Although a fish poacher is handy for large fish, any pot that is large enough to contain the fish *with* its cooking liquid will do. Wrapping the fish in cheesecloth or placing it on a rack with handles, facilitates its removal at the end of the poaching period.

A classic poaching medium is a court bouillon made from water flavored with wine, vinegar, or lemon juice, herbs and spices. Use vinegar in the court bouillon for cooking a strong-flavored fish with high oil content. Plain salted water or fish stock is often used for simple poaching, while a combination of water, milk, and thinly sliced lemon enhances delicate fishes.

Poaching techniques differ for small fillets or steaks from that used for thick pieces or whole fish. The latter should be immersed in the poaching liquid *before* it is brought to the simmering point. On the other hand, small fillets or steaks should be placed directly in the heated and simmering liquid. Using the Canadian Guideline for length of cooking, timing should start when the liquid starts to simmer. If the fish is to be served cooled, reduce the cooking time by several minutes and let the fish cool slightly in the poaching liquid before removing it. (Save the poaching liquid for soups, or reduce it to use in sauces.)

Moist Heat: Braising

Because the fish is not completely immersed in the cooking liquid or ingredients (which is an important part of the completed dish), braising combines the techniques of both steaming and poaching. As a method, it is particularly suitable for strongly flavored fish, whole fish, steaks, and even shellfish.

Essentially, braising calls for sautéing diced vegetables in a small amount of butter until soft, then placing the fish on top of the vegetables and adding a small amount of stock or other cooking liquid. The pot is covered and as always, the Canadian Guideline is used to determine the cooking time. Delicate fish should be braised with mildly flavored vegetables such as celery and carrots, while mackerel or bluefish will do well with the stronger flavors of peppers, garlic, and tomatoes. Many different and unusual flavors will result by experimenting with a variety of mixtures in the braising pot.

Moist Heat: Soups and Chowders

Seafood soups range from delicate consommes to hearty chowders. Simple clam broth with a few clams, refined stock for lobster consomme, a rich shrimp bisque, or a creamy New England fish chowder all start off with a good base of fish stock or broth. By utilizing a variety of vegetables, milk, or seasonings and seafood, many different soups can be made. As always, it is important not to overcook the seafood.

Moist Heat: Stewing

Stewing is similar to braising, but a larger amount of liquid is used in proportion to the vegetables and fish. In general, chunks of fish rather than whole fish are used, and sometimes shellfish is added as well. Cioppino and bouillabaisse are two of the more familiar seafood stews, and they combine a wide variety of fish and shellfish.

Stews should have a good fish stock base before the vegetables and seafood are added. Variety makes stews interesting. Take care not to overcook the fish, as it is important to the success of the dish for each ingredient to retain its own flavor and texture. A hot garlicky sauce and toast rounds often accompany seafood stews.

Another form of stew, popular in New England, is a simple combination of seafood, milk, and cream. Lobster stew and oyster stew are two favorites.

Oil or Fat: Pan Frying and Sautéing

Small whole fish, steaks, or fillets are excellent choices for pan-frying or sautéing. A small amount of oil or a combination of oils—roughly ¼ inch—should be heated to the bubbling stage in a skillet that is large enough to hold the pieces of fish without crowding. Care should be taken with the temperature of the oil. If it is smoking, it is too hot. However, if the oil is not hot enough, the fish, if it is coated with flour or bread crumbs, will absorb too much fat.

For proper frying time, use the Canadian Guideline.

When the fish is nicely browned on both sides, carefully remove it from the oil and drain it well on brown paper before serving.

Oil or Fat: Deep-Frying

Fried fish, coated in batter or bread crumbs and cooked to a golden brown in hot oil, is a great American favorite. Small whole fish or individual portions are best suited to this method of preparation. The oil should be heated in a deep fryer or a wok to a temperature of 375 degrees. The fish should be coated in either a batter (such as the Beer Batter used for our Fish and Chips) or a traditional bread crumb mixture. Following the Canadian Guideline, the cooking time should be determined by the thickness of the fish. Always fry the fish in small amounts, as overcrowding causes the temperature of the oil to drop too low and the fish will not cook properly. (If using frozen fish, it is better to partially thaw it before frying to avoid the same problem.)

When the fish is cooked, remove it from the fryer and drain well on brown paper or paper towel before serving.

Oil or Fat: Stir-Frying

Stir-frying, utilizing high heat, relatively little oil, and constant stirring, is an Oriental cooking technique that has gained many enthusiastic advocates in recent years. Seafood in combination with vegetables, both cut into small pieces, is well suited to this technique of rapid cooking.

Determine the relative cooking time for the seafood and vegetables, as it is important to start with the item that requires the longest cooking. Some, like carrots, take far longer than others, such as snow peas. Add just enough oil to the heated wok or large skillet to cook all the fish and vegetables being prepared. Have all the ingredients close at hand and ready to cook once you start the process. Seasonings and liquids should be added near the end of the cooking time.

Suggestions For Left-Over Cooked Seafood

Leftover seafood may be combined with other ingredients to make another meal, such as a soup, hash, or a salad. Pieces of leftover shellfish may be used as garnishes. Most simply prepared fish—broiled, baked, steamed or poached—lend themselves to leftover dishes. However, more elaborate seafood in a sauce is good over pasta.

Note: Leftover seafood may be frozen. However, it is not advisable to refreeze leftovers once they have been used in any of the following methods.

Soups for Two

These soups are easy to make and a good way to use up leftover seafood. The basic recipe consists of 2 cups of liquid, a few vegetables, and the seafood. The amount of seafood added will depend on the supply. It does not really make a great deal of difference whether it measures 1/2 cup or 1 cup, as the point of these recipes is to use up the leftover food.

☐ Combine a 10-to 12-ounce can of tomato/vegetable juice with a 10- to 12-ounce can of clam broth in a small saucepan. Throw in a handful of chopped celery, a pinch of thyme, a slice of lemon rind stuck with a couple of cloves, and a grind of black pepper. Heat to the boiling point, then reduce heat and add leftover seafood. Simmer for 5 minutes and serve. Different varieties of fish will lend different flavors.

☐ Heat 2 cups of chicken broth, homemade or out of a can. Add thinly sliced carrots, celery, chopped lettuce leaves, a pinch of ground ginger, and a drop of hot pepper sauce. Add leftover seafood and simmer for 5 minutes. Serve sprinkled with crunchy Chinese noodles.

☐ Heat 2 cups of fish stock. Add 1/4 cup sliced carrot, 2 tablespoons sliced onion, and 1/2 cup diced, peeled potato. Simmer until vegetables are soft. Puree in food mill or processor. Add salt and pepper to taste. Light cream may be added to enrich this soup, if desired. Serve hot or cold, garnished with pieces of leftover shrimp, crabmeat, or lobster.

☐ Heat 1 cup of fish stock or canned clam broth with 1 cup of milk. Add leftover diced potato along with leftover fish to the simmering mixture and heat for 5 minutes. Not as rich as "Grandmother's," but a simple way to use leftovers. Serve with oyster crackers.

Salad

☐ Combine any plain leftover seafood with mayonnaise or a mayonnaise-based salad dressing. Add some minced celery and/or sweet onion, salt and pepper to taste, and an herb such as minced fresh basil. Serve on a bed of lettuce, in a scooped-out tomato half, or make a sandwich.

Quiche

☐ Add leftover fish or shellfish to a favorite quiche recipe instead of the ham or other meat.

Casseroles

☐ Substitute any leftover fish for the tuna in the traditional tuna casserole.
☐ Leftover white or light fish added to a crabmeat or lobster Newburg stretches the casserole to serve more people.

Seafood Stew

☐ Freeze leftover seafood until several varieties have been collected. Then make a seafood stew with all the frozen leftovers.

Pasta

☐ Add leftover shellfish to a small amount of garlicky olive oil. Heat through, then pour over freshly cooked pasta. Toss and serve.

Fishcakes

Leftover fish makes excellent fish cakes. Use a favorite recipe or try the following.

2 *tablespoons butter*
2 *tablespoons flour*
$^1/_2$ *cup milk or fish stock*
1 *egg, beaten*
Pinch *of thyme*
$^1/_4$ *teaspoon black pepper*
$^1/_8$ *teaspoon dry mustard*
1 *teaspoon white wine vinegar*
3 *tablespoons chopped celery*
1 *tablespoon minced scallion*
1 *tablespoon minced fresh parsley*
1 *cup flaked cooked fish*
4 *tablespoons dry bread crumbs, plus additional*
   crumbs for coating
2 *tablespoons vegetable oil for cooking*

1. In a small saucepan melt butter over medium heat. Stir in flour until the mixture is smooth. Gradually stir in the milk or stock. Remove from heat and whisk in the beaten egg. Return the pan to the heat and continue to whisk the mixture. Remove pan from heat.
2. Add the thyme, pepper, and mustard. Stir in the vinegar. Add the celery, scallion, parsley, fish, and the 4 tablespoons of bread crumbs. Mix well. Place the mixture in a small bowl and refrigerate for 2 hours or until well chilled.
3. Divide the mixture into 4 cakes and coat with bread crumbs.
4. Heat the oil in a heavy skillet. Fry the fishcakes over moderately high heat until golden brown on both sides, about 4 to 5 minutes per side. Serve with a tartar sauce or Dijon-style mustard.

Chapter 2

Shellfish:
The Ocean's
First Bounty

"Shellfish" is a general nonscientific name for a variety of aquatic animals—none of which are fishes at all! Of all the seafood that we eat today, shellfish were the first to evolve. Ancestors of these venerable invertebrates (animals without backbones) lived in the oceans at least 600 million years ago.

The term "shellfish" usually refers to mollusks and crustaceans, especially the species that man enjoys eating. The shell is actually a skeleton that the animal wears on the outside as protection. Although mollusks and crustaceans have numerous similarities, like their hard outsides and soft insides, they also have many differences. Most edible crustaceans, for instance, have jointed bodies and belong to a group known as decapods, meaning ten-footed. Count the legs on a crab, crayfish, lobster, or shrimp. You'll find ten. The shells of crustaceans do not expand, so these animals must shed or "molt" periodically in order to grow.

Mollusks, on the other hand, enlarge their shells by making calcium carbonate from lime in the water and simply adding it on. Thus the tiny whorl at the small end of a snail's shell is the original home it possessed when it was just starting out in life. Squid and octopus, also mollusks, lost their external shells during the course of evolution. The stiff internal "pen" of the squid is a vestigial remnant of an ancestral shell. Mollusks that we eat can be divided into three main groups: bivalves, or two-shelled, such as clams, mussels, oysters, and scallops; gastropods, or "stomach foots," of which conchs and snails are familiar examples; and cephalopods, or "head-foots," which include squid and octopus.

Of all the currently popular seafood, shellfish have the most universal appeal. There is a shellfish recipe for almost any occasion, and often one kind of shellfish may be freely substituted for another with fortuitous results. Whether it's a regal banquet for fifty or a quick supper for two, shellfish can satisfy the most demanding of palates. From hors d'oeuvres to salad to entree, shellfish run a glorious gamut.

Several centuries ago, in coastal France, when a fishing fleet came home, each man threw a share of his catch into a huge copper pot called *la chaudière*. The community then shared in a feast celebrating the safe return of the fishermen. The tradition found its way to New England where *la chaudière* became chowder.

CLAMS

CONCH

MUSSELS

OCTOPUS

OYSTERS

SCALLOPS

SQUID

Mollusks: Clams, Conch, Mussels, Octopus, Oysters, Scallops, and Squid

We find mollusks nearly everywhere. There are snails in the sea, snails in fresh water, and snails on the land. Clams burrow in the mud flats, mussels cling to the rocks, and squid patrol the open ocean. A scallop "swims" across the floor of a bay by clapping its shells together, while a baby oyster cements itself to one spot for the rest of its life.

But our favorite place to find a mollusk is lying tenderly on the plate, hidden in the pasta or enriching the chowder bowl.

New England Clam Chowder

This version of traditional New England clam chowder has a lovely light consistency because it is not flour-thickened. Using salt pork instead of bacon produces a flavor that is especially complementary to the briny quality of clams.

12–15 *medium chowder clams (quahogs), well scrubbed*

2–4 *cups water*

4 *ounces "streak of lean" salt pork, cut in ¹/₂-inch dice (about ³/₄ cup)*

5 *medium onions, sliced (about 3 cups)*

³/₄ *cup crumbled Vermont common crackers, or unsalted soda crackers*

6 *medium boiling potatoes, peeled and cut into ¹/₂-inch dice (about 3 cups)*

1 *bay leaf*

1 *cup milk*

2 *cups light cream*

Freshly ground black pepper

2 *teaspoons butter*

1. Place the clams in a large kettle and pour in 2 to 4 cups water, enough to cover the bottom of the kettle to a depth of one inch. Cover and bring to a boil; steam the clams for 5 to 10 minutes, or until they open.
2. With a slotted spoon, remove the clams from the broth. Discard any clams that did not open. Remove the meat from the clam shells, chop, and set aside. Strain the broth through a fine mesh sieve and measure. Add enough water to make 4 cups. Set aside.
3. Bring 1 ½ quarts of water to a boil in another saucepan and simmer the salt pork for 5 to 10 minutes to remove the salt. Drain and pat dry with paper towels.
4. In a large heavy kettle, sauté the salt pork over medium-low heat until it starts to brown. Add the onions and sauté, covered, over low heat until they are tender, but not browned. Stir in the crumbled crackers. Add the reserved clam broth and water mixture to the onions, then add the potatoes and the bay leaf. Simmer, partially covered, for 20 minutes. Stir in the milk, cream, and chopped clams, and heat through, but do not let boil. Taste for seasoning.
5. Let the chowder cool, then cover and refrigerate at least several hours or, preferably, overnight.
6. Just before serving, heat the chowder. Add the butter and let it melt. Serve immediately.

Serves 6
Must be prepared in advance

Down Easters were so upset that anyone would make a tomato and clam chowder (Manhattan clam chowder) that the Maine Legislature once introduced a bill to outlaw forever the mixing of clams and tomatoes.

Clams are one of the most popular edible bivalves. The two valves or shells come together to protect the clam inside. Thus, "to clam up"—a familiar phrase, means to shut up.

Littleneck clams were named after Little Neck Bay on Long Island, New York.

Cherrystones are named for Cherrystone Creek in Virginia.

The familiar quahog, or hard-shell clam, is found along our Atlantic coastline in sandy bays from the Gulf of St. Lawrence south into the Gulf of Mexico. These clams grow rapidly and may live twenty years or more. They are marketed according to size: "Littlenecks," about 1 to 1 ½ inches, "Cherrystones," about 2 inches; and "chowder" size quahogs, which measure 3 inches or more.

Cherrystone Clams

This old classic is a festive way to begin an evening. For variety, we suggest you serve half the clams as described below and the other half according to the variation.

½ cup unsalted butter (1 stick)
1 ½ teaspoons minced garlic
¼ cup finely chopped green pepper (about ½ small pepper)
1 tablespoon fresh strained lemon juice
6 tablespoons fine fresh bread crumbs
¼ teaspoon salt
Freshly ground black pepper to taste
24 cherrystone clams
Lemon wedges for garnish

1. In a medium saucepan, melt 4 tablespoons of the butter over medium heat and sauté the garlic and green pepper for 2 or 3 minutes, stirring frequently. Add the lemon juice, bread crumbs, salt, and pepper. Add the remaining butter and stir until well combined. Taste and correct seasoning, adding more salt and pepper if desired. This step may be completed up to 6 hours in advance; keep the mixture in the refrigerator, covered.
2. When you are ready to finish preparation, preheat oven to 450 degrees.
3. Open the clams, discarding the top shells. Arrange the clams in a shallow baking dish on a bed of crumpled aluminum foil or rock salt to prevent tipping.
4. Place a teaspoonful of stuffing on top of each clam, patting it down well, and bake in the preheated oven for 10 minutes. Serve immediately with lemon wedges.

Variation: For Bacon Baked Clams, proceed as above, adding 2 tablespoons minced scallions and ¼ cup chopped mushrooms to the sauté pan. Omit the final 4 tablespoons butter and place a piece of bacon on top of each clam. Bake until the bacon is crisp.

Serves 6
May be partially prepared in advance

How to Open a Clam
First wash hard-shell clams in several changes of water. Then cover them with cold salt water and let them soak for several hours to get rid of any sand or mud that remains. About ¼ to ½ cup of cornmeal can be added to the soaking water to aid in bringing out any sand or mud.

1: Hold the clam in the palm of your hand with the rounded edge facing out. Insert a sharp strong knife between the halves of the shell and cut around the clam, twisting the knife to pry open the shell. Cut the clam away from the shell but leave the clam on the half shell for serving.
2. If the clams are to be cooked, placing them in the freezer for 5 to 10 minutes will make them easier to open. Then proceed as in Step 1.

Shuck clams for "half-shell" presentation as close to serving time as possible.

Always keep fresh clams cold. Never put them in sunlight or fresh water. Properly stored clams will live for several days.

Clams with Black Bean Sauce

There are countless variations of this popular Chinese dish. We like this version with its occidental touch of lemon.

1 tablespoon fermented black beans*
1 cup water
2 tablespoons Chinese rice wine or dry sherry
20 littleneck clams, well scrubbed
3 tablespoons peanut or vegetable oil
1 tablespoon minced gingerroot
2 teaspoons minced garlic
1 teaspoon dried red pepper flakes, crushed
3 tablespoons oyster sauce*
1 tablespoon light soy sauce*
1 tablespoon cornstarch, dissolved in 2 tablespoons water
1 tablespoon grated lemon rind (zest)
Slivered lemon peel for garnish (optional)

*Available in Chinese markets or specialty section of your supermarket.

1. Rinse the black beans under running water and then soak them for 10 to 15 minutes in ½ cup of water. Drain, then cover with the rice wine or sherry and mash lightly with a spoon.
2. Steam the clams open in a pot with the remaining ½ cup water. Drain, reserving 1 cup of strained clam broth. Set clams aside, keeping them warm.
3. Place the oil in a wok or skillet and warm over medium heat. Stir-fry the ginger, garlic, and crushed pepper flakes for 1 minute. Add the oyster sauce, soy sauce, reserved clam broth, the fermented beans, and their soaking liquid. Bring to a boil and cook over high heat for 1 minute.
4. Slowly add the cornstarch mixture, reduce heat, and stir until thickened. Add the grated lemon rind and stir until combined.
5. Place the clams on a warm platter and pour the sauce over them. Garnish with the lemon peel.

Serves 4

"Steamers" are a uniquely East Coast clam. While all types of clams can be interchanged in clam recipes, New Englanders tend to prefer steamers, also known as Ipswich clams or *Mya arenaria.*

How to Steam Clams

The best clams to use for steaming are soft-shell clams, otherwise known as "steamers." Because of their long double siphon (neck), they are unable to close completely, which causes the clams to be sandy. It is a good idea to soak them in a pail of salted water with ½ cup cornmeal for several hours before preparation. In other parts of the country, little neck clams are also used for steaming. They should also be soaked before preparation.

Place the clams in a kettle large enough to hold them to a depth of 4 to 5 inches. Add about 1½ to 2 inches of one of the following: water, beer, dry white wine, or a combination of water and beer, or water and wine. Cover the kettle and bring to a boil over high heat. Steam 8 to 10 minutes, or until the shells have opened. Discard any that do not open.

Serve the clams with melted butter. The steaming liquid can also be served in mugs and used for rinsing the clams before dipping them in the butter. Many people drink the clam broth as well.

Linguine with White Clam Sauce

A quick, healthy, and tasty dish. For visual and gastronomic interest, experiment with a colored pasta, such as spinach or carrot. Both will provide a striking background for the pale, creamy clams. Another variation would be to use steamed mussels instead of clams.

6 *pounds cherrystone clams (about 36–40 clams),*
  well scrubbed
2–4 *cups liquid (water, beer, dry white wine, etc.)*
1/4 *cup olive oil*
4 *teaspoons minced garlic*
5 *tablespoons minced fresh parsley*
1/4 *cup dry white wine*
1/2 *teaspoon freshly ground black pepper*
1 *pound uncooked linguine*

1. Place the clams in a large kettle. Pour the liquid you have selected over them to a depth of about one inch. Cover and bring to a boil; then steam 10 minutes until the clams have opened. Discard any clams that do not open. With a slotted spoon, remove the clams, reserving 6 clams for garnish. Remove the remaining clams from the shells, chop, and set aside. Refrigerate both the whole clams and the chopped clams, covered, if not proceeding immediately.
2. In a large skillet, heat the oil over low heat. Add the garlic and cook until soft, 4 to 5 minutes, stirring frequently. Add the parsley and cook just until the garlic begins to turn golden.
3. Drain the steamed clams, reserving 1 cup liquid. Add the liquid to the skillet, along with the wine and pepper. Bring to a boil and cook, uncovered, over medium-high heat for 5 minutes.
4. The recipe may be prepared to this point up to 24 hours in advance. Cover the oil, garlic, parsley, and clam broth mixture and refrigerate. Bring back to a boil before proceeding.
5. Cook the linguine according to package directions. Meanwhile, bring the broth mixture to a boil and add the chopped clams. Cook for 2 minutes, uncovered. Remove from heat, cover, and keep warm until the linguine is cooked and drained.
6. Toss the linguine with the chopped clam mixture,

The name Quahog is a corruption of the Pequot word "P'*quaughaug*" meaning thick or tightly closed shell.

The Latin name for the hard shell Quahog clam is *Mercenaria mercenaria*, meaning money.

Wampum beads, carved from Quahog or chowder clam shells, were used as money in the 1700s, when the colonists bartered with the Indians. Those beads which had more purple coloration were considered of higher monetary value.

A lot of clams = a lot of money.

heap onto a serving platter, and garnish with the whole clams. Serve immediately.

Serves 6
May be partially prepared in advance

Spaghetti Squash with Tomato-Clam Sauce

The unique quality of spaghetti squash lends itself to interesting sauces. This recipe minimizes calories and fats while maximizing taste. For a little color add some julienned zucchini.

1 3-pound spaghetti squash
4 large tomatoes, peeled, seeded, and chopped (about 2 pounds)
1 teaspoon minced garlic
2 tablespoons olive oil
1 small dried red hot pepper, seeds removed
¼ cup chopped fresh basil
24 littleneck or cherrystone clams, well scrubbed
Basil sprigs for garnish

Canned chopped or minced clams, as well as frozen clams, may be used in our recipes—but *fresh* is always best.

1. With a large fork, pierce the squash in several places. Cook the squash in a large pot of boiling water for 45 minutes, or until the skin can be pierced easily. Drain, cut in half, and scrape out the pulp. The pulp will come out in strands similar to spaghetti. The squash may be prepared up to 24 hours in advance and reheated in a microwave oven, according to the manufacturer's instructions.
2. In a skillet over medium heat, sauté the tomatoes and garlic in the oil for about 5 minutes. Crumble the red pepper into very small pieces and add, along with the basil, to the skillet. Cook 1 more minute.
3. In another pan, steam the clams, covered, in about 1 inch of water until they open (about 10 minutes). Discard any that do not open. Reserve 6 clams for garnish; shuck the remainder and add them to the tomato mixture; with their juices collected as you shuck them. Heat through and serve over the spaghetti squash, garnished with the reserved clams and sprigs of basil.

Many clams live in the intertidal zone, where predators have a hard time getting at them. This means they can only eat on a high tide. Hence, a truly contented person is said to be *"happy as a clam at high tide."*

Serves 4
May be partially prepared in advance

Conch Chowder

Conch chowder, another adaptation from the Caribbean, is a hearty meal in itself. Spiced with hot sauce or spiked with dark rum or sherry, this chowder makes a perfect cool-weather dish.

6 *slices bacon*
2 *cups chopped onion (about 2 large onions)*
1/2 *cup chopped carrot (about 1 large carrot)*
1 *cup chopped green pepper (about 1 large pepper)*
1 *pound frozen minced conch, thawed (about 2 cups)*
3 *medium tomatoes, peeled, seeded, and chopped (about 1 1/2 cups)*
1 *6-ounce can tomato paste*
3 *medium potatoes, peeled and cut in 1/2-inch dice (about 1 pound)*
4 *cups water*
1 *teaspoon salt*
1/2 *teaspoon freshly ground black pepper*
1/2 *teaspoon dried thyme*
1/2 *teaspoon Tabasco sauce*

Familiar edible marine gastropods (stomach foots) include periwinkles, whelks, conch, and abalone.

Sometimes the names whelk and conch are used interchangeably, and indeed, one may be substituted for the other in some recipes, although they belong to two distinct families of gastropod mollusks.

1. Fry the bacon in a large kettle until crisp. Remove and drain on paper toweling and reserve.
2. Sauté the onion, carrot, and green pepper in the bacon drippings until softened, about 5 minutes. Add the conch and mix well. Cover and simmer for 5 minutes.
3. Add the tomatoes, tomato paste, potatoes, water, salt, pepper, thyme, and Tabasco. Cover and simmer for 2 hours.
4. The chowder may be prepared up to 24 hours in advance and stored, covered tightly, in the refrigerator.
5. Before serving, bring the chowder back to a boil, taste for seasoning and adjust if necessary. Serve topped with the crumbled bacon.

Variation: Substituting minced clams in this recipe for the conch will produce a "Manhattan" Clam Chowder.

Serves 6
May be prepared in advance

Conch Fritters

These delicious fritters will be the hit of any party. This recipe, an adaptation from the Caribbean, is easy to prepare. In fact, the fritters may be made ahead and frozen. To freeze, allow the fritters to cool on a cookie sheet, then place the whole sheet in the freezer. When the fritters are frozen, transfer them to a plastic freezer bag and seal. They may be stored this way for several months. To serve, place the frozen fritters on a cookie sheet in a 450-degree oven. Heat until sizzling, about 10 to 15 minutes. Drain on a paper towel before serving. Clams or squid may be substituted for the conch.

> 1 cup flour
> 1 teaspoon baking powder
> 1/4 teaspoon cayenne pepper
> 2 eggs
> 1/2 cup milk
> 1 pound frozen minced conch, thawed (about 2 cups)
> 1 small onion, chopped
> 1/4 cup finely chopped green pepper (about 1/3 pepper)
> 2 tablespoons minced fresh parsley
> 1/2 teaspoon salt
> 1/4 teaspoon freshly ground black pepper
> 2–3 drops Tabasco, according to taste
> 4 cups oil for deep-frying
> Cocktail Sauce (see page 258)
> Lime wedges for garnish

1. In a large bowl, combine the flour, baking powder, and cayenne. In another bowl, beat the eggs and milk together, and add slowly to the flour mixture, blending well. Let stand 30 minutes. Stir in the conch, onion, green pepper, parsley, salt, pepper, and Tabasco, and combine thoroughly.
2. Heat the oil to 375 degrees.
3. Drop the batter by the teaspoonful into the hot oil and fry, turning once or twice, until golden brown, about 5 to 7 minutes. Drain on paper towels and serve as an hors d'oeuvre with Cocktail Sauce and lime wedges.

Yield: 30 fritters
May be prepared in advance

The secret to delectable conch is tenderizing the meat. This can be accomplished by breaking down the connective tissue, either with a mallet and your muscles, or by grinding and mincing, then marinating.

The Queen conch, Strombus gigas, is found in Florida waters as well as in the Caribbean. Native residents of Key West, Florida, nickname themselves "Conchs," and many tasty dishes utilizing conch meat are served in Key West restaurants. The conch shells, with their beautiful pearly pink insides, are then sold to tourists.

Linguine alla Marinara

FROM THE QUARTERDECK RESTAURANT, MAYNARD, MASSACHUSETTS

The Quarterdeck Restaurant and Fishmarket, owned and operated by four of the Basile brothers, serves some of the freshest seafood west of Boston. A fifth brother owns the "Felony," a fishing boat that supplies much of the fish for the family business. This recipe is one of their favorites and is also a favorite at their restaurant.

2 *small cloves garlic*
¼ *cup olive oil*
¼ *cup clarified butter (see page 273)*
½ *cup parsley leaves, stems removed*
½ *cup dry white wine*
20 *mussels, scrubbed and beards pulled off*
20 *large shrimp, peeled and deveined (about 1 pound)*
4 *small squid, cleaned and cut into rings*
20 *bay scallops or small sea scallops*
1 *pound uncooked linguine*

1. In a food processor fitted with the steel knife, process the garlic, olive oil, butter, and parsley until smooth. Set aside.
2. In a large enameled skillet, over medium heat, heat the white wine and ½ cup of the garlic mixture. Add the mussels, cover, and cook until the mussels open. Discard any that do not open. Add the shrimp, squid, and scallops, and sauté, uncovered, for about 5 minutes, until just cooked.
3. The recipe may be prepared 24 hours in advance up to this point. With a slotted spoon, transfer the mussels, shrimp, squid, and scallops to a separate container. Pour the remaining cooking liquid into another container. Cover both containers and refrigerate.
4. Bring the broth to a boiling point. Add the mussels, shrimp, squid, and scallops to the broth. Meanwhile, cook the linguine according to package directions. Drain, then divide evenly among 4 bowls and top with the seafood.

Serves 4–6
May be partially prepared in advance

The most abundant of all mollusks, mussels live in dense colonies along the shore. They attach themselves firmly to rocks and piers with byssus threads, commonly called "beards." Debearding, or removing these fibers, is part of the cleaning process before cooking.

Mussels Remoulade

This remoulade sauce is so good, we're tempted to bottle and sell it. Use it to bind almost any fish, from tuna flakes to mahi mahi.

8 *pounds mussels, scrubbed, beards pulled off*
1/4 *cup thinly sliced scallions, including 2 inches of the green section*
1/2 *cup capers, rinsed and drained*
3/4 *cup minced fresh parsley*
3 *hard-boiled eggs, shelled and coarsely chopped*
1/4 *cup salad oil*
1 *cup mayonnaise, preferably homemade*
2 *tablespoons fresh strained lemon juice*
2 *tablespoons Dijon-style mustard*
Salt and freshly ground black pepper to taste
18 *slices white bread, toasted and cut in "points"*

1. Pour 2 inches of water in the bottom of an 8- to 10-quart steaming kettle. Add the mussels. Cover and bring to a boil over high heat. Reduce heat to medium and steam the mussels, stirring once or twice to redistribute, until their shells have opened, about 5 to 7 minutes. Discard all unopened ones. Drain.
2. When the mussels are cool enough to handle, remove the body meat and discard the shells. There should be about 4 cups of meat. If there is substantially more or less, increase or reduce the proportion of the remaining ingredients accordingly. (If the amount is anywhere from 3 1/2 to 4 1/2 cups, retain the amounts listed.)
3. With a pair of kitchen shears, cut each mussel in thirds, transferring them to a medium-size mixing bowl. Add the scallions, capers, parsley, and chopped eggs, and toss well.
4. In a separate bowl, blend the oil into the mayonnaise to lighten it. Beat in the lemon juice and mustard and mix thoroughly. Pour the dressing over the mussel mixture and toss until all the pieces are well coated. Taste for seasoning and adjust. Cover with plastic wrap and refrigerate for 30 minutes or up to 24 hours.
5. Serve with toast points.

Serves 12 as an appetizer
Must be prepared in advance

Mussels have been cultivated for 300 years in Europe. They are farmed in the United States in Maine and Rhode Island. Cultured mussels are usually grown in racks set above the ocean sand, so they come to market with less grit between the shells than wild mussels.

Le Pot-au-Feu de Poissons à Ma Façon

FROM DOMAINE CHANDON, YOUNTVILLE, CALIFORNIA

This elegant entree for "Fish Stew in My Style" was given to the New England Aquarium by Chef de Cuisine Philippe Jeanty. The aroma is irresistible. Make sure you have plenty of warm sourdough or French bread for soaking up the broth.

24 *mussels, cleaned and debearded*
24 *littleneck clams, well scrubbed*
4 *shallots, chopped*
1 *cup champagne*
½ *cup water*
2 *teaspoons minced garlic*
½ *cup peeled, seeded, and chopped tomato (about 1 medium)*
1 *tablespoon fresh thyme leaves*
6 *medium prawns or large shrimp, shelled*
2 *ounces scallops, cut into ¾-inch cubes*
2 *ounces salmon, cut into ¾-inch cubes*
12 *tablespoons unsalted butter (1½ sticks)*
2 *tablespoons fresh strained lemon juice*
Salt and freshly ground black pepper to taste

Well-washed fresh mussels can be stored in the refrigerator in an aerated plastic bag for up to three days.

Mussels are a favorite meal for seagulls and starfishes.

1. Put the mussels, clams, shallots, champagne, and water in a large saucepan. Steam, covered, until the mussels and clams have opened. The mussels will open in 2 to 4 minutes; the clams will take from 5 to 10 minutes. Remove the mussels and clams with a slotted spoon. When they are cool enough to handle, remove the meat from the shells; discard the shells. Strain the broth through several layers of cheesecloth and reserve. The recipe can be done to this point 24 hours in advance; store the broth, mussels, and clams in tightly covered separate containers in the refrigerator.
2. Bring the broth to a boil in a medium-size saucepan. Add the garlic, tomato, and prawns. Reduce the heat to a simmer and add the scallops and salmon. Poach, covered, until just cooked, 3 to 5 minutes. Immediately remove the prawns, scallops, and salmon and set aside.
3. Over low heat, whisk the butter into the broth, one tablespoon at a time. Return the salmon, mussels, scallops, shrimp, and clams to the broth and heat

through. Add the lemon juice, taste, and add salt and pepper if necessary. Serve immediately in shallow soup bowls.

Serves 6
May be partially prepared in advance

Basic Steamed Mussels

Serve these mussels with French bread and a green salad for a simple and satisfying meal.

    8 *pounds mussels, scrubbed and beards pulled off*
    ¹/₂ *cup sliced onion (1 medium)*   *garlic*
    4 *sprigs parsley, plus 2 tablespoons minced parsley*
        for garnish
    1 *cup dry white wine*
    1 *cup water*
    4 *tablespoons unsalted butter (¹/₂ stick), optional*

1. Place the onion, parsley sprigs, wine, and water in a large kettle. Bring to a boil over high heat.
2. Add the mussels. Cover and bring to a boil again. Reduce heat and simmer, shaking the pan occasionally for 5 to 7 minutes, until the mussels open. Drain, reserving the broth. Discard any mussels whose shells have not opened.
3. Strain the broth into a saucepan through a sieve lined with a double layer of cheesecloth. Add the optional butter and warm over low heat.
4. Mound the mussels into 4 wide bowls. Serve accompanied by smaller bowls of broth. Or serve the mussels and their broth in deep soup bowls. Sprinkle with the minced parsley.

Variations: Use 1 cup beer or hard cider instead of the wine, or 2 cups of wine and omit the water, or 2 cups of water.

Reduce the strained mussel broth (without the optional butter) over high heat for 5 minutes. Add 1 cup crème fraîche and cook 2 minutes over medium heat. Add parsley and serve as above.

Serve with Rouille, Pesto, or any of the warm tomato sauces (see chapter 7).

Serves 4

Always discard mussels that have not opened during the steaming process.

Be suspicious of any mussel that is noticeably heavy: in all probability it contains sand or mud.

Wild Rice and Mussel Salad

This recipe is an excellent base for almost any firm-fleshed, cooked fish. Other grains, such as bulgur wheat or couscous, can be used instead of the rice.

> 5 pounds mussels, scrubbed and beards pulled off
> 1/2 small cucumber, peeled, seeded, and chopped (about 1/2 cup)
> 1 teaspoon salt
> 1 cup raw wild rice
> 3/4 cup finely chopped mixed herbs, such as basil, mint, and parsley
> 1/4 cup thinly sliced scallions, including 2 inches of the green section
> 3 medium tomatoes, peeled, seeded, and coarsely chopped (about 1 pound)
> 1 teaspoon minced garlic
> 1 teaspoon Dijon-style mustard
> Pinch of black pepper
> 1 tablespoon olive oil
> 1/2 cup toasted nuts, such as pignolia (pine nuts) or almonds
> Large lettuce leaves

The shell of the blue mussel, *Mytilus edulis*, may grow to a length of 3 to 4 inches and, with optimum conditions, may reach its full growth within a year.

1. Prepare the mussels by following directions in the Basic Steamed Mussels recipe through step 2, dividing the ingredients approximately in half. Cool. Remove the meat from the shells and refrigerate. Discard the shells.
2. Over high heat, reduce the mussel broth to 1/2 cup. The recipe may be prepared 24 hours in advance up to this point. Refrigerate the mussels and broth, tightly covered.
3. Sprinkle the cucumber pieces with the teaspoon of salt and let stand 20 minutes.
4. Cook the wild rice according to package directions until it is done. Drain and transfer to a mixing bowl. Add as much mussel broth as the rice will absorb without becoming soggy, about 2 or 3 tablespoons.
5. Rinse the cucumber slices and add them to the rice along with the herbs, scallions, and tomatoes.
6. In a small bowl, whisk together the garlic, mustard, pepper, and olive oil. Add salt and pepper to taste.
7. Pour the dressing over the rice mixture. Add the mussels and nuts and toss to mix. The recipe may be prepared up to 4 hours in advance to this point.

8. To serve, arrange the lettuce leaves on a large serving platter. Mound the wild rice and mussel salad on top.

Serves 6
May be prepared in advance

Cocktail Mussels

Almost all the preparation for this hors d'oeuvre may be done 24 hours in advance. Cocktail Mussels are a visual delight, flavored with a variety of savory sauces.

2 pounds mussels, scrubbed and beards pulled off
Mustard Salad Dressing (see page 255)
Red Pepper Mayonnaise (see page 252)
Pesto Salad Dressing (see page 255)
1 2-ounce jar red salmon roe
Lettuce or alfalfa sprouts

1. Prepare the mussels by following the directions in the Basic Steamed Mussels recipe through step 2. Let the mussels cool, then discard the top shells. The broth may be strained and frozen for a future use.
2. Top one third of the mussels with a scant spoonful of Mustard Salad Dressing, another third with Red Pepper Mayonnaise, and the final third with Pesto Salad Dressing. Garnish all the mussels with 3 or 4 grains of the salmon roe.
3. Arrange on a bed of lettuce or sprouts to prevent the shells from rocking.

Serves 6–8
May be prepared in advance

Mussels and beef have one characteristic in common: They are both good sources of protein. While a one-pound T-bone steak supplies 59 grams of protein, the same amount of mussel meat offers 65 grams. An acre of land can grow 300 pounds of beef, while an acre of sea can produce 300,000 pounds of mussel meat.

How to Prepare Octopus

Be sure to select an octopus under two pounds, as it will be more tender than a larger, more mature animal. It is likely to be sold cleaned; in some cases its thin purple skin will also have been removed.

Wash the octopus thoroughly and cut the eight arms away from the body. If the skin has not been removed, use a very sharp knife and your fingers to peel it away. The skin covering the suckers does not come off. Don't worry if bits of skin remain, as you can peel them off after cooking. Cut the arms into one-inch-long rings, discarding the very thin ends. Cut the body into bite-size pieces, and score the undersides of the pieces.

Bring a large pot of water to a boil, and drop in the pieces of flesh. Gently boil for 15 to 20 minutes. The water will turn a light purple, and the octopus pieces will become light pink. The meat will show some resistance and spring, almost like a cooked chicken heart. Drain and refresh under cold water. Peel away any remaining purple skin and fragments of membrane.

The octopus is now ready for marinating or for use in a stew.

Octopus and Squid Salad

FROM RISTORANTE TOSCANO, BOSTON

Chef Vinicio Paoli's recipe for seafood salad has been on the restaurant menu for several years. It might be one of the most unusual seafood salads you have ever tasted.

> 1 *pound octopus, prepared according to directions (see sidebar)*
> 1 *pound squid, cleaned and sliced into rings, tentacles left intact if small*
> 1 *pound shucked littleneck clams*
> 1 *cup fresh strained lemon juice*
> 1 *cup olive oil, preferably extra-virgin*
> *Lettuce leaves*

1. In 2 quarts of water in a 6-quart kettle, boil the octopus and clams until almost tender, 2 to 3 minutes, depending upon size. Add the squid and boil an additional 30 to 60 seconds until tender. Drain.
2. Mix the octopus, squid, clams, lemon juice and olive oil in a ceramic bowl. Refrigerate overnight.
3. Serve on beds of lettuce.

Serves 8

Fried Oysters

One of the best fried oyster recipes we tested! It is also good with octopus prepared according to direction on page 34.

> 6 ounces plain crackers, such as saltines, finely crushed (about 3 cups)
> 2 eggs
> 2 tablespoons milk
> 2–3 drops Tabasco
> 28 freshly shucked oysters, drained
> 1/2 cup vegetable oil
> 1/2 cup clarified butter (see page 273)
> Tartar Sauce (page 269), optional

1. Place the cracker crumbs on a large plate. In a medium bowl, beat the eggs, milk, and Tabasco until well blended. Add the oysters and toss thoroughly.
2. Remove the oysters, one at a time, and roll in the cracker crumbs to coat well. Place the oysters on a wire rack and refrigerate for 1/2 hour to help the crumbs adhere to the oysters.
3. Preheat oven to 200 degrees.
4. Heat a heavy skillet over medium-high heat until it is very hot. Add 1/4 cup oil and 1/4 cup clarified butter and heat. Add half the oysters, being careful not to overcrowd the pan. Cook gently 1 to 2 minutes. With a slotted spoon, turn the oysters and cook an additional 1 to 2 minutes.
5. With a slotted spoon, remove the oysters and drain on brown paper. Reserve in the warm oven. Cook the rest of the oysters in the remaining oil and butter. Serve as is or accompanied by Tartar Sauce.

Serves 4
Must be partially prepared in advance

How to Open an Oyster

Method 1: Use a folded towel or potholder to protect your hand. Place the thick side of the oyster down on a flat surface. Push the tip of an oyster knife between the halves of the shell, near the hinge. Pry upward. Slide the knife around the top shell to release the muscle holding the shells together. Be careful not to puncture the oyster itself. Remove and discard the top shell. Slide the knife under the oyster to sever the bottom muscle.

Method 2: If the oysters are to be served cooked, placing them in the freezer for about 10 minutes will make them easier to open. Remove and shuck immediately, following Method 1.

Method 3: Hold the oyster in your left hand, hinged end pointing out. Insert the pointed end of an ordinary can opener into the hinge and pry up until the muscle releases the top and bottom shells. Finish separating the shells with an oyster knife and then slide the knife under the oyster to sever the bottom muscle.

Few foods are better nutritionally balanced than oysters. Six oysters will supply more than the U.S. RDA of copper and iron and half the RDA of iodine.

Ostriche con Polenta

FROM SPIAGGIA RESTAURANT, CHICAGO

Oysters on the Half Shell
Oysters on the half shell
should be opened
immediately before serving,
according to the directions
on page 35. Place the
oysters on a bed of chipped
ice or divide them among
individual serving plates.
They may be served with
Cocktail Sauce (page 258),
another sauce of your
choice, or just a squeeze of
lemon juice. Count on at
least six oysters per
serving, but in our
experience, true oyster
lovers will eat upwards of a
dozen. At one formal party
we gave, eight people ate
10 dozen oysters! This was
only hard on the person
who was shucking the
oysters.

No single food item has
more legend or love tales
connected with it than the
oyster. Known as the
ultimate aphrodisiac, it is
rumored that Casanova ate
fifty per day.

"It was a bold man that first
ate an oyster." —Jonathan
Swift

This delicious recipe for Oysters with Polenta comes from
Chef Anthony Mantuano. The pleasant mingling of flavors is
complemented by the simple taste of the polenta. Serve it
as an appetizer at a special dinner. To make the polenta, a
heavy saucepan and a wooden spoon are essential.

> ¼ cup unsalted butter (½ stick), plus 2 tablespoons
> at room temperature
> 1 cup sliced shiitake mushrooms
> 2 tablespoons finely chopped leeks, white part only
> 2 tablespoons minced oil-preserved sun-dried
> tomatoes
> 2 tablespoons minced fresh parsley
> ¼ cup dry vermouth
> ¼ cup dry white wine
> 12 freshly shucked oysters
> Salt and freshly ground black pepper to taste
> 1 recipe Polenta (see recipe below)

1. In a large skillet, melt ¼ cup butter over medium
   heat. Add mushrooms and leeks and sauté briefly
   until the leeks are lightly colored. Add the tomatoes,
   parsley, vermouth, and white wine. Simmer until the
   mixture is reduced to about ½ cup. The recipe may
   be prepared 24 hours in advance up to this point.
   Keep the mixture tightly covered in the refrigerator;
   gently reheat before continuing.
2. Add the oysters and continue to cook, stirring, until
   the edges of the oysters begin to ruffle, about 2 to 3
   minutes. Taste and add salt and pepper to taste. Remove from the heat and add the remaining 2 tablespoons butter.
3. To serve, ladle about ¼ cup polenta onto each of 4
   warm serving plates. Divide equal amounts of the
   oyster mixture over the polenta.

Polenta

> ½ cup water
> ⅓ cup yellow cornmeal
> 1 ⅓ cups chicken stock

1. Combine the cornmeal and water in a small bowl.
2. Bring the stock to a boil in a small saucepan over
   high heat. Reduce heat to low and stir in the cornmeal mixture. Continue stirring and do not leave un-
   attended for more than a minute or it will stick to

the pan. After 15 to 20 minutes the polenta will pull away from the bottom of the pan while you are stirring. Serve immediately, as it will begin to set quickly. This recipe makes 1 cup of polenta.

Serves 4
May be partially prepared in advance

Broiled Oyster and Mushroom Appetizer

This delicious appetizer uses duxelles, a classic French recipe used in combination with many meat, game, or fish dishes. The duxelles may be made whenever mushrooms are a good buy and frozen for up to 2 months.

> 1 *recipe Duxelles (see recipe below)*
> 24 *freshly shucked oysters left on half-shell*
> 1/2 *cup freshly grated Gruyère cheese*

1. Preheat broiler to medium-high. Arrange the oven rack so that the oysters will be 4 inches from the heating element.
2. Arrange the oysters in a large pan or pans on a bed of rock salt or crumpled aluminum foil to prevent them from tipping over.
3. Place 1 teaspoon of duxelles on top of each shucked oyster. Sprinkle grated cheese on top, evenly divided between the oysters.
4. Broil until the cheese is lightly browned and the oysters are bubbly. Serve at once.

Serves 4

Duxelles

> 3 *tablespoons unsalted butter*
> 1/2 *cup finely chopped onion (about 1 medium)*
> 1 *pound minced mushrooms, including stems*
> 1/4 *teaspoon freshly ground black pepper*
> 1 *tablespoon fresh strained lemon juice*
> 2 *teaspoons minced shallots*
> 1/4 *cup Madeira wine*
> 1/2 *cup heavy cream*

1. Melt the butter in a large skillet over moderately high heat until the foam subsides. Add the onion and sauté until transparent, stirring occasionally.

Charcoal-grilled oysters are easier to cook than a hamburger. As with all grilling, however, cooking time depends on the intensity of the heat and the distance of the grill from the coals. We recommend the grill be positioned 3–4 inches above red-hot, but not flaming, coals. The oyster shells will open after 4 to 8 minutes. Serve with one of our emulsified butter sauces.

Larousse Gastronomique defines duxelles as a kind of mushroom hash. It has many uses in cooking and can easily be kept on hand in the refrigerator for up to 10 days or frozen for up to 2 months.

"Seeing is deceiving; it's eating that's believing" —James Thurber

2. Stir in the mushrooms, pepper, lemon juice, and shallots. Cook over medium-high heat, stirring frequently until quite dry, being careful not to burn the mixture. Stir in the Madeira and let it evaporate.
3. Reduce the heat to medium, add the cream, and mix well. Continue to cook over medium-low heat, stirring frequently. When most of the liquid has evaporated, the mixture is ready to use or freeze. You will have ³/₄ to 1 cup of duxelles.

Note: If you wish to freeze the duxelles, cool it first. Spoon rounded teaspoonfuls onto a cookie sheet or aluminum foil and place them in the freezer. When hard, transfer to a plastic bag or box. Seal securely and freeze.

Serves 4
May be partially prepared in advance

Oysters Jezebel

Jalapeño peppers and oysters are a winning combination to serve as an appetizer. For variation try recipe with other mollusks.

    1 *small green pepper*
    3 *small jalapeño peppers, or 3 tablespoons minced*
      canned jalapeños
    1 *tablespoon minced garlic*
    ¹/₄ *cup pine nuts (pignolia) or slivered almonds*
    6 *tablespoons freshly grated Parmesan or Romano*
      cheese
    6 *tablespoons minced fresh cilantro*
    1 *tablespoon fresh strained lime juice*
    ¹/₂ *cup vegetable oil*
    Freshly ground black pepper (optional)
    16 *freshly shucked oysters, left on the half-shell*

1. Roast the green pepper and fresh jalapeño peppers under a broiler or over a gas flame, turning until the skin is charred on all sides. Immediately pop into a brown paper bag and close. Leave for 20 minutes, then slip the skins off, remove seeds, and cut into 1-inch squares. (If using canned jalapeños, omit the charring.)
2. In a food processor or blender, puree the peppers,

No need to purge oysters of sand: just open and eat.

Oysters are fully cooked when their edges begin to ruffle. N*ever, never* overcook.

The old adage about not eating oysters during the months that have no R's makes sense on two counts. First, summer is the time when oysters are spawning. As a conservation measure, they should not be eaten at this time. A second reason for avoiding them from May to August is that this is the season when red tide occasionally occurs in the waters off New England. Red tide is a population explosion, or bloom of toxic phytoplankton (single celled plants), which affects mussels, oysters, and clams. Although the toxin does not harm the shellfish that accumulate it, it is extremely dangerous to humans who consume the affected species.

garlic, nuts, 3 tablespoons of the cheese, coriander, and lime juice. Add the vegetable oil in a thin slow stream. Taste and add black pepper if desired. The sauce may be prepared up to 24 hours in advance.

3. Before serving, preheat oven to 400 degrees. Preheat the broiler if it is separate from the oven unit.

4. Arrange the oysters in a large pan on a bed of rock salt or crumpled aluminum foil to prevent tipping over. Spoon a tablespoon of sauce over each oyster and bake in the preheated oven for 6 minutes. Remove and sprinkle the remaining 3 tablespoons cheese evenly over the oysters. Switch the thermostat to broil or transfer the oysters to the broiler unit. Broil 3 inches from the heat source for 1 to 2 minutes, or until the oyster tops begin to brown. Serve immediately.

Variation: The oysters can be prepared without their shells by substituting 1/2 pint of oysters. Place 3 or 4 oysters with a spoonful of their liquor in 4 small oven proof ramekins. Top with the sauce and proceed with the recipe. Serve with French bread for soaking up the sauce.

Serves 4
May be partially prepared in advance

Oyster Stew

For some reason, oyster stew is synonymous with cozy Sunday night suppers. Accompany the soup with a bowl of crisp oyster crackers and a tossed green salad. Complete your hassle-free menu by serving fruit and cheese for dessert.

1/4 *cup unsalted butter (1/2 stick)*
1 *pint shucked oysters, undrained*
1 *cup milk*
1 *cup light cream*
1/2 *teaspoon salt*
1/8 *teaspoon freshly ground black pepper*
2 *tablespoons minced fresh parsley for garnish*

1. Place the butter, oysters, milk, cream, salt, and pepper in the top of a double boiler over boiling water. Heat until the butter is melted and the oysters float on top. The stew is done when the edges of the oysters are ruffled.

2. Sprinkle with parsley and serve hot.

Serves 4

"No matter how good the oyster stew, it's not worth eating with the wrong people." —Anon.

Oyster stew is best cooked in a double boiler to prevent overcooking.

The rough, heavy shells of the oyster are unequal in size; the bottom shell is cupped to contain the animal, while the top shell is flatter and forms a tight seal with the lower shell. During the first stages of an oyster's development, it is a microscopic free-swimming animal. When it reaches the "spat" stage, no bigger than the head of a pin, it finds a hard surface, such as an old oyster shell, and cements itself down for life.

Virginia Ham and Oyster Pie

Traditionally, scalloped oysters are served as an accompaniment to "Virginia" or "country dry cured" ham, but this pie combines the flavors very neatly all in one dish.

The thick-shelled Atlantic oyster (*Crassostrea virginica*) is a bivalve found along the Atlantic coast from the Gulf of Saint Lawrence to the Gulf of Mexico. The oyster's size and shape are determined by local conditions, and its name is often different depending on its location. There are Canadian Malpeques, Cape Cod Cotuits, Long Island Blue Points, Chesapeake Chincoteagues, and Florida Apalachicolas.

¼ *pound cooked Virginia ham, cut in ½-inch dice*
3 *tablespoons unsalted butter*
2 *cups sliced mushrooms (about ½ pound)*
½ *cup chopped onion*
½ *cup chopped scallions, including 2 inches of the green portion*
¼ *cup flour*
½ *teaspoon salt*
¼ *teaspoon cayenne pepper*
1 *pint shucked oysters, drained*
¼ *cup minced fresh parsley*
1 *tablespoon fresh strained lemon juice*
1½ *cups flour*
2¼ *teaspoons baking powder*
¼ *teaspoon salt*
3 *tablespoons unsalted butter*
½ *cup milk*

Oysters attach themselves to rocks or lie on the sea bottom where they form large oyster beds. They are unable to move, but they can be dislodged by wave action.

1. Melt 3 tablespoons in a large skillet. Add the diced ham and sauté until heated through. Remove the ham with a slotted spoon and drain on paper towels. Add the mushrooms, onions, and scallions to the butter remaining in the pan. Cover and simmer 5 minutes, or until tender. Blend in the ¼ cup flour, ½ teaspoon salt, and cayenne. Stir in the oysters, ham, parsley, and lemon juice. Transfer the oyster mixture to a greased 9-inch pie plate and reserve. The recipe can be prepared to this point 6 hours in advance.

In general, oysters reach market size in three to four years.

2. Preheat oven to 400 degrees.
3. Sift 1½ cups flour, baking powder, and salt together. Cut in the 3 tablespoons of butter until the mixture resembles coarse crumbs. Add the milk all at once. Mix until a soft dough forms. Turn onto a lightly floured surface and knead gently 5 or 6 times. Shape into a ball.
4. Roll the dough into a 9-inch circle to fit on top of the pie plate. Cover the oyster mixture with the topping. Score the topping.

Approximately 90 million pounds of oysters are harvested annually in the the U.S.

5. Bake for 20 to 25 minutes, or until the topping is lightly browned. Cut the pie in wedges and serve immediately.

Serves 6
May be partially prepared in advance

Seviche

Using scallops in this recipe instead of fish brings a new flavor and texture to Seviche.

 1 *pound bay scallops, rinsed, drained, and patted dry*
 2 *hot green chili peppers, seeded and thinly sliced (about 2 tablespoons)*
 2 *hot red chili peppers, seeded and thinly sliced (about 2 tablespoons), or 1 teaspoon dried red pepper flakes*
 1/3 *cup finely sliced onion (about 1 medium)*
 1 *cup fresh strained lime juice*
 1 *teaspoon salt*
 Lettuce leaves
 3 *tablespoons minced fresh cilantro (optional) for garnish*

1. In a glass bowl, combine the scallops, red and green chilies, onion, lime juice, and salt. Toss to coat the scallops thoroughly with the lime juice mixture, cover with plastic wrap, and refrigerate overnight or up to 24 hours.
2. Drain, taste and correct seasoning, and arrange on a bed of lettuce. Sprinkle with coriander and serve.

Variations: Shortly before serving, add 1/3 cup of peeled, seeded, and chopped tomato and 1/2 cup of cubed avocado.

Try this recipe with a variety of fin fish.

Serves 4
Must be prepared in advance

There are three varieties of scallops found along our East Coast—the sea scallop, the calico scallop, and the bay or cape scallop. Of these the first two are mechanically harvested. The latter can be hand-harvested since they live close to shore.

The small calico scallop (*Argopecten gibbus*) is a close relative of the bay scallop and is gaining popularity in the seafood market. Thousands of pounds of this scallop are harvested off the coast of Florida and northward to South Carolina. Calicos have become a plentiful substitute for bay scallops, but their small size requires that you are careful not to overcook. They are available fresh in retail markets throughout most of the year.

Scallop and Mussel Soup

This shellfish soup offers two unexpected bonuses. It can be prepared the night ahead through step 3. And, in spite of tasting so rich, it only requires one-half cup of cream—a mere smattering of calories.

1 *pound sea scallops, rinsed and drained*
4 *pounds mussels, scrubbed and beards torn off*
3 *tablespoons unsalted butter*
1/2 *cup finely chopped onion (about 1 medium)*
3 *tablespoons minced shallots*
1/2 *cup finely chopped carrot (about 1 medium)*
1/8 *teaspoon dried thyme*
1 *bay leaf*
2 *teaspoons salt*
1 *pinch cayenne pepper*
2 *medium tomatoes, peeled, seeded, and chopped*
  (about 1 pound)
Fish stock (see page 277) or bottled clam juice
1/2 *cup whipping cream*
1/2 *teaspoon saffron, crumbled*

1. Cut the scallops in half crosswise, retaining round shape. Place them in a container, cover, and refrigerate until ready to use.
2. Prepare the mussels following the Basic Steamed Mussels recipe through step 2 but dividing the quantities in half. When cool, remove the meat from the shells, cover with plastic wrap, and refrigerate. Reserve the mussel broth and discard the shells.
3. Meanwhile, in a 6-quart kettle, melt the butter over low heat. Add the onion, shallot, and carrot, and cook, stirring, until they are soft but not brown. Add the thyme, bay leaf, salt, cayenne pepper, and tomatoes, and continue to cook, partially covered, over low heat, until most of the juices have evaporated. Remove and discard the bay leaf.
4. Strain the mussel stock through a fine-meshed sieve and measure; add enough fish stock or clam juice to make 2 1/2 cups. Pour the stock over the vegetables and bring to a boil. Reduce heat and mix in the cream and saffron. Simmer, partially covered, for 20 minutes.
5. Add the scallops and simmer about 5 minutes. Taste and adjust seasoning. Add the mussels and simmer about 3 minutes or until just heated through. Ladle into soup bowls and serve with warm French or sourdough bread.

The large Atlantic sea scallop (*Placopecten magellanicus*) is found in deep water from Labrador to North Carolina. Generally, these scallops are shucked at sea and processed on the fishing vessel. The edible white muscle of this scallop freezes well, which makes it available year-round.

Variations: This soup is equally successful using a combination of shellfish and fin fish, or using just fin fish. It is best to use mild-flavored fishes such as haddock, cod, or monkfish. Poach the fish briefly before adding it to the soup base in step 5. Be sure to save the poaching liquid and use it to make up the 2 1/2 cups of stock.

The soup may also be prepared without the cream, if desired.

Serves 6 as an entree; 8 as an appetizer
May be partially prepared in advance

Scallop and Mussel Soup en Croute

Puff pastry makes a dramatic presentation of our soup. It is surprisingly easy to stage if you use one of the excellent commercial frozen puff pastries available at the supermarket.

1 *recipe Scallop and Mussel Soup, chilled*
1 *17-ounce package frozen puff pastry, defrosted according to package directions*
2 *eggs*
4 *tablespoons water*

1. Divide the cold soup among 6 one-cup ovenproof soup bowls, making sure it does not come higher than 3/4 inch from the top of the bowl.
2. Roll the pastry out to 1/8-inch thickness on a floured surface and cut 6 rounds 1 1/2 inches larger than the diameter of the soup bowls.
3. Make an egg wash by beating together the eggs and water. Brush the pastry lightly with the wash and place it over the top of the bowls, egg side down. Press firmly to the sides of the bowls, being careful not to break the pastry. Brush the remaining egg wash on top of the rounds and place the bowls on a baking sheet.
4. Refrigerate at least 1 hour, or up to 2 hours.
5. Preheat oven to 425 degrees.
6. Bake for 20 minutes, or until the pastry is puffed and golden brown. Serve immediately.

Serves 6 as an entree; 8 as an appetizer
Must be prepared in advance

"Soup of the evening, beautiful soup."—*Alice's Adventures in Wonderland* by Lewis Carroll

43

Hunan Scallop Soup

The combination of tastes—the brandy, gingerroot, and sesame oil—gives the scallops a unique flavor. This soup is especially attractive when served in clear glass bowls. Try the recipe with firm-fleshed white fish, such as members of the cod family, instead of, or in combination with, the scallops.

1 *pound bay scallops, rinsed and drained*
4 *tablespoons cornstarch*
6 *cups chicken stock*
2 *peeled slices fresh gingerroot (size and thickness of a quarter)*
4 *tablespoons brandy*
$1/2$ *teaspoon salt*
$1 1/2$ *cups Chinese cabbage, shredded (about $1/2$ cabbage)*
$1/2$ *teaspoon oriental sesame oil**
Freshly ground black pepper
2 *tablespoons sliced scallion, including green section*
$1/4$ *cup shredded ham (about $1/8$ pound)*
$1/4$ *cup sliced fresh mushrooms, sliced paper-thin (about $1/8$ pound)*

*Available in Chinese market or specialty section of your food store.

1. Dredge the scallops in cornstarch and shake in a strainer to remove the excess.
2. In a 3-quart saucepan, heat the chicken broth, ginger, brandy, and salt. Bring to a boil and add the cabbage. Reduce heat and simmer, uncovered, for 2 minutes. Return to a boil and add the scallops, stirring until bubbles begin to appear on the surface. Remove from heat and whisk in the sesame oil. Cover the pan and let sit for 2 minutes. Taste for seasoning and add pepper and additional salt, if desired.
3. Pour the soup into a heated tureen and scatter the scallion, ham, and mushrooms decoratively on top.

Serves 6

Bay scallops inhabit relatively shallow water and can often be found in sandy bays hiding in the eel grass.

Small bay scallops (A*rgopecten irradians*) are harvested from Canada south to the Gulf of Mexico; those that grow in the waters around Cape Cod and the islands of Nantucket and Martha's Vineyard, called "cape" scallops, are the sweetest and tastiest. Cape scallops command a high price but are well worth it, as their season is short (from November through March) and availability is limited.

Warm Scallop Salad

Bursting with fresh flavors, this salad is a marvelous warm weather entree. Cooking is minimal and the contrast of warm scallops on crunchy cool greens flavored with mint is utterly refreshing.

1/3 cup olive oil
2 teaspoons minced shallots
2 tablespoons fresh strained lemon juice
3/4 teaspoon salt
1/2 teaspoon freshly ground black pepper
2 medium tomatoes, peeled, seeded, and chopped (about 3/4 pound)
3 tablespoons minced fresh mint leaves
1 pound bay scallops or halved sea scallops, rinsed, drained, and patted dry
2 tablespoons unsalted butter
1 bunch watercress, large stems removed
1 bunch arugula, large stems removed
1 Belgian endive, leaves separated

1. Heat the olive oil in a 10-inch skillet. Add shallots and sauté over moderately low heat for 2 minutes, or until soft. Add the lemon juice, 1/2 teaspoon salt, and pepper. Remove from heat and add the tomatoes and mint. Set the dressing aside. The recipe may be prepared 2 hours in advance to this point. Hold the dressing at room temperature.
2. When you are ready to finish cooking, melt the butter in another skillet over medium-high heat. Sauté scallops for 3 to 5 minutes, depending upon their size, turning often. When they are slightly translucent in the middle, remove them from heat. Pour half the dressing over the scallops and toss to coat. Taste for seasoning and add the additional 1/4 teaspoon salt and pepper to taste, if desired.
3. Divide the watercress, arugula, and endive among individual serving plates. Mound the scallops into the center of each plate. Spoon additional dressing around the scallops and serve.

Serves 6 as an appetizer; 4 as an entree
May be partially prepared in advance

A scallop lives 20 to 26 months, unless it falls prey to one of its few natural enemies, or to a human.

There are numerous religious and literary references to scallops. The Greek goddess, Aphrodite, rose from the sea in a scallop shell, which symbolizes her beauty. Botticelli's famous *Birth of Venus* depicts this mythological event.

Broiled Garlicked Scallops

Scallops, broiled with a touch of garlic, are pleasing to any palate. The use of lemon juice and sherry, which combine with the cooking juices, adds just the flavor we were looking for.

7 *tablespoons unsalted butter*
1 *teaspoon minced garlic*
1 *tablespoon minced shallots*
2 *teaspoons fresh strained lemon juice*
1 *tablespoon dry sherry*
3/4 *cup fine, fresh, untoasted bread crumbs,*
  preferably homemade
1/3 *cup minced fresh parsley*
1/4 *teaspoon salt*
Freshly ground black pepper
1 *pound bay scallops or quartered sea scallops,*
  rinsed and drained

1. Preheat the broiler. Adjust the oven rack about 6 inches from the broiler element.
2. In a small skillet, melt 4 tablespoons butter over medium heat, then sauté the garlic and shallot until wilted, about 5 minutes. Add the lemon juice and sherry. Cook 1 minute and remove from the heat.
3. Combine the garlic mixture with the bread crumbs, parsley, salt, and pepper in a large shallow bowl. Mix well. Roll the scallops in this bread crumb mixture to coat them on all sides.
4. Place the scallops in a lightly oiled, shallow 8-inch pan, or 4 lightly oiled scallop shells. Melt the remaining 3 tablespoons butter and drizzle it over the scallops.
5. Broil the scallops 5 minutes. If the crumbs brown too quickly, lower the oven rack and cover the pan loosely with aluminum foil. Serve hot.

Serves 4

The shell of the scallop is closed by a single large muscle, which is the only portion eaten in the U.S. In many other countries, scallop roe is considered a delicacy.

Scallops Provençal

Robust Mediterranean flavors spike this scallop dish. Serve it with pasta or rice and a green salad garnished with oil-cured black olives. Other shellfish, such as shrimp or squid, would be equally delicious in this recipe. We also think it would be excellent with small chunks of pollock, red snapper, swordfish, or shark.

3 tablespoons unsalted butter
2 teaspoons minced garlic
2 teaspoons minced shallots
1 tablespoon fresh strained lemon juice
1/2 cup dry white wine
3 medium tomatoes, peeled, seeded, and chopped
    (about 1 pound)
1/4 teaspoon salt
1 1/2 pounds bay scallops or quartered sea scallops,
    rinsed and drained
Freshly ground black pepper
Minced fresh parsley for garnish

1. Melt the butter in an enameled 12- to 14-inch skillet over medium heat. Sauté the minced garlic and shallots until tender, about 5 minutes. Add the lemon juice, wine, tomatoes, and salt and cook 2 minutes. Add the scallops and cook until just opaque, about 3 to 5 minutes. Taste for seasoning and add black pepper, if desired.
2. Serve sprinkled with parsley.

Serves 4

Scallops are hermaphrodites; that is, both sexes are present in the same individual.

Scallops with Red Pepper Sauce

The ease of preparation, the color, and wonderful flavor combine to make this a favorite for a dinner party. The sauce may be made in advance or even frozen.

> 2 *tablespoons unsalted butter*
> 2 *pounds sea scallops, rinsed and drained*
> 1/4 *teaspoon salt*
> 1/4 *teaspoon freshly ground black pepper*
> 3/4 *cup dry white wine*
> 2 *tablespoons medium-dry sherry*
> 1 *cup heavy cream*
> 1/2 *cup Red Pepper Sauce (see recipe below)*

1. Melt the butter in a 12-inch skillet over medium-high heat. Add the scallops, salt, and pepper, and cook, stirring, until just opaque, up to 5 minutes. With a slotted spoon, transfer the scallops to a bowl and keep warm.
2. Pour the wine and sherry in the skillet and reduce until slightly syrupy, about 7 minutes. Whisk in the cream and juices from the scallop bowl. Boil until slightly thickened, stirring occasionally. Whisk in the Red Pepper Sauce and heat thoroughly. Return the scallops to the pan, adjust the seasonings, and serve immediately.
3. The scallops may also be served on top of a pool of sauce, arranged on warm plates.

Red Pepper Sauce

> 2 *pounds sweet red peppers*
> 1/4 *cup unsalted butter (1/2 stick)*
> 2 *tablespoons sugar*
> 2 *tablespoons cider vinegar*
> 1/8 *teaspoon cayenne pepper*
> 1 *teaspoon Hungarian paprika*
> *Pinch of salt*

1. Roast the peppers under a broiler or over a gas flame, turning until the skin is charred on all sides. Immediately place the peppers in a brown paper bag and seal tightly. Leave for 20 minutes. Slip the skins off, remove the seeds, and cut into 2-inch dice.

The delicate, sweet scallop is delicious raw, so it follows that overcooking will only diminish its succulence. Sauté bay or calico scallops no longer than 3 minutes and the larger sea scallops no more than 5 to 7 minutes.

2. Melt the butter in a skillet over low heat. Add the peppers, sugar, vinegar, cayenne, paprika, and salt, and cook, covered, until the peppers are soft, about 50 minutes. Stir occasionally. Uncover the pan, increase heat to medium, and stir until all liquid evaporates. Watch carefully so the peppers do not brown.

3. In a food processor fitted with a steel knife, puree the peppers until smooth.

4. The sauce may be stored, covered, in the refrigerator for one week or frozen for up to 3 months. You will have 1 1/2 cups of sauce.

Variation: Make Scallops in a Pastry Scallop Shell using the recipe and your favorite pie crust dough. Roll the dough 1/8-inch thick and press it into 6 large shells. Trim edges. Press 6 more large shells into the pastry-lined shells. Refrigerate 1/2 hour. Bake at 400 degrees for 20 minutes. Carefully remove the top shells and bake 5 minutes longer or until the pastry is golden. Cool, then remove pastry from shells. To serve, reheat pastry shells for 5 minutes at 275 degrees and fill them with the Scallops in Red Pepper Sauce.

Serves 6
May be partially prepared in advance

It is always a good idea to rinse any fresh fish product in cold water, and then pat dry with paper toweling before proceeding with a recipe.

Szechuan Squid Salad

This squid salad will delight those who enjoy food with a hint of peppery heat. The colorful combination of yellow and red peppers with the white squid is at its most appealing when served on a glass plate.

1-¼ pounds prepared squid
1 large stalk celery, diagonally sliced in ¾-inch sections
2 tablespoons red wine vinegar
2 teaspoons fresh strained lemon juice
2 tablespoons soy sauce
2 tablespoons oriental sesame oil*
¾ teaspoon chili oil*
2 teaspoons grated gingerroot
2 teaspoons minced garlic
½ teaspoon sugar
¼ teaspoon salt
½ sweet red pepper, cored, seeded, and cut in thin strips
½ sweet yellow pepper, cored, seeded, and cut in thin strips
2 tablespoons minced fresh cilantro leaves**
Lettuce leaves

*Available in Chinese markets or the specialty section of your supermarket.

1. Cut each squid in half lengthwise and score each piece. Cut into pieces about 1 inch square. If the tentacle clusters are large, separate them; leave them whole if they are small. The squid may be prepared up to 4 hours in advance to this point.
2. Boil 2 quarts of water and add the squid. Boil 1 to 3 minutes or until just opaque, then remove with a slotted spoon, drain in a sieve or colander, and refresh under cold water. Lightly pat dry with paper toweling, place in a covered container, and refrigerate several hours or overnight.
3. Bring the water back to a boil and add the celery. Boil 30 seconds, remove with a slotted spoon, drain in a sieve or colander, and refresh under cold water. Transfer to a covered container and refrigerate several hours or overnight.
4. In a small bowl, blend together the vinegar, lemon juice, soy sauce, sesame oil, and chili oil. Add the gingerroot, garlic, sugar, and salt. Stir until the sugar and salt dissolve. Set aside.

Squid is a highly specialized member of the phylum Mollusca. The remnants of its shell, a thin, chitinoid, pen-shaped structure, is found embedded in the squid's body.

5. One hour before serving, toss the squid, celery, and peppers together with the soy–vinegar mixture. Add the coriander and toss again.
6. Serve the salad on lettuce leaves.

**Note: If you cannot find fresh cilantro, you may substitute Italian parsley. Cucumber may be substituted for the celery, but remove the seeds and do not blanch.

Variations: Soak 3 or 4 dried Chinese mushrooms or cloud ears in warm water to soften for 20 minutes. Drain and cut out tough stems. Slice in strips and add to recipe in step 5.

Cut 10 wonton skins into strips ¼-inch wide. Heat enough vegetable oil in a wok or skillet to deep-fry them, and fry until golden brown, about 15 seconds. Toss into salad just before serving.

Shrimp, mussels, surimi, and scallops, used separately or in combination, are also excellent choices for this salad, as are the firm-fleshed fish of chapters 4 & 5.

Serves 4 as an entree; 6 as an appetizer
Must be prepared in advance

How to Clean Squid
1. Place the squid on a flat surface and peel off the thin spotted skin from the body section. Pull the head, tentacles, and intestines from the body; they should all come out in one piece.
2. With a sharp knife, sever the tentacles from the head and intestines. Remove the hard beak from the middle of the tentacles. Discard the head and intestines.
3. Remove the translucent cartilage or "pen" from the center of the body and discard.
4. Rinse the body and tentacles well. Cook as is, or slice the body into rings and separate the tentacles if they are large.

Hoover's Squid Salad

Hoover was the New England Aquarium's famous talking seal who loved squid. He lends his name to this ideal summer meal. All the cooking can be done several hours in advance, and the squid can be prepared the night before. Although we love the texture and taste of fresh pasta, we recommend dry pasta for this dish because it stands up better to all the tossing of ingredients.

1 *pound prepared squid, sliced into rings, tentacles separated if large*
1 *pound fusilli or cavatelli pasta*
1 *tablespoon vegetable oil*
1/2 *cup celery, cut in matchsticks (about 1 stalk)*
1 *small zucchini, cut in matchsticks (about 1/3 pound)*
1/2 *cup diced sweet red or yellow pepper, cored and seeded (about 1/2 medium)*
1/2 *cup Vinaigrette (see page 256)*
1/4 *cup chopped fresh basil, or 1 teaspoon dried basil**
3 *tablespoons minced fresh parsley*
1/2 *cup black olives, pitted and sliced in half*
1/4 *cup freshly grated Parmesan cheese*
Salt and freshly ground black pepper to taste
Basil sprigs for garnish

1. Cook squid in 2 quarts of boiling water for 1 to 3 minutes until opaque. Drain, and when cool, refrigerate and cover.
2. Cook pasta "al dente" (barely tender), according to package directions. Drain and rinse with cold water. Place in a bowl of cold water with the tablespoon of vegetable oil and set aside.
3. Blanch celery and zucchini in boiling salted water for 30 seconds. Drain and immediately refresh with cold water. Blot dry with paper towels. The recipe can be prepared to this point several hours in advance.
4. Drain the pasta and blot dry with paper towels. Toss with the vinaigrette, in a large bowl. Add the celery, zucchini, red or yellow pepper, fresh basil, parsley, olives, and cheese and toss again, thoroughly. Taste for seasoning and add salt and pepper, if desired. Add squid and toss again.
5. Serve on a large platter, garnished with the basil sprigs.

Although we love the texture and taste of fresh pasta, we recommend dry for this dish, because it stands up better to all the tossing.

Squid are the favorite food of the New England Aquarium seals.

*Note: If you are using dried basil, add it to the vinaigrette 2 hours before serving.

Variations: This recipe works well with shrimp, or a combination of squid, shrimp, and scallops. Or, be adventuresome and use leftover chunks of cooked swordfish, mahi mahi, tuna, salmon, or shark.

Browned pine nuts (pignolia) sprinkled over the salad just before serving complements the other ingredients. Use about 6 tablespoons.

Serves 4–6
May be partially prepared in advance

Carib Calamari

This carefree entree is a breeze to prepare. The bean sprouts give an unexpected and welcome crunch.

1/4 cup vegetable oil
1 cup thinly sliced scallions, including 2 inches of the green section
3 tablespoons soy sauce
1/2 teaspoon sugar
1 teaspoon minced garlic
3 or 4 drops Tabasco sauce, or more if you like "heat"
1 pound cleaned squid, sliced into rings
1 cup fresh bean sprouts
Hot cooked rice

1. Heat the oil in a heavy skillet over moderate heat. Stir in the scallions, soy sauce, sugar, garlic, and Tabasco. Add the squid and sauté about 3 minutes, until it is firm and opaque.
2. Stir in the bean sprouts and cook 2 more minutes, stirring occasionally.
3. Serve with hot rice.

Variation: Use one pound of cleaned octopus, cut into small pieces, as a substitute for the squid. The tastes will be similar.

Serves 4

The fastest-swimming of all invertebrates, the squid has a large head with strong jaws and a relatively large brain. It will shoot out a cloud of dark ink when threatened.

Artists have used squid ink in sepia drawings for ages. A recent use has been in the production of a black pasta, using the ink for flavoring and color.

Stuffed Native Squid with Linguine and Marinara Sauce

FROM APLEY'S RESTAURANT, BOSTON

Jeffrey Worobel of Apleys Restaurant in The Sheraton Boston sent us this recipe. An innovative combination of sausage, lobster, and squid produces a hearty meal guaranteed to lift spirits on the most formidable of winter nights. Although this recipe may seem involved, almost all of it can be prepared at least 24 hours in advance.

6 tablespoons olive oil
1 teaspoon minced shallot
$^1/_2$ teaspoon minced garlic
$^1/_4$ pound small white mushrooms, finely chopped
2 tablespoons dry white wine
12 prepared squid, unsliced, tentacles chopped
$^1/_4$ pound smoked sausage such as chorizo, cut in small dice
$^1/_4$ pound cooked lobster meat, cut in small dice
$^1/_4$ pound bread cubes, cut in $^1/_4$-inch dice, lightly toasted
2 tablespoons strained fresh lemon juice
1 egg yolk, slightly beaten
$^1/_2$ teaspoon salt (optional)
$^1/_2$ teaspoon freshly ground black pepper (optional)
1 recipe Linguine with Garlic Butter (see recipe below)
1 recipe Marinara Sauce (see recipe below)

Frozen squid is available in the supermarket, already cleaned. It is as good as fresh, and lots easier.

1. In a 12-inch skillet, heat 2 tablespoons olive oil over moderate heat and lightly sauté the minced shallots and garlic. Add the mushrooms and white wine. Heat through. Add the chopped squid tentacles, moving them around the pan with a wooden spoon, just until they become opaque.
2. Add the sausage, lobster, bread cubes, and lemon juice, stirring continuously until the lemon juice is absorbed. Quickly add the egg yolk to bind the mixture. Remove from heat. Season with salt and pepper to taste. Allow to cool.
3. Stuff the squid bodies with the sausage and lobster mixture about half full, as they will shrink in cooking. The recipe may be completed to this point 24 hours in advance. Refrigerate the stuffed squid.

4. When you are ready to finish cooking, preheat oven to 350 degrees.
5. In a large skillet, heat the remaining ¹/₄ cup olive oil. Place the stuffed squid in the pan, leaving enough room for them to roll about. Keep tossing until all sides are lightly brown.
6. Transfer the skillet, covered, to the oven and bake for 7 minutes. Serve the stuffed squid on a bed of the linguine and topped with the sauce.

Linguine with Garlic Butter

1 *pound linguine*
¹/₂ *cup unsalted butter (1 stick)*
2 *teaspoons minced garlic*
¹/₄ *cup minced fresh parsley*

1. Cook the linguine in boiling salted water "al dente" (barely tender), according to package directions.
2. While the linguine is cooking, melt the butter in a small skillet over low heat. Sauté the garlic until soft. Stir in the parsley. Remove from heat.
3. Drain the linguine into a large bowl. Pour the garlic/parsley butter over it and toss well.

Marinara Sauce

2 *tablespoons olive oil*
1 *teaspoon minced garlic*
2 *tablespoons finely chopped onion*
1 *tablespoon chopped fresh basil, or 1 teaspoon dried basil*
1 *16-ounce can Italian tomatoes, chopped, undrained*
Salt and freshly ground black pepper to taste

1. In a small saucepan, warm the olive oil over moderate heat. Sauté the garlic and onion until transparent, about 5 minutes. Add the basil, oregano, and can of tomatoes. Stir well and cook for 15 minutes over medium heat. Season to taste with salt and pepper.
2. Refrigerate up to 48 hours, if you wish. Gently reheat in a saucepan prior to serving.

Serves 4–6
May be partially prepared in advance

Contrary to a common misconception, squid never has a rubber-band consistency unless it is overcooked.

Calamari Vinaigrette

FROM THE DAILY CATCH, BOSTON

The original family-owned Daily Catch, a tiny restaurant in Boston's Italian North End, has always specialized in calamari or squid. Although the restaurant has now given birth to several branch operations, it is still known best for its excellent ways with this mollusk.

4 tablespoons butter (¹/₂ stick)
2 tablespoons olive oil
2 teaspoons minced garlic
2 medium onions, cut in half lengthwise, sliced thin
    and separated (about 1 ¹/₂ cups)
15–20 medium-size mushroom caps (stems removed
    and reserved for another use)
¹/₄ cup dry white wine
Freshly ground black pepper
2 pounds prepared squid, sliced into rings, with
    tentacles
1 teaspoon unseasoned soft bread crumbs, preferably
    homemade
1 tablespoon freshly grated Romano cheese
4 teaspoons red wine vinegar

1. In a 12-inch skillet, over moderate heat, melt the butter with the oil. Add the garlic and sauté until lightly browned, being careful it does not burn. Toss in the onion slices and mushroom caps and sauté until lightly browned, stirring frequently.
2. Pour in the white wine, raise the heat, and cook, stirring constantly, until the liquid is reduced by half. Season with black pepper to taste. The recipe can be prepared to this point up to 24 hours in advance and refrigerated. If so, bring back to a gentle simmer before continuing.
3. Reduce the heat and gently stir in the squid. Add the bread crumbs, a pinch at a time, until the liquid thickens. Cook gently for 3 minutes. Sprinkle in the grated cheese and vinegar. Continue cooking until the squid appears opaque and firm, about 3 minutes. Do not overcook or the squid will toughen.

Serves 4
May be partially prepared in advance

Squid has many virtues. It is high in protein and relatively inexpensive, and while it is plentiful, it is underutilized. Popular in Mediterranean cultures, squid is beginning to develop a following in the United States.

Backfin or lump crabmeat consists of whole pieces of meat from the large body muscles that operate the swimming legs. It is the most prized and most expensive portion of the crab.

Crustaceans: Crabs, Crayfish, Lobster, and Shrimp

CRAB

The hard outer parts of such crustaceans as shrimp, lobster, and crabs are not really made up of true shell. Of the "shellfish," only the mollusks (clams, snails, etc.) deserve the name. The protective exoskeletons of crustaceans are made of chitin, a material similar to our fingernails.

Most crustaceans dwell in the sea, but a few, such as crayfish, live in fresh water. Several tropical crabs and the common gray "pill bugs" of our back yards are the only land-living crustaceans.

The sweet white meat of lobsters, shrimp, and crabs comes from the parts where powerful muscles are needed: the tails of the shrimp and lobsters and the claws of lobsters and crabs.

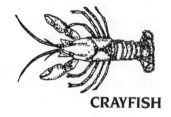

CRAYFISH

St. Michael's Crab Salad

This recipe comes from St. Michael's, Maryland, a lovely town on the eastern shore of the Chesapeake Bay, where the Maryland, or blue, crab has been prized for centuries. If you cannot get blue crab, any fresh crabmeat will do.

LOBSTER

1 *pound fresh Maryland lump (backfin) crabmeat, picked over, shells and cartilage removed*
3/4 *cup diced celery (about 2 stalks)*
2 *tablespoons fresh strained lemon juice*
1 *teaspoon salt*
1/4 *teaspoon freshly ground black pepper*
1 *teaspoon capers (more, if desired), rinsed and drained*
3 *tablespoons minced fresh parsley*
3 *tablespoons mayonnaise*

SHRIMP

1. In a large bowl, combine the crabmeat and celery, gently tossing with your hands. In another bowl, thoroughly mix the lemon juice, salt, pepper, capers, parsley, and mayonnaise.
2. Add the mayonnaise mixture to the crabmeat and toss gently. Cover and refrigerate until serving time. The salad can be made 10 to 12 hours in advance, if you wish.

Serves 2
May be prepared in advance

Why is a crab so crabby? She grows 1/3 of her size in a couple of hours, sheds out of her skin and has to walk around in her bones 15 or so times in her lifetime. She only has a lifespan of 2–3 years and then someone is likely to throw her in boiling water while still alive. Anyone would be crabby after that. —*Beachcombers Handbook* by Hugh Zachary

57

Madras Seafood Salad

Crabmeat may be used in this salad, but the donor of this recipe advises us to use surimi, which is sometimes sold as seafood legs or imitation crab. Do not spare the curry powder. The incendiary powder of the curry tends to diminish slightly when the salad is refrigerated.

> $1^{1}/_{2}$ pounds crabmeat, fresh, frozen, or canned,
>   picked over, shell and cartilage removed
> $^{3}/_{4}$ cup mayonnaise, preferably homemade
> $1^{1}/_{2}-2$ teaspoons curry powder
> $^{3}/_{4}$ cup finely chopped sweet red or green pepper
>   (about 1 pepper)
> $^{1}/_{4}$ cup minced fresh cilantro
> 8 drops Tabasco sauce
> 1 tablespoon chopped chutney
> $^{1}/_{4}$ cup slivered blanched toasted almonds
> Lettuce leaves
> 2 oranges, peeled and sectioned
> 6 small bunches of grapes, red seedless preferred

1. In a large bowl, combine the crabmeat, mayonnaise, curry powder, pepper, coriander, Tabasco, and chutney. Taste and add more curry powder if needed. Refrigerate for up to 4 hours.
2. Just before serving, stir in the almonds. Make a bed of salad greens on each plate and spoon a mound of crab salad in the center. Decorate the salads with orange sections and grapes.

Variations: Use Madras Crab Salad as an hors d'oeuvre. Serve on crackers or as a dip with vegetables.

Present the salad on a slice of cantaloupe. Cut a crosswise slice of melon, about $^{1}/_{4}$ inch thick, seeds removed, and pile the salad into the center.

For an added touch, freeze the small bunches of grapes. You will find they are a refreshing companion to the spicy curry, and an interesting textural contrast.

Serves 4
Must be prepared in advance

The blue crab is found from Massachusetts to northern South America and has been introduced in the Mediterranean. Its scientific name, *Callinectes sapidus*, is perfectly suited, for it means tasty beautiful swimmer. A pair of paddle-shaped legs at its rear allow it to swim, rather than walk as the other crabs do. Its meat is generally thought to be best of all the species of crabs.

The Japanese have made surimi for hundreds of years. It usually is made from Alaskan pollock. After the fish is minced and cooked, salt, sweeteners, flavors, and flavor enhancers are added that may mimic scallops, crab, lobster, or shrimp. The surimi is then extruded into various shapes and tinted with color. In the United States, surimi is usually marketed as imitation crabmeat, seafood legs, or ready-to-heat-and-eat fried products.

Surimi is generally low in calories and fat, yet high in protein. It is relatively inexpensive and sold frozen in most markets. Persons with shellfish allergies should check the label carefully, as some surimi products may contain crab, lobster, or shrimp essence to give a more authentic flavor.

Maryland Crab Soup

Old Bay Seasoning is a must for this soup. It is made in Baltimore and contains a mixture of seasonings—celery salt, mustard, bay leaves, cloves, ginger, paprika, and more.

> 8 *cups beef stock, preferably homemade*
> 2 *teaspoons Old Bay Seasoning (or more, to taste)*
> 1/2 *teaspoon dried crushed red pepper flakes*
> 1/2 *teaspoon salt*
> 1/2 *teaspoon black pepper*
> 1 *cup diced carrots (about 2)*
> 1/2 *cup chopped onion (about 1 medium)*
> 1 *cup chopped celery (about 2 stalks)*
> 1 *cup inch-long sliced green beans*
> 3 *tablespoons tomato paste*
> 1 *teaspoon Worcestershire sauce*
> *Leftover steamed crab legs, claws, and outer shells*
> 1 *pound fresh or frozen crabmeat, picked over, shells and cartilage removed*
> 1 *cup fresh or thawed frozen peas*

1. In a 6-quart kettle, heat the beef stock, Old Bay Seasoning, red pepper flakes, salt, black pepper, carrots, onion, celery, beans, tomato paste, Worcestershire sauce, and leftover crab legs, claws, and shells. Bring to a boil, reduce heat, and simmer, uncovered, for 30 minutes. Add extra stock if necessary. The recipe can be prepared 24 hours in advance up to this point. Keep tightly covered in the refrigerator and return to the boiling point before proceeding with the recipe.
2. Add the crabmeat and peas, and continue to simmer until the peas are cooked through, about 5 to 7 minutes. Taste and correct seasoning. Remove shells before serving.

Serves 6
May be partially prepared in advance

Steamed Crabs
Add 2 cups of vinegar, a bay leaf, and some peppercorns to a large kettle of boiling water. If you like a spicy taste, add a "crab boil mixture" to the pot. Toss in 24 Atlantic blue crabs and bring the water back to boil. Cook for 10 minutes or until crabs are bright red.

The shelf life of fresh steamed crab is three to five days. Pasteurized crabmeat has a shelf life of six months.

Eating fresh crab is part of the summertime culture in coastal Maryland. Fresh crabs are in season from April to December, although the summer months produce the most prolific catch. Crabbers rise at 4:00 A.M. to set their trot lines (long cords baited with salted eel), and they continue their runs until 10:00 A.M. Their catch is then transported in wicker bushel baskets to the dock where it is sold to retail markets. Local stores have the freshly caught crab for sale by early afternoon.

Sautéed Soft-Shell Crabs

FROM THE HARVEST RESTAURANT, CAMBRIDGE,
MASSACHUSETTS

How to Prepare Soft-Shell Crabs
Kill the crab by sticking the point of a sharp knife into the body between the eyes. Lift and fold back the tapering points on each side of the back shell and remove the spongy substance underneath. Then, turn the crab on its back and remove the piece of shell that ends in a point, called the apron. The crab is now ready to be cooked.

For commercial purposes, soft-shell crabs must be caught before they begin to molt. Called "peelers" by the watermen, they are placed in special shedding floats and checked every four to five hours. Once they molt, they are immediately plucked from the float, packed in ice and eel grass, and shipped to fine restaurants and fish markets, where they are available fresh or frozen.

Both hard- and soft-shell blue crabs are marketed. The entire body of the soft-shell crab, including the shell, may be eaten after dressing and cooking.

This crab recipe with Lime Coriander Beurre Blanc was created by Chef Michael Hann. Using this recipe through step 4 is a good basic method for cooking soft-shell crabs.

1–1½ cups milk
8 medium soft-shell crabs, cleaned
1½ cups flour
1 teaspoon salt
½ teaspoon white pepper
3 tablespoons unsalted butter, plus ½ cup butter, cut in ½-inch pieces
3 tablespoons vegetable oil
1 teaspoon minced shallot
½ teaspoon minced garlic
¼ cup packed fresh cilantro leaves
3 tablespoons fresh strained lime juice
3 tablespoons white wine
Freshly ground black pepper to taste

1. Preheat oven to 250 degrees.
2. Pour the milk into a flat dish large enough to hold the crabs in one layer, and soak them for 15 minutes. Drain the crabs, discard the milk, and lay the crabs on paper toweling to drain some more.
3. Combine the flour, salt, and white pepper in a large shallow bowl. Lightly dredge the crabs in the flour mixture, shaking off any excess.
4. In a heavy 12-inch skillet or sauté pan, melt 3 tablespoons butter over low heat. Add the oil, mix well, and increase the heat to medium-high. Place the crabs on their backs in the pan and sauté until golden, about 4 minutes. (Do not crowd the crabs in the pan.) Turn and sauté about 4 more minutes. Transfer to a baking sheet lined with paper toweling and hold in the oven while sautéing the rest of the crabs. Discard any cooking oils remaining in the pan.
5. Add the shallots, garlic, cilantro, lime juice, and white wine to the pan. Cook until the liquid is reduced to 1 tablespoon, about 10 minutes. Remove from the heat and swirl in the remaining butter, piece by piece, whisking continuously, until the sauce thickens. Taste and adjust the seasoning if necessary. Add black pepper if desired. Arrange the

crabs on a preheated platter and serve the sauce over them.

Serves 4

Deviled Crab

An old favorite and easy to make. May be frozen!

4 tablespoons unsalted butter (¹/₂ stick)
¹/₂ cup fresh bread crumbs, preferably homemade
2 tablespoons flour
1 cup milk, scalded
Dash cayenne pepper
1 tablespoon Worcestershire sauce
1 teaspoon fresh strained lemon juice
2 egg yolks, lightly beaten
¹/₄ cup dry sherry
1 pound crabmeat, fresh, frozen, or canned, drained, picked over, shells and cartilage discarded

1. Melt 1 tablespoon of the butter in a small skillet, add the bread crumbs, and cook over moderate heat, stirring frequently. When golden brown, set aside.
2. In a large skillet, melt the remaining 3 tablespoons of butter over moderate heat. Add the flour and cook, stirring, for 2 minutes. Add the milk and stir until the sauce thickens. Mix in the cayenne pepper, Worcestershire sauce, and lemon juice.
3. Remove the sauce from heat, add the beaten egg yolks, and blend well. Return to heat and cook for 3 minutes. Do not boil. Stir in the sherry. Remove the pan from heat and gently fold in the crabmeat.
4. Divide the crabmeat mixture evenly among 4 individual buttered ramekins or small baking dishes. Refrigerate several hours or freeze if desired. Thaw before baking.
5. When ready to cook, preheat oven to 450 degrees.
6. Sprinkle the reserved bread crumbs on top of the crabmeat and bake for 20 minutes.

Serves 4
May be prepared in advance

Jonah crabs and rock crabs are closely related and similar in appearance and taste. The Jonah crabs, however, have larger claws that are sometimes sold separately.

The red crab is red to deep orange before cooking. An underexploited species, it is generally sold as cooked, picked, frozen meat.

King crab inhabit very cold waters; Alaska is the most important fishing territory for this species.

Crab/Shrimp Boil
This is a combination of seasonings to add flavor to the cooking water for crab or shrimp. Tie the seasonings in a cheesecloth bag yourself, or buy a packaged mix. The following spices are usually in the mix: mustard seed, coriander seed, red pepper flakes, bay leaves, dill seed, cloves, and allspice.

Crab Cakes

Crab cakes are good anytime, especially with cole slaw and beer. We suggest the following simple guidelines to make our crab cakes truly sublime. (1) Use only the best-quality lump (backfin crabmeat. (2) If you don't sauté the cakes over too high a heat or cook them longer than necessary, you will have very tender crab cakes.

3 eggs
1 tablespoon mayonnaise
1 tablespoon sour cream
2 tablespoons minced fresh chives
1/2 teaspoon salt
1/4 teaspoon freshly ground black pepper
1 tablespoon grated onion
2 cups cracker crumbs
4–5 drops Tabasco or hot pepper sauce
1 pound lump (backfin) crabmeat, picked over,
    cartilage and shells discarded
1/2–1 cup vegetable oil
1/2 cup unsalted butter (1 stick)
Lemon wedges
Tartar Sauce (see page 269)

1. Beat 1 egg. Combine it with the mayonnaise, sour cream, chives, salt, pepper, grated onion, 1 cup of the cracker crumbs, and hot sauce. Mix well. Gently fold in the crabmeat, handling it as little as possible. With your hands, form the mixture into cakes approximately 2 inches in diameter and 3/4 inch thick.
2. In a shallow dish, beat the remaining 2 eggs. Dip the crab cakes into the eggs on all sides, then roll them in the remaining cracker crumbs. Arrange on a tray lined with wax paper and chill the cakes at least 1/2 hour, or up to 4 hours.
3. In a heavy 12-inch skillet, heat the oil and butter together over moderately high heat. (There should be about 1/4 inch of fat in the skillet.) When the butter begins to foam, add the crab cakes. (Do not crowd them; do them in two batches, if necessary.) Sauté the cakes about 3 minutes per side, until golden. Drain on paper towels and serve immediately, with lemon wedges and tartar sauce.

Serves 4
Must be partially prepared in advance

Male and female blue crabs migrate up bays or estuaries during the spring and summer. In late summer, after mating takes place, the female swims back downstream to spawn. She will lay 2 million eggs, of which only two or three will grow to maturity.

Male crabs, also called jimmys, are used to prepare steamed crab. Female crabs, called she-crabs or sooks, are usually sent to the crab houses to be sold as picked meat.

Seafood Gumbo

FROM CAJUN YANKEE RESTAURANT, CAMBRIDGE, MASSACHUSETTS

This hearty peppery soup from Chef John Silberman is a splendid winter chill-chaser. Serve it with a garlicky green salad and a loaf of chewy bread.

Roux

3/4 cup vegetable oil
3/4 cup flour
1 cup chopped onion (about 1 large)
1/2 cup chopped celery (about 1 large stalk)
3/4 cup chopped green pepper (about 1 small)
2 bay leaves

1. In a heavy cast-iron skillet, heat the oil until it is very hot. Slowly add the flour, stirring constantly. Cook the roux over medium heat until it is a dark reddish brown, stirring constantly. This will take about 25 minutes. Be very careful not to let it burn.
2. Remove from heat and add the chopped onion, celery, and pepper. Return to the heat and cook 1 minute, stir in the bay leaves, and set aside.

Soup

3/4 cup unsalted butter (1 1/2 sticks)
2 cups chopped onions (about 2 large)
2 cups chopped celery (about 4 large stalks)
2 cups chopped green peppers (about 2 large)
2 cups chopped fresh okra, or 2 10-ounce packages of frozen orka, thawed and chopped
5 cups fish stock (see page 277)
1 cup pureed canned tomatoes
1 teaspoon minced garlic
1 1/2 teaspoons paprika
1–1 1/2 teaspoons cayenne pepper
1/2 teaspoon freshly ground black pepper
1/2 teaspoon white pepper
1/2 teaspoon dried thyme
1/2 teaspoon dried oregano
3 bay leaves
1 Recipe Roux (see recipe above)
1 pound crabmeat, fresh, frozen, or canned, drained, picked over, shells and cartilage discarded
1 1/2 pounds crayfish, heads removed, shelled and deveined, or shrimp, shelled and deveined

Until recently, no one thought of cultivating crayfish. However, spurred by a rising demand for this crustacean, it is now farmed very successfully in several southern states. Many thousands of pounds are shipped abroad to Sweden for their annual crayfish festival in August.

1. Melt the butter over medium heat in a 4-quart stock-pot. Add onions, celery, green peppers, and okra. Cook about 15 minutes, stirring occasionally until softened. Add the fish stock and tomatoes and simmer for 30 minutes. Add the garlic, paprika, 1 teaspoon of cayenne, white and black pepper, thyme, oregano, and bay leaves. Cook 15 minutes.
2. Bring the mixture to a rolling boil and blend in the roux with a whisk. Reduce heat and simmer 15 minutes. Add the crabmeat and crayfish or shrimp and simmer for 3 to 5 minutes. Taste and add additional cayenne if desired.
3. Serve in large soup bowls. The Cajun Yankee serves their Seafood Gumbo over cooked white rice.

Variations: Gumbo may also be made with oysters, substituting ½ pint shucked oysters for the crabmeat.

Any leftovers can be thinned out with the addition of fish or vegetable stock and served as a first course.

Serves 6

Freshwater crayfish resemble their lobster relatives but are smaller. They live in freshwater rivers and streams where they burrow into banks and feed on live and decaying animals and plants.

In France they are called *écrevisse* and the term *Nantua* indicates their presence in a recipe. In the United States they are called both crayfish and crawfish. Whatever the name, they are small freshwater crustaceans similar in looks to a miniature lobster.

Penne Con Scampi

FROM MICHELA'S RESTAURANT, CAMBRIDGE, MASSACHUSETTS

Chef Todd English calls for langoustine in this recipe. We think that crayfish or large shrimp will work just as well, and they are more easily available. The creative vegetable sauce, featuring beans, is an unusual, delicious, and healthy way to sauce the penne pasta and the crustaceans.

¼ cup plus 2 tablespoons extra-virgin olive oil
8 ounces dried beans (6 ounces navy beans, 2 ounces pinto beans)
1 large carrot, chopped (about ¾ cup)
1 medium onion, chopped (about ½ cup)
2 stalks celery, chopped (about ½ cup)
2 teaspoons chopped garlic (about 2 cloves)
2 tablespoons chopped fresh rosemary or 1½ to 2 teaspoons dried rosemary
1½ quarts chicken stock
Salt and freshly ground black pepper to taste

1 tablespoon dried red pepper flakes (optional)
2 tablespoons butter
16 langoustine (or crayfish tails or large shrimp,
    shelled and deveined)
1 pound penne, cooked according to package
    directions
3/4 cup freshly grated Parmesan cheese
3 tablespoons chopped Italian parsley

1. In a large kettle heat the 2 tablespoons of olive oil over medium heat. Add the beans, carrots, onion, celery, garlic, and rosemary. Cook 3 to 5 minutes. Add the chicken stock and simmer until the beans break apart, about 1 1/2 hours.
2. Transfer the mixture to a food processor fitted with the steel knife and process until smooth. Blend in the remaining 1/4 cup olive oil. Sprinkle in salt and pepper to taste and red pepper flakes. The recipe may be prepared to this point in advance.
3. When you are ready to complete preparation, melt 1 tablespoon of the butter in a large skillet over medium heat. Lightly sauté the langoustine (or crayfish tails or shrimp) about 2 to 4 minutes, until just opaque. Sprinkle in salt and pepper to taste. Add the bean sauce and then the cooked and drained penne. Toss well to blend thoroughly. If the sauce needs to be thinned, add a little of the pasta water.
4. Remove from the heat and stir in the Parmesan, the remaining 1 tablespoon butter, and the parsley. Serve immediately.

Serves 6
May be partially prepared in advance

Langoustine, a tiny lobster that is imported from Europe, is also known by several other names. They include Norway lobster, Dublin Bay prawn, Danish lobster, and scampi—all members of the family *Nephropidae*. To add to the confusion, in the United States, scampi usually refers to large shrimp prepared with garlic and butter.

Crayfish Etouffé

A wonderful do-ahead entree, Crayfish Etouffé's flavors mellow if it is made 12 to 14 hours in advance. A deep brown roux is essential to the success of the dish.

Crayfish or Shrimp Stock

Heads and shells from 2 pounds crayfish or large
    shrimp (save meat for main body of recipe)
1 cup white wine
1 cup fish stock, clam juice, or water
¹/₂ cup coarsely chopped onion (1 small)
¹/₂ cup coarsely chopped celery (1 large stalk)
Herbal bouquet of 4 sprigs parsley, ¹/₈ teaspoon
    dried thyme, 3 peppercorns, and 1 clove smashed
    garlic, tied together in a cheesecloth sack

1. At least 1 hour before preparing the étouffé recipe, place all the stock ingredients in a nonaluminium saucepan and bring to a boil. Reduce heat to a simmer and cook for 45 minutes, skimming off the foam occasionally. Strain through a fine-mesh sieve, pressing hard on the solids to extract all the liquid. Measure stock and add additional wine, fish stock, or clam juice to equal 2 cups.

Yield: 2 cups

Etouffé

1 cup unsalted butter (2 sticks)
¹/₄ cup vegetable oil
¹/₄ cup flour
³/₄ cup sliced scallions, including green section
1 cup finely chopped onion (about 1 large)
¹/₂ cup chopped green pepper (about ¹/₂ large)
¹/₂ cup chopped celery (about 1 large stalk)
4 teaspoons minced garlic
¹/₄ teaspoon dried thyme
1 teaspoon dried basil
1 8-ounce can tomato sauce
¹/₂ teaspoon pepper
2 teaspoons salt
2 cups Crayfish or Shrimp Stock (see recipe above)
1 tablespoon Worcestershire sauce
Dash Tabasco sauce
2 tablespoons cognac (optional)

1 tablespoon fresh strained lemon juice
2 teaspoons grated lemon rind
2 pounds crayfish or large shrimp, heads removed, shelled, and deveined
1/4 cup minced fresh parsley

1. In a heavy skillet, melt 1/2 cup butter with the oil. Slowly add the flour and stir constantly over medium heat until the mixture or roux becomes dark brown, about 25 minutes. Be careful that the roux does not burn.
2. Add the remaining 1/2 cup butter, 1/2 cup of the scallions, onion, pepper, and celery. Cook until tender, about 15 minutes. Add the garlic, thyme, basil, tomato sauce, pepper, salt, stock, Worcestershire sauce, and Tabasco. Simmer uncovered, stirring occasionally, for 1 hour. Replenish the liquid if necessary, using wine, water, or fish stock. Add the cognac, lemon juice, and lemon rind and cook for 5 more minutes.
3. The recipe may be prepared in advance up to this point. Refrigerate mixture up to 24 hours. Gently reheat before proceeding.
4. Add the crayfish or shrimp and simmer until cooked, about 3 to 5 minutes. Serve over white rice and sprinkle with the minced parsley and the remaining 1/4 cup scallions.

Serves 8
May be partially prepared in advance

Lobster Bisque

FROM MAISON ROBERT, BOSTON

The American or Maine lobster, *Homarus americanus*, is found in the wild from Labrador to North Carolina. This popular crustacean is easily distinguished from the spiny lobster of California, Florida, and Africa by its two large claws. These big claws are used for crushing and tearing food, while the other four pairs of slender legs are used for walking.

Usually a mottled green and reddish brown, the Maine lobster may have a light tan and brown coloration called calico. The rarest color is the blue lobster, occurring in one in twenty million lobsters.

In most states, the minimum size of a lobster that can be legally taken from the sea is 3³/₁₆ inches. However, the size soon will be increased by a small increment. The measurement is taken from the eye socket back to the point where the tail begins.

This recipe comes from Chef Lucien Robert, owner of Maison Robert, a French restaurant in Old City Hall, in Boston. The delicate flavor of this bisque may be spiced up with more cayenne pepper.

6 tablespoons unsalted butter
¹/₂ cup finely diced carrots
¹/₃ cup finely diced onion
¹/₂ cup finely diced celery
¹/₄ teaspoon dried thyme
1 small bay leaf
3 sprigs parsley
6 lobster carcasses*
¹/₂ teaspoon salt
¹/₄ teaspoon freshly ground black pepper
2 tablespoons cognac
¹/₂ cup white wine
4 cups fish stock (see page 277)
¹/₃ cup raw rice
³/₄ cup cream
Cayenne pepper

*The term lobster carcass refers to the front part of the lobster, the portion that is left when the claws and tail have been removed. Chef Robert uses fresh uncooked carcasses in his restaurant; however, cooked carcasses are more readily available in fish markets. When using cooked carcasses, use an additional 2 or 3 carcasses.

1. In a large skillet, melt 1 tablespoon of the butter and cook the carrots, onion, celery, thyme, bay leaf, and parsley until the vegetables are soft. Add the lobster carcasses and cook over high heat until they become red. Season with the salt and pepper and splash with the cognac and white wine. Ignite the liquid and continue to cook until reduced by two-thirds. Add ¹/₂ cup of the stock and cook for 10 minutes.
2. Meanwhile, in a separate pan, cook the rice in 2 cups of the stock.
3. Remove the lobster carcasses from the kettle reserving the liquid, and pound in a mortar, or sieve in a food mill until they are well crushed. Combine the crushed carcasses, rice, vegetables, and cooking liquid. Rub through a sieve by pressing it with a wooden spoon, collecting as much puree as possible. Discard the shells and solids.

4. Pour the puree into a saucepan along with the remaining 1½ cups of stock and bring to a boil. Remove from the heat and strain through a fine sieve. The recipe can be prepared 24 hours in advance up to this point. Keep the mixture tightly covered in the refrigerator. Return to the boiling point before continuing.
5. To finish, just before serving, add the 5 remaining tablespoons of butter, one at a time, swirling until melted. Enrich with the cream. Correct the seasoning and add a large or small pinch of cayenne according to your preference. You may also garnish with pieces of fresh lobster meat.

Serves 6
May be partially prepared in advance

Lobster Salad

A good traditional way to serve lobster on a warm summer night or as an elegant luncheon dish at anytime of the year.

> ³/₄ *pound cooked lobster meat, cut into bite-size*
>   *pieces (about 1½ cups)*
> 1 *cup chopped celery (about 3 large stalks)*
> 2 *tablespoons thinly sliced scallion*
> 1 *3-ounce jar pimientos, drained and chopped*
> ¹/₄ *cup mayonnaise, preferably homemade*
> 2 *chopped hard-boiled eggs*
> *Freshly ground black pepper to taste*
> *Lettuce leaves*

1. In a bowl, combine the lobster, celery, scallion, and pimientos. Add the mayonnaise and mix thoroughly. Fold in the hard-boiled eggs. Taste for seasoning, adding pepper if necessary. Chill, covered, for at least 2 hours or up to 24 hours.
2. Serve on beds of lettuce leaves, or on French rolls or hot dog rolls that have been lined with lettuce leaves.

Serves 4
Must be prepared in advance

How to Boil Lobster

In an 8- to 10-quart pot, over high heat, bring about 8 inches of water to a full, rolling boil. A bay leaf, 1 teaspoon salt, and 8 to 10 peppercorns may be added. Put the live lobsters in the boiling water, one at a time, head first. Cover and return to a boil. Lower the heat so the lobsters are gently boiling and cook 12 to 15 minutes, until the lobsters are bright red. They are done when a leg detaches easily.

Four to six 1¼-pound lobsters can be cooked simultaneously in this manner. If you want to cook more, do not drain the water, but just remove the lobsters. Return the water to a boil, adding more water if necessary. Repeat the process with the additional lobsters.

After cooking, the broth can be strained through several layers of cheesecloth in a fine sieve and then reduced to one quart. The resulting reduction is a richly flavored stock base, which may be frozen in 1-cup containers and used when a rich shellfish stock is required.

Cold Lobster and Spinach Linguine Salad

FROM ALLEGRO RESTAURANT, WALTHAM, MASSACHUSETTS

This wonderful salad was contributed by Owner-Chef James Burke. The popularity of this restaurant encouraged James Burke to open a second Allegro on Boylston Street in Boston. The combination of fresh herbs, virgin olive oil, and lemon juice brings out the best in lobster.

2 1 1/4 pound live lobsters
1/4 pound fresh spinach linguine
2 tablespoons plus 1/2 cup virgin olive oil
salt and freshly ground black pepper to taste
2 tablespoons red wine vinegar
2 tablespoons fresh strained lemon juice
1/4 cup peeled, seeded, chopped, and drained tomato
    (about 1 small)
1 tablespoon chopped fresh basil
1 teaspoon minced fresh chervil
1/4 teaspoon minced garlic

1. Plunge the lobsters in a 6- to 8-quart pot of boiling water and cook, uncovered, for 6 minutes. Remove the lobsters and chill in ice water. When cool enough to handle, remove the meat from the tails and claws. Cut the tails in half, lengthwise. (Save the bodies for use in such recipes as Lobster Bisque.) Coat the pieces with 1 tablespoon of olive oil. Grill briefly over a charcoal or gas grill, allowing less time for the smaller pieces. Cut into bite-size pieces and refrigerate.

2. Place the pasta in a 6-quart pot of rapidly boiling water and stir with a fork to prevent sticking. Cook for 2 or 3 minutes, or until just tender or "al dente." Drain and transfer to ice water to chill. As soon as the pasta is cool, drain again and pat dry with paper towels. Place in a large serving bowl, toss with the remaining 1 tablespoon olive oil, and season to taste with the salt and pepper.

3. Meanwhile, prepare the vinaigrette. Whisk the remaining 1/2 cup olive oil, vinegar, and lemon juice in a small bowl. Stir in the tomato, basil, and chervil. Add the garlic and salt and pepper to taste, using more garlic if desired. The recipe can be prepared to this point one hour in advance. Leave the pasta and vinaigrette at room temperature.

"On unadulterate wine we here regale, and strip the lobster of his scarlet mail." —Gay, 1720

It takes more than six years for the lobster to reach its allowed market size.

There is no basis in fact of the belief that a large lobster (over 3 pounds) is tough. It will be tough only if overcooked.

70

4. Just before serving, add the lobster pieces to the pasta and toss to mix. Add only enough vinaigrette to lightly coat the pasta and lobster without soaking it. Toss well and serve.

Serves 4
May be prepared in advance

Charcoal-Grilled Lobster

Enjoy your summertime lobster without enduring a steamy kitchen! Grilled lobster is simple and quick. The aroma and taste are irresistible.

  2 *1 1/2 pound live lobsters*
  1 *cup simple butter sauce of your choice (see page 270)*

1. Prepare barbeque for grilling and light the coals.
2. Kill the lobsters either by severing the spinal cord at the juncture of chest and tail, or by dropping them into boiling water for 2 minutes, then transferring them to ice water to stop their cooking.
3. Split each lobster in half lengthwise and remove the stomach, tomalley, and coral.
4. Adjust the grill to 4 inches above the coals. Grill the lobster, cut-side down, for 6 to 7 minutes. Turn cut-side up, baste lightly with the butter sauce, and continue to grill 5 more minutes or until the flesh is firm and opaque.
5. Arrange two lobster halves on each plate and generously spoon the butter sauce over each piece.

Serves 2

Lobster Stew

A "pure" Maine lobster stew has only a few ingredients: lobster, butter, milk, and seasoning. It is very rich and very satisfying.

> 4 1¹/₄ pound live lobsters
> ¹/₂ cup unsalted butter (1 stick)
> 1 quart whole milk, or 2 cups milk and 2 cups
>   light cream
> Salt and freshly ground black pepper

1. Boil the lobsters as described on page 69. Remove the meat immediately, reserving the coral and tomalley. Cut the meat into large chunks.
2. Melt the butter in a heavy kettle, and sauté the coral and tomalley for 7 to 8 minutes. Add the lobster meat and cook 1 to 2 minutes. Remove from heat and cool slightly.
3. In a separate pan, heat the milk, or the milk and cream, but do not let it boil. Add the milk very slowly to the slightly cooled lobster, stirring constantly until the stew turns a rich salmon color.
4. Cool the stew, then "age" it in the refrigerator at least 5 hours but as long as 48 hours.
5. To serve, bring the stew slowly to just below a boil. Taste and add salt and pepper. Ladle into heated bowls and serve immediately.

Serves 4
Must be prepared in advance

A 2-¹/₂ pound lobster will yield less than ¹/₂ pound lobster meat, or about 1 cup.

The American lobster lives for about fifteen years, unless it is caught. It averages 10 inches in length and usually weighs between 2 and 5 pounds, although the record is 45 pounds. The female lays many thousands of eggs, usually every two years.

Chinese-Style Shrimp and Snow Peas

Stir-frying is the ultimate in fast food, if slicing, chopping, and mincing are done ahead of time. The foods can then be stored, covered tightly, in separate containers in the refrigerator.

> 2 tablespoons soy sauce
> 2 tablespoons sweet or cream-style sherry
> 3 tablespoons vegetable or peanut oil
> 1 tablespoon minced garlic
> 1 tablespoon minced gingerroot
> 1 pound medium shrimp, shelled and deveined (an equal amount of scallops or squid can be substituted, or a combination of all three)
> 1/2 pound mushrooms, thickly sliced
> 1 pound snow peas, ends trimmed ★ ✳
> 1/2 cup thinly sliced scallions, including 2 inches of green section
> 1 1/2 teaspoons cornstarch

1. Combine the soy sauce and sherry and set aside.
2. Heat the oil in a wok or a large skillet over moderate heat, until it is hot. Add the garlic and ginger and cook 30 seconds, stirring. (Do not allow to burn.) Raise heat to medium-high and add the shrimp. Stirring constantly, cook just until the shrimp turns opaque, 1 to 2 minutes. Add half of the sherry–soy mixture and the mushrooms. Cover and cook 2 minutes. Add the peas and scallions. Stir, cover, and cook an additional 2 minutes.
3. Blend the cornstarch into the remaining sherry–soy mixture, add to the shrimp and stir well. Cook until the sauce thickens, about 15 to 30 seconds. Serve immediately.

Serves 4

✳ could Substitute:
asparagus
regular peas
red pepper

How to Boil Shrimp
To cook one pound of unshelled shrimp, bring a quart of water to a boil. Drop the shrimp into water and cook until they begin to curl and the shells turn pink, about 3 to 5 minutes, according to size. Remove from heat, drain, and refresh with cold water. Do not overcook or the shrimp will toughen.

Shell and devein. To devein, cut a slit about 1/16-inch deep along the long curved outside edge of the shrimp, exposing the intestinal vein. Lift out the vein with a knife, and cleanse the area with cold running water. Pat the shrimp dry with paper towels and store in the refrigerator, covered, for no longer than 24 hours.

Shrimp Jambalaya

For years jambalaya has been a mainstay of the Cajun diet. Its name is derived from *laya*, an African word meaning rice, and *jamon*, which is Spanish for pork. It originated as a dish to use leftovers, with rice as a stretcher. Giant cauldrons were hauled to the Louisiana sugarcane fields where jambalaya was cooked and served to the people working there. This recipe is our version of this well-known stew—a hearty dish that can be prepared and served direct from the stove in a large enameled casserole or Dutch oven.

> ¹/₄ *cup vegetable oil*
> 6 *ounces smoked sausage, such as kielbasa, cut in* ¹/₄*-inch slices*
> 6 *ounces cooked ham, cut into* ¹/₂*-inch cubes*
> 1 *cup chopped onion*
> 1 *cup chopped green pepper (1 large)*
> 1 *cup chopped celery (about 2 stalks)*
> 1 *cup thinly sliced scallions, including 2 inches of green stem*
> 1 *tablespoon minced garlic*
> 1 *16-ounce can peeled tomatoes, drained, juice reserved*
> 1 *teaspoon dried thyme, crushed*
> 1 *teaspoon freshly ground black pepper*
> ¹/₄ *teaspoon cayenne pepper*
> 1 *teaspoon salt*
> 1 *cup raw white rice*
> 2 *cups chicken broth*
> 2 *tablespoons Worcestershire sauce*
> 2 *pounds large shrimp, shelled and deveined*

1. In a heavy enameled 6-quart casserole dish or Dutch oven, heat oil over moderate heat. Add the sausage and ham and brown, stirring frequently. Remove the meat with a slotted spoon, and set aside on paper toweling to drain.
2. Sauté the onion, pepper, celery, scallions, and garlic in the oil remaining in the casserole until soft, stirring occasionally.
3. Chop the drained tomatoes, then add them to the vegetable mixture. Stir in the thyme, black pepper, cayenne, and salt. Cook for 5 minutes over medium heat. Stir in the rice.
4. Combine the juice drained from the tomatoes, chicken broth, and Worcestershire sauce in a large measuring cup. If it does not amount to 2¹/₂ cups, add water. Pour into the casserole, bring to a boil,

Shrimp are sold according to size, based on the number of shrimp, with heads removed, per pound. Sizes suggested by the Massachusetts Division of Marine Fisheries are as follows:

Size Category	Count per Pound	
	Shell On	Peeled
Colossal	10/15	13-18
Jumbo	21/25	25-30
Extra large	26/30	31-36
Large	31/35	37-42
Medium	43/50	51-60
Small	51/60	61-72

then reduce heat, cover, and simmer for 15 minutes.

5. Add the sausage and ham and mix well. Simmer, covered, for 10 minutes. The recipe may be prepared 24 hours in advance up to this point. Tightly cover the dish and refrigerate. When you are ready to finish cooking, return the casserole to a simmer.

6. Add the shrimp and cook, covered, for another 5 minutes. Serve in shallow bowls or soup dishes.

Serves 8–10
May be prepared in advance

Shrimp New Orleans

This recipe was created for its donor by a New Orleans chef, for her engagement party over 50 years ago.

1 *clove garlic*
1/2 *cup finely chopped celery (about 1 medium stalk)*
1 *teaspoon minced fresh parsley*
2 *tablespoons thinly sliced scallion, including 2 inches of green section*
2 *teaspoons Dijon-style mustard*
2 *tablespoons prepared horseradish*
2 *tablespoons olive oil*
10 *drops Tabasco sauce (1/4 teaspoon)*
1/4 *teaspoon paprika*
1/2 *teaspoon salt*
2 *tablespoons fresh strained lemon juice*
1 *pound cooked large shrimp, shelled and deveined*

1. Cut the garlic in half and rub the cut sides against the sides of a large glass bowl.

2. Combine the celery, parsley, scallion, mustard, horseradish, olive oil, Tabasco, paprika, salt, and lemon juice in the bowl; stir to mix. Add the shrimp and toss well. Cover with plastic wrap and marinate in the refrigerator for at least 12 hours or for as long as 24 hours.

3. Bring to room temperature. Toss again and serve with toothpicks.

Serves 4–6
Must be prepared in advance

Save shrimp and lobster shells, storing them in the freezer until you are ready to make a stock.

There is no clear distinction between the terms "shrimp" and "prawn." If you see prawns on a menu in the United States, it is likely to mean large shrimp.

Scallop-Stuffed Shrimp

Delicate scallops and shrimp team up to make an elegant dinner entree, which can be prepared the night before. Potato chips are a surprise Ingredient here. Buy the best-quality salted brand you can find. Calico, or Florida, scallops are easy to use in this recipe, as they do not have to be chopped. Because the completed dish is rich, you need only a watercress salad with our Vinaigrette dressing (see page 256) and a colorful steamed vegetable to complete the meal.

2 *pounds jumbo shrimp, shelled and deveined*
1 *pound sea or bay scallops, coarsely chopped (or whole calico scallops)*
1 *cup cracker crumbs*
6 *tablespoons unsalted butter (3/4 stick), melted*
6 *tablespoons freshly grated Parmesan cheese*
6 *tablespoons crushed potato chips*
1 *tablespoon minced fresh cilantro for garnish*

Shrimp consumption in the U.S. is exceeded only by the consumption of tuna. Americans love shrimp.

Should shrimp be boiled shelled or unshelled? Is it necessary to devein shrimp? We prefer to cook shrimp unshelled as the shell imparts considerable flavor; and while eating the vein will bring you no harm, we prefer to devein the shrimp for aesthetic reasons.

1. Butterfly the shrimp by cutting them lengthwise through the center of their bodies just to the tail section and pressing the two sides open. Lightly butter a round baking dish and line with the shrimp, tails pointing toward rim. Top with the chopped scallops. The recipe may be prepared 24 hours in advance up to this point. Cover the dish and refrigerate.
2. When you are ready to cook, preheat oven to 350 degrees.
3. Sprinkle with the cracker crumbs and drizzle the melted butter over the top. Sprinkle with the grated Parmesan and crushed potato chips.
4. Bake, uncovered, for 30 minutes. Serve sprinkled with the cilantro.

Serves 4
May be partially prepared in advance

Shrimp Salad with Tomatoes and Goat Cheese

This recipe combines an interesting variety of flavors and texture. It may also be served as an appetizer, serving 8.

4–6 tomatoes, peeled (about 2 1/2 pounds)
1 recipe Pesto Sauce, made without Parmesan cheese (see page 262), or 1 cup sauce
2 tablespoons fresh strained lemon juice
3 tablespoons olive oil
24 imported small black olives, pitted
2 teaspoons thinly sliced scallion, including 2 inches of green stem
1 1/2 pounds cooked large shrimp (about 30), shelled and deveined
8 ounces mild goat cheese, such as Montrachet or Bucheron
1 head of Romaine lettuce, trimmed
4 tablespoons chopped fresh herbs, such as parsley, dill, or basil, in any combination
Freshly ground black pepper

1. Cut the tomatoes into quarters or sixths, depending upon their size. Set aside.
2. In a large bowl, combine the pesto, lemon juice, 2 tablespoons of the olive oil, olives, and scallion; mix until well blended. Gently fold in the tomatoes and shrimp. Crumble the cheese over the mixture. Cover with plastic wrap and refrigerate 2 to 4 hours.
3. Toss the lettuce with the remaining 1 tablespoon oil. Arrange the lettuce on 6 plates and divide the shrimp mixture evenly among them. Sprinkle with the fresh herbs and a grind of black pepper.

Serves 6
Must be prepared in advance

Shrimp is truly a universal seafood. Almost every coastal nation supports wild or cultured stocks.

Almost all shrimp sold in New England retail markets have been flash frozen aboard fishing vessels with the heads removed to make them less perishable. In New England, Maine shrimp are the only ones available fresh from December to March.

Grilled Shrimp with Basil, Saffron, and Tomatoes

FROM DEVON, WORLD TRADE CENTER, BOSTON

Combining a palette of warm colors—orange, pink, and red—Chef Daniel Weisel showcases simple grilled shrimp with a variety of sauces. For increased visual appeal, serve this dish on black plates.

4 tablespoons olive oil
2 bay leaves
1 tablespoon minced fresh parsley
1 tablespoon cracked black peppercorns
1 tablespoon coarsely chopped fresh basil
1 tablespoon coarsely chopped fresh thyme (or substitute celery leaves)
2 teaspoons minced garlic
3 tablespoons slivered shallots
1 1/2 teaspoons coarse salt
24 jumbo shrimp (about 2 1/2 pounds), shelled and deveined, shells reserved for Saffron Sauce
Cooked rice for 4
1 recipe Sautéed Fennel (see recipe below)
1 recipe Tomato Fondue (see recipe below)
1 recipe Saffron Sauce (see recipe below)
4 whole, unblemished basil leaves for garnish

1. Combine the olive oil, bay leaves, parsley, peppercorns, basil, thyme, garlic, shallot, and salt. Blend well.
2. Place the shrimp in a shallow container and cover with the marinade. Toss to coat the shrimp. Cover, refrigerate, and marinate for 5 to 6 hours.
3. Preheat broiler.
4. Remove the shrimp from the marinade with a slotted spoon, and drain. Discard the marinade. Thread the shrimp on skewers and broil about 3 to 4 inches from the heat for 2 or 3 minutes per side. Do not overcook.
5. Divide the boiled rice between 4 dinner plates. Lay 6 shrimp on top of each bed of rice. Arrange a portion of Sautéed Fennel and Tomato Fondue to each side. Spoon Saffron Sauce over the shrimp and garnish each plate with one perfect basil leaf.

Most people think of shrimp as pinky-orange in color. However, in their raw state they may be pink, brown, gray, dark green, or white.

Sautéed Fennel

1 *bulb fresh fennel (about ³/₄ cup sliced)*
1 *tablespoon olive oil*
1 *clove garlic, smashed*
1 *tomato (about ¹/₂ pound), peeled, seeded, and chopped*
Salt and freshly ground black pepper to taste

1. Cut the top from the fennel, and core. Slice into thin pieces and then cut into slivers. (Use scraps in Saffron Sauce.)
2. In a 10- to 12-inch skillet, heat the olive oil over moderate heat and add the garlic. Cook 2 or 3 minutes, making sure the garlic does not brown. Add the fennel and cook until tender, about 10 minutes, tossing frequently. Remove and discard the garlic. Add the tomato, season to taste with the salt and pepper, and cook until the tomato is heated through, about 2 minutes.
3. Keep warm until ready to serve. Or, if you choose, you may prepare the fennel up to 24 hours in advance and refrigerate, covered. Fifteen minutes before serving, warm in a covered pan over low heat or in a microwave oven. If you do make the fennel in advance, the tomato will look fresher if you add it as you rewarm the fennel.

Tomato Fondue

4 *medium-size tomatoes (about 1 ¹/₂ pounds), peeled, seeded, and coarsely chopped*
1 *sprig of fresh thyme, or ¹/₄ teaspoon dried thyme*
1 *clove garlic, smashed*
1 *teaspoon salt*
1 *teaspoon freshly ground black pepper*
1 ¹/₂ *tablespoons coarsely chopped fresh basil*

1. In a small, heavy saucepan combine the tomatoes, thyme, garlic, salt, and pepper. Cook over moderate heat, covered, for 3 to 4 minutes. Remove the cover and cook until most of the juices have evaporated, about 7 to 10 minutes. Add the basil.
2. Remove from heat. Discard the garlic and thyme sprig. Keep warm until ready to serve. Or, you may make it up to 24 hours in advance and refrigerate, covered. Fifteen minutes before serving, warm it gently in a covered pan over low heat or in a microwave oven. The recipe makes ³/₄ to 1 cup.

To many Americans, scampi is shrimp broiled with garlic and oil or butter. To a fishmonger or marine biologist, scampi is a Norwegian lobster with an Italian name.

Saffron Sauce

1 tablespoon olive oil
Reserved shrimp shells
1 cup chopped vegetables (onions, celery, carrots,
  and the fennel scraps)
1 cup port wine
1 cup white wine
1 cup fish stock (see page 277)
1 clove garlic, smashed
1 tablespoon coarsely chopped fresh basil leaves
1 tablespoon coarsely chopped fresh parsley
1 teaspoon coarsely chopped bay leaf
1 teaspoon coarsely chopped fresh thyme, or ¼
  teaspoon dried thyme
1 tomato, coarsely chopped (about ⅓ pound), or ¼
  cup canned Italian tomatoes, drained and chopped
½ cup heavy cream
½ cup unsalted butter (1 stick), softened
1½ teaspoons saffron threads, soaked in 1
  tablespoon white wine

The edible yield of shrimp is 50 percent. Crab and lobster are 20 percent. Shrimp are unusually rich in minerals and have a high iodine content.

1. Heat the oil over moderate heat in a 10- to 12-inch skillet. Sauté the shrimp shells for 3 minutes. Add the chopped vegetables and sauté for 3 more minutes.
2. Add the port and white wine. Boil until the liquid is reduced by half. Add the fish stock, garlic, basil, parsley, bay leaf, thyme, and tomato. Simmer ½ hour, skimming the stock of any gray foam as it cooks. After ½ hour, strain the stock into a separate pan, and reduce it over high heat, to 1 cup. The sauce may be prepared 24 hours in advance up to this point and kept tightly covered in the refrigerator. Heat it to a simmer before continuing.
3. Over low heat, whisk in the cream. Whisk in the butter, one tablespoon at a time, ensuring that each addition of butter is fully incorporated before adding the next. Add the saffron soaked in wine.
4. Keep warm until ready to serve. Do not make the sauce more than ½ hour before serving. The recipe makes 1 cup.

Serves 4
Must be partially prepared in advance

Skewered Shrimp with Cilantro and Salsa Verde

The flavorful sauce is perfect for these shrimp. They make a delicious hors d'oeuvre.

2 pounds jumbo shrimp, shelled and deveined
3 tablespoons minced fresh cilantro
2 teaspoons minced garlic
3 tablespoons fresh strained lime juice
3 tablespoons olive oil
$1/4$ teaspoon salt
Freshly ground black pepper
8 lettuce leaves
12 cherry tomatoes
1 cup Salsa Verde (see page 266)

1. In a glass bowl, combine the shrimp, cilantro, garlic, lime juice, olive oil, and salt; toss to mix well. Cover with plastic wrap and marinate in the refrigerator for at least 30 minutes, or up to 4 hours.
2. Preheat broiler or light charcoal in a barbecue grill.
3. Drain the shrimp, discarding the marinade, and season with pepper. Thread lengthwise on skewers, pushing the skewer through each shrimp near the ends but leaving the center free.
4. Grill over red-hot but not flaming charcoal, or in broiler, about 3 inches from flame, for 2 minutes per side or until just firm and pink.
5. Arrange on lettuce leaves and garnish with cherry tomatoes. Serve accompanied by the Salsa Verde.

Serves 6
Must be partially prepared in advance

Shrimp are backward swimmers: it is the curved tail muscle that we eat.

Shrimp farming is becoming a major source of freshwater shrimp. The farmed shrimp can reach a weight of 6 ounces.

Chapter 3

Sharks and Skates: No Bones About Them

Man eats sharks, and it's about time! Modern sharks and skates are descended from some of the world's earliest fishes, which appeared about 400 million years ago—200 million years before the age of dinosaurs. Although these ancient fishes have been around for a long time, they have only recently become common in American fish markets. Nevertheless, cooks in other parts of the world consider them delicacies because of their exceptional taste and texture.

Probably the most unique characteristic of sharks and skates is their lack of calcified bones; their entire skeleton is composed of cartilage. Long ago their ancestors stopped producing bones as we know them. Perhaps this was a response to the need for increased buoyancy, or perhaps it was to allow their supple bodies to move through the water more efficiently.

Sharks have thousands of toothlike scales on their skin, which gives them a rough, sandpapery feeling. It is the teeth in their jaws, however, which give some of them their bad reputations. These are arranged in rows, and new teeth continuously replace old ones. This way, a shark always has a full set of sharp, functional teeth ready for action.

Sharks come in two basic models: warm-bodied (like mako and great white) and cold-bodied (like dogfish). Because the warm-bodied sharks are not as sensitive to changes in water temperature as the cold-bodied sharks, they have greater swimming ranges. Their meat has a wonderful steaky quality, part white and part dark. Cold-bodied sharks generally have shorter swimming ranges, and they yield a firm, white flesh that is easily cut into nuggets for shish kebab and salads.

Skates are flat, kite-shaped fishes that live on the bottom of the sea. Their wings have firm white meat with a sweet flavor that some people think is similar to scallops. Sharks and skates deserve to be regarded as culinary treats, not fearsome beasts of the deep. The following recipes will introduce you to just how delicious they can be.

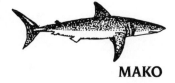

MAKO

GREAT WHITE

DOGFISH

Shark's Fin Soup

Chinese culture awards this soup an exalted status on a menu. It is reserved for special occasions and special people. Producing a proper shark's fin soup is a bit tricky, but the creamy, fragrant result is well worth the effort.

$^1/_2$ *pound dried skinless shark's fin**

3 *dried black mushrooms**

$^1/_2$ *pound skinned and boned chicken breast, cut in*
   $^1/_4$ x 2-inch strips

$^1/_4$ *cup cornstarch*

6 *cups rich chicken stock, preferably homemade*

$^1/_2$ *cup thinly sliced bamboo shoots*

1 *teaspoon peeled and minced fresh gingerroot*

1 *tablespoon minced scallions, including 1 inch of*
   green

$^1/_4$ *teaspoon salt*

$^1/_8$ *teaspoon freshly ground black pepper*

$^1/_4$ *cup julienne strips of cooked ham*

**Available in Chinese markets.*

Dried shark's fin, the cartilage portion of the fin, is sold as threadlike filaments. Although it is available either with or without the skin, we strongly recommend purchasing the skinless variety. It is more expensive but far easier to prepare. All dried shark's fin must be soaked first and/or simmered before using it in a recipe.

1. Prepare the shark's fin: Rinse the fin thoroughly in cold water, place in a bowl, and cover with warm water. Let soak overnight. Wash again, place in a saucepan, cover with water, and bring to a boil. Lower heat and simmer, covered, for 2 hours. Drain the fin and set aside.
2. Soak the mushrooms in warm water for 30 minutes. Drain and set aside.
3. Dredge the chicken strips in cornstarch and shake off any excess.
4. Bring the chicken stock to a boil and add the shark's fin. Cover and simmer over low heat for 30 minutes. Add the chicken and simmer, covered, for 5 minutes longer. Remove from heat.
5. Gently squeeze the mushrooms to remove any excess moisture. Cut off stems and discard. Thinly slice the caps. Combine them in a bowl with the bamboo shoots, gingerroot, scallion, salt, and pepper. Toss to mix. Add to the soup, along with the ham.
6. The soup may be prepared up to 12 hours in advance and refrigerated. Before serving, return the soup to the heat and simmer for 10 minutes, uncovered, over low heat. Taste and add more salt and pepper if needed.

Serves 4
May be prepared in advance

Shark Steaks with Tomato-Caper Sauce

During her catering career, Jane Lavine created this delightful recipe. The robust quality of the colorful tomato and caper sauce works nicely with tuna and swordfish as well as with shark.

   4 tablespoons olive oil
   1/2 cup chopped onion
   2 teaspoons minced garlic
   1 1/2 teaspoons dried oregano
   4 1/2 teaspoons capers, rinsed and drained
   1 14-ounce can Italian tomatoes, undrained
   1 teaspoon salt
   4 mako shark steaks, 3/4- to 1-inch thick, 6 to 8
      ounces each
   1/4 cup fresh strained lemon juice
   Freshly ground black pepper to taste

1. Preheat oven to 500 degrees or as high as it will go.
2. Heat the oil in a 10- to 12-inch skillet and sauté the onion and garlic until soft, about 5 minutes. Stir in the oregano and capers and sauté for 1 minute more.
3. Coarsely chop the tomatoes and add them, with their liquid, to the onion and garlic. Add 1/2 teaspoon salt and simmer, uncovered, over low heat approximately 20 minutes, until the oil starts to separate. Set aside, cover, and keep warm.
4. Place the fish steaks in a shallow buttered baking dish. Sprinkle with the lemon juice, the remaining 1/2 teaspoon salt, and pepper. Cover with buttered wax or parchment paper. Bake 5 to 8 minutes, depending upon thickness. Cut into a small section of one steak; it is done when the flesh is just opaque. Remove the steaks from the oven.
5. Remove and discard the skin. Arrange the fish steaks on a heated platter and serve topped with the sauce.

Variation: This recipe may also be prepared using swordfish or tuna steaks, or thicker fillets, such as sea trout, monkfish, wolffish, snapper, or tilefish. Adjust the cooking time according to thickness of fish.

Serves 4

Mako shark has a taste and texture very similar to swordfish, but it costs less. The cost differential is partly due to the economics of supply and demand. Another reason is that shark yields more meat per pound than its bony counterpart, swordfish. However, the good news about shark is traveling fast, and prices for it are creeping upward.

Mako en Brochette

Juicy chunks of shark and squares of sweet peppers make a vibrant entree, which is effortless to prepare and very low in fats. We think it is best cooked over the coals, but it can also be broiled in your oven. For a substantial hors d'oeuvre, make mini-brochettes using small bamboo skewers.

1   1-inch piece of peeled gingerroot, cut in quarters
3   cloves garlic, cut in thick slices
1   cup soy sauce
1/2   cup dry white wine
2   tablespoons vegetable oil
1/2   cup fresh strained lemon juice
4   pounds mako shark, cut in 1 1/2-inch cubes
2   sweet red peppers, cored and seeded, cut into
      1 1/2-inch pieces
2   sweet yellow peppers, cored and seeded, cut into
      1 1/2-inch pieces
24   mushroom caps, 1 1/2 inches across, stems
      discarded
24   small white onions (about 1 1/2 to 2 pounds)

1. Drop the gingerroot and garlic through the feed tube of a food processor fitted with the steel knife and, with the motor running, process on and off until finely minced. Add the soy sauce, wine, oil, and lemon juice and process again until well combined into a marinade.
2. Place the shark cubes in a glass bowl and pour the marinade over them. Marinate, covered, in the refrigerator for up to 1 hour.
3. Blanch the peppers in boiling water for 1 minute, then immediately refresh under cold water to stop the cooking.
4. Remove the shark from the marinade and let drain. (Reserve the marinade.) Alternate cubes of shark, pieces of peppers, mushroom caps, and whole onions on skewers. The amount on each skewer will depend on whether you wish to use the brochettes for entrees or for hors d'oeuvres.
5. Prepare charcoal grill or preheat broiler. The coals should be red but not flaming when you begin cooking.
6. Grill until the fish is opaque, but not falling off the skewer, about 5 to 7 minutes. Turn the skewers 2 or 3 times during the cooking process. Serve the brochettes on a heated platter as an hors d'oeuvre or on individual plates as an entree.

7. If desired, transfer the marinade to a saucepan and place it over high heat. Bring it to a boil and cook rapidly for 7 to 10 minutes, until it is reduced by half and slightly thickened. Serve it as a sauce with the brochettes.

    Variation: This recipe may be prepared using chucks of any firm-fleshed fish, such as monkfish, halibut, tuna, or swordfish. Shrimp and sea scallops would also work.

    Serves 8 as entree, or yields 40 small brochettes for hors d'oeuvres
    Must be partially prepared in advance

Mako Shark with Three Peppercorns

The meaty quality of mako shark led us to create a sauce based on a meat reduction. The result is an elegant entree, especially if it is accompanied by a rich California Chardonnay or white Burgundy wine.

> 6   slices (³/₄- to 1-inch thick) mako shark, 6 to 8 ounces each
> 1   tablespoon coarsely crushed peppercorns, a mixture of black, white, and green
> 3   tablespoons vegetable oil
> ³/₄ cup rich chicken stock
> 2   tablespoons minced shallots
> ¹/₄ cup Calvados or cognac
> ¹/₄ cup unsalted butter, at room temperature
> 1   teaspoon fresh strained lemon juice

1. Sprinkle each side of the steaks with the crushed peppercorns, pressing them into the flesh until they adhere. The recipe should be prepared at least 30 minutes or up to 4 hours in advance and refrigerated, covered, before proceeding.
2. When you are ready to complete the preparation, preheat oven to 350 degrees.
3. Heat 2 tablespoons of the oil in a large nonstick skillet over medium-high heat. Working in batches if necessary, sauté the shark steaks until they are crusty and golden brown on both sides, about 2 to 3 minutes per side. Add the remaining 1 tablespoon

Warm-bodied sharks—mako, great white, and porbeagle, to name a few—may be substituted for each other in recipes in this book. At this time, however, great white and porbeagle are less likely to be sold at retail than mako shark.

Shark skin is very difficult to remove before cooking. However, this is a more elegant recipe than our other shark recipes, and the skin easily comes off midway through cooking.

oil if it is needed. Remove the skin from the steaks at this time, and place the steaks on an ovenproof serving platter that is large enough to hold all of them in one layer. Cover with foil and place in the oven. They will continue to cook while the sauce is being made.

4. Wipe out the skillet and add the stock and shallots. Bring to a boil over high heat and reduce to $^1/_4$ cup. Add the Calvados or cognac and reduce by half. Turn the heat to low and swirl in the butter, one tablespoon at a time. Stir in the lemon juice.

5. Remove the shark from the oven and add any juices accumulated on the platter to the sauce. Spoon the sauce over the shark and serve immediately.

Variation: This recipe may be made without the sauce by preparing it only through step 3. When the fish is opaque and flakes easily, remove from the oven. Serve the steaks garnished with chopped fresh parsley and lemon wedges.

Serves 6
Must be partially prepared in advance

Grilled Great White Shark Steaks

This recipe comes from John Prescott, executive director of the New England Aquarium, who was once presented with thirty pounds of great white shark. He decided that a straightforward presentation was the best choice when grilling. If you are very careful not to overcook the fish, the results will be moist and toothsome. Any fish steak can be prepared in this manner.

4 *shark steaks, ³/₄- to 1-inch thick, 6 to 8 ounces*
  each
¹/₂ teaspoon salt
Freshly ground black pepper to taste
¹/₂ cup unsalted butter (1 stick), melted
2 tablespoons minced fresh parsley
¹/₂ cup fresh strained lemon juice
1 lemon, sliced in rounds for garnish
Parsley sprigs for garnish

1. Prepare the charcoal for grilling. The coals should be red but not flaming when you begin cooking.
2. Sprinkle both sides of the steaks with the salt and pepper. Combine the melted butter with the parsley and lemon juice. Paint one side of the steaks with the butter mixture and place, buttered side down, on the hot grill rack positioned 5 inches above the coals.
3. Grill for 4 to 5 minutes. Watch for flaming and sprinkle the coals with a little water if necessary. Paint the top of the steaks with the butter mixture; turn them over. Grill the second side for 4 minutes, or until the fish flakes easily but is still moist. Remove skin and discard.
4. Arrange the steaks on a heated platter and garnish with the parsley sprigs and lemon slices.

Serves 4

It is always a good idea to rinse any fresh fish product in cold water, and then pat dry with paper toweling before proceeding with a recipe.

Oriental Dogfish Salad

When the amateur fisherman presents you with dogfish, present him or her with this salad. The spicy aromatic qualities of the Oriental ingredients provide a zesty warm weather entree. The flavors and ingredients work nicely with almost any cooked fish.

1/2 cup snow peas, stems removed and strings torn off
4 tablespoons soy sauce
1/4 cup dry sherry
1/2 teaspoon sugar
2 teaspoons minced garlic
1 1-inch piece gingerroot, crushed
2 teaspoons oriental sesame oil*
2 whole star anise*
1 pound prepared dogfish, cut into 1/2-inch cubes
1 cup mung bean sprouts
1/2 cup sliced water chestnuts
3 tablespoons thinly sliced scallions, including 2 inches of green section
1/2 cup thinly sliced red radishes
1 tablespoon sesame seeds, toasted
1/2 cup vegetable oil
1 teaspoon water
2 tablespoons dry white wine
2 tablespoons white wine vinegar
1 10-ounce bag fresh spinach, washed, dried, and tough stems discarded
1 lemon, sliced in thin rounds for garnish

*Available in Oriental markets or in the specialty section of your supermarket.

1. Bring a small saucepan of water to a boil. Drop in the snow peas. When the water returns to a boil, immediately drain the peas and refresh them under cold water to stop their cooking. Cut the peas crosswise in 1/2-inch slices and reserve.

How to Prepare Dogfish

Dogfish, shark, and skate all maintain a high level of urea in their systems, which produces the smell of ammonia right after they are killed. Commercially caught sharks and skates are processed before they reach the market. Since dogfish are almost always caught by the amateur, they have to be processed at home.

When the fish is caught, cut off and discard the head and eviscerate the fish. As soon as you reach home, cut the fish into fillets, steaks or chunks. Soak it for 6 hours in the refrigerator in a mild acidic bath, using 1 tablespoon vinegar to 1 quart of water. The fish can be left in the bath for up to 24 hours and then drained and wrapped. Refrigerate, if desired, for no more than 3 days.

2. In a medium-size glass bowl, combine 2 tablespoons of the soy sauce with the sherry, sugar, garlic, ginger-root, 1/2 teaspoon sesame oil, and star anise. Stir thoroughly. Add the dogfish pieces, toss to coat on all sides, and marinate at room temperature for 30 minutes.

3. Transfer the fish and marinade to a saucepan, cover with water, and bring to a boil. Reduce heat and cook 2 minutes, or until the fish is opaque and cooked through. Drain the fish and transfer to a large mixing bowl. Add the snow peas, bean sprouts, water chestnuts, scallions, radishes, and toasted sesame seeds to the fish. Toss to mix.

4. In a pint jar, combine the vegetable oil, remaining 1 1/2 teaspoons sesame oil, 1 teaspoon of water, remaining 2 tablespoons soy sauce, white wine, and vinegar. Cover tightly and shake well. Pour enough of the dressing over the fish mixture to moisten it. Toss thoroughly, adding more dressing if necessary. Cover loosely with plastic wrap and chill for at least 30 minutes, or up to 1 hour.

5. When ready to serve, toss again briefly and taste for seasoning, adding salt and pepper if desired.

6. Arrange spinach leaves on individual plates and mound the salad on top. Garnish with lemon slices.

Serves 4
Must be prepared in advance

Dogfish Florentine

There are no last-minute kitchen duties with this recipe since all but the baking can be done up to 4 hours in advance. Serve with wild rice and a salad for a cozy dinner for four. This recipe is also good with fillets of hake, cusk, ocean pout, ocean perch, sea trout, wolffish, or tilefish.

> 2 10-ounce bags of fresh spinach, washed, dried, and tough stems discarded, or 3 packages frozen chopped spinach
> 1 tablespoon minced shallots or scallions
> 2 teaspoons vegetable oil
> 2 teaspoons minced garlic
> 2 eggs, lightly beaten
> 2 teaspoons fresh strained lemon juice
> 1 teaspoon salt
> 1/2 teaspoon freshly ground black pepper
> 1/2 cup grated Swiss cheese
> 1 1/2 pounds prepared dogfish fillets, cut into 4 pieces of equal size
> 3 tablespoons fine fresh bread crumbs, toasted
> 1 tablespoon unsalted butter
> Freshly grated nutmeg or paprika

Dogfish are very high in Omega-3 acids, which are very good for reducing blood cholesterol levels.

Dogfish is often called "sand shark." Fishermen catch it all the time and regard it as a pest. Ask for it from your friendly angler.

1. Steam the spinach until barely tender. (If using frozen spinach, cook according to directions on the package.) Squeeze out all the moisture, then chop coarsely. Set aside.
2. In a skillet over medium heat, sauté the shallots or scallions in the oil for 3 or 4 minutes. Add the garlic, cook for 1 minute, and remove from heat..
3. Combine the spinach, shallot-garlic mixture, eggs, lemon juice, salt, pepper, and 6 tablespoons of the cheese. Mix well and taste for seasoning. Transfer the spinach mixture to a buttered 9-inch pie plate or round baking dish, and smooth evenly. Arrange the dogfish fillets like spokes on a wheel on top of the spinach. If the fillets are too wide, cut them lengthwise into 8 pieces.
4. Combine the remaining 2 tablespoons of cheese and the bread crumbs and sprinkle over each fillet. Dot the entire surface with the tablespoon of butter. The recipe may be prepared 4 hours in advance up to this point. Keep the dish covered in the refrigerator. Remove 10 minutes before baking.
5. When ready to cook, preheat oven to 375 degrees.
6. Sprinkle the dish lightly with nutmeg or paprika and bake, uncovered, for 20 minutes or until the fish is

just opaque. If desired, run under a preheated broiler for 1 minute to brown the top.

Serves 4
May be partially prepared in advance

Fish and Chips

This recipe is most authentic if the fish and chips are served wrapped first in wax paper, then in newspaper, and sprinkled with malt vinegar. They may also be put on a platter and served with lemon wedges.

1 1/2 *cups flour*
3/4 *cup beer*
1 1/2 *teaspoons salt*
1/2 *teaspoon freshly ground black pepper*
6 *medium potatoes, peeled (about 2 pounds)*
Vegetable oil for deep frying
2 *pounds prepared dogfish fillets, cut in pieces 4 to*
   6 inches long and 2 to 3 inches wide
Lemon wedges for garnish
Malt vinegar (optional)

1. Set oven at lowest possible temperature.
2. Mix 1 cup flour, beer, 1 teaspoon salt, and 1/4 teaspoon pepper together until well blended. Let rest for 5 minutes.
3. Cut the potatoes lengthwise in 1/4-inch-thick slices, and then again in 1/4-inch slices crosswise. Soak in ice water for 5 minutes.
4. Heat the oil to 375 degrees. Drain and dry the potatoes thoroughly with paper towels. Drop into the oil and fry until almost brown, about 5 minutes. Remove with a slotted spoon and drain on folded brown bags or paper towels.
5. In a shallow bowl, combine the remaining 1/2 cup flour, 1/2 teaspoon salt, and 1/4 teaspoon pepper. Mix well, using your fingers. Dredge the dogfish in the seasoned flour, shaking off any excess, and then dip into the beer batter.
6. Fry about four or five pieces of fish at a time in the deep fat, for about 5 minutes, turning the pieces once or twice. The fish will be pale in color. With a slotted spoon, remove the fish pieces and drain on paper towels or brown bags. Repeat until all the fish is fried.

The British are famous for their "fish and chips," often made with dogfish. Its firm white flesh, typical of cold-bodied sharks, is delicious. And the wonderful, crispy, crunchy coating is due to frying the fish twice.

7. Make sure the oil has returned to 375 degrees. Return the fish to the oil in batches and fry again until golden brown, about 3 minutes. Do not overcrowd the pieces of fish in the oil. Drain and keep warm.
8. Again, check the oil's heat, making certain it is 375 degrees. Add all the potatoes to the oil and fry until golden brown, about 2 minutes. Drain, and sprinkle with salt, if desired. Arrange fish and chips on a platter and garnish with lemon wedges. Accompany with a small pitcher of malt vinegar.

Serves 6

Dogfish Provençal

Bright red tomato sauce enlivened with black olives makes this an attractive presentation. Serve this dish on rustic earthenware along with French bread and a tossed green salad.

> 2 *cups thinly sliced onion (about 2 large)*
> 1 *14-ounce can Italian plum tomatoes, drained and chopped*
> 6 *tablespoons minced fresh parsley*
> 2 *teaspoons minced garlic*
> 1 *teaspoon dried thyme*
> 1 *crumbled bay leaf*
> 1/4 *teaspoon salt*
> *Freshly ground black pepper to taste*
> 2 *pounds prepared dogfish fillets*
> 1 *cup dry white wine*
> 1 *cup water*
> 2 *tablespoons tomato paste*
> 6 *lemon slices*
> 12 *pitted black olives*
> 2 *teaspoons cornstarch*
> 2 *tablespoons fresh strained lemon juice*
> 2 *tablespoons unsalted butter*

1. Combine the onion, tomatoes, 4 tablespoons of the parsley, garlic, thyme, and bay leaf in a mixing bowl. Add the salt and pepper and toss to mix.
2. Grease a flameproof baking dish and spread half the tomato mixture in the dish. Place the dogfish fillets on top and cover with the rest of the mixture. The recipe may be prepared 2 hours in advance up to this point. Bring the dish to room temperature before proceeding with the recipe.
3. Preheat oven to 350 degrees.
4. Blend the wine, water, and tomato paste and pour over the dogfish. Arrange the lemon slices of the fish.
5. Place the baking dish on the range and bring the liquid to a boil over moderately high heat. Remove from heat and immediately cover securely with buttered aluminum foil. Bake in the oven for 10 minutes.
6. Briefly remove the foil and add the black olives. Secure the foil and continue to bake for another 10 minutes, or until the fish just flakes when tested with a fork.
7. With a slotted spoon, transfer the dogfish and vegetables to a heated platter and keep warm. Reduce the cooking juices in the baking dish over high heat for 3 minutes. Dissolve the cornstarch in the lemon juice and whisk into the sauce. Stir over high heat until slightly thickened.
8. Remove the dish from heat. Add the butter and stir until melted. Pour the sauce over the dogfish and garnish with the remaining 2 tablespoons of parsley.

Serves 4–6
May be partially prepared in advance

Skate au Beurre Noir

Although this recipe's name translates literally as "Skate in Black Butter," "black" is really a misnomer. The sauce should not contain any black particles that would give the sauce a burned and acrid flavor. Rather, the butter should be a deep brown, which adds a delicious nutty taste to the fish. For superior results, we suggest using clarified butter.

> 2 sprigs parsley
> 1 bay leaf
> 1/2 teaspoon dried thyme
> 2 pounds skate wings
> 2 tablespoons white vinegar
> 1/2 cup clarified butter (see page 273), or 1/2 cup
>   unsalted butter
> 1 tablespoon capers, rinsed and drained
> Salt
> Freshly ground black pepper to taste
> 1 lemon, sliced into thin rounds for garnish
> 2 tablespoons minced fresh parsley for garnish

1. Prepare a bouquet garni: Place the parsley sprigs, bay leaf, and thyme in a cheesecloth square, and tie.
2. Place the skate wings in a fish poacher or large skillet. Add water to cover them by 1/2 inch. It is preferable to poach the fish in one layer, but because of the unusual shape of skate wings, you may need to overlap slightly. Add 1 tablespoon of the vinegar and the bouquet garni. Cover and bring to a boil over high heat, then immediately reduce the heat to simmer the fish gently for 10 minutes, or until the flesh is opaque. Remove the skate from the poaching liquid and scrape off the gelatinous membrane. Carefully transfer the skate to a heated serving dish, cover loosely with foil, and keep warm.
3. Melt the butter over medium heat. Add the remaining vinegar and cook until the butter turns brown, being careful not to burn it (about 1 minute). Add the capers, salt, and pepper and taste for seasoning.
4. Drain any excess liquid from the skate and pour the sauce over the fish. Garnish with lemon rounds and minced parsley.

Serves 4

If you ever walk beaches, you have doubtless encountered the small, black, rectangular-shaped pouches called mermaids' purses. This little pouch housed the skate egg during its incubation.

Skate has a sweet mild taste some think is similar to scallops. Its meat shreds into filaments when removed from the cartilage, giving it a crablike texture. Poached skate may be substituted for crab in most crab salad recipes when mayonnaise is the binder.

Skate with Red Pepper, Mustard, and Tarragon Sauce

FROM L'ESPALIER RESTAURANT, BOSTON

Snow-white skate wings, served with red pepper sauce, become an entree with high visual impact. The red pepper sauce can be prepared 24 hours in advance. The recipe was created by Moncef Meddeb, the chef/owner of the restaurant.

4 skate wings
Sea salt
1/2 cup red wine vinegar
2 sweet red peppers, cored, seeded, and cut into
coarse chunks
2 tablespoons minced onion
1/4 cup white wine
3 tablespoons heavy cream
1–2 tablespoons whole-grain mustard
1 teaspoon minced fresh tarragon
Salt and freshly ground black pepper to taste
Capers, rinsed and drained, for garnish

1. Rinse the skate wings under running water to remove any film. Place them in a kettle and cover with 6 quarts of water. Add 3 to 4 pinches of sea salt and the vinegar. Bring slowly to a low simmer and poach 10 minutes. Drain carefully and skin (if not already skinned by fishmonger). Set aside and keep warm.
2. Place the red peppers, onion, and wine in a small skillet. Cover and simmer over low heat for about 15 minutes until soft. Pour into a blender and blend at top speed until smooth. Transfer to a saucepan over medium heat.
3. Add the heavy cream to the pepper mixture and heat through, but do not let boil. Add 1 to 2 tablespoons mustard and tarragon, and salt and pepper to taste. (If you have prepared the sauce in advance, gently reheat before serving.)
4. Divide the sauce among 4 heated serving plates and arrange the skate wings on top. Garnish the skate with a few capers and serve.

Serves 4
May be partially prepared in advance

Besides being both economical and delicious, skate has an additional, most unusual asset. If quite fresh, it will keep in the refrigerator on a draining pan filled with ice, covered with a dampened tea towel, for up to 48 hours with a distinct improvement in flavor.

Grecian Wings

Entertain a crowd with ease by preparing and freezing this light and crispy hors d'oeuvre several weeks in advance. The sweet meat of the skate makes them popular at any gathering. When you make them, you will find that working with fillo dough is a time-consuming process, so be certain to set aside a couple of hours for this recipe's preparation.

1 *pound prepared skate wings (see directions, sidebar)*
4 *tablespoons unsalted butter (¹/₂ stick)*
2 *tablespoons flour*
1 ¹/₂ *cups milk or light cream*
¹/₄ *cup dry sherry*
¹/₂ *teaspoon paprika*
1 *teaspoon salt*
¹/₂ *teaspoon freshly ground black pepper*
1 *egg yolk*
3 *tablespoons minced fresh parsley*
1 *16-ounce package fillo pastry, defrosted according to package directions*

How to Prepare Skate

How to Prepare Skate

Place the skate wings in a single layer in a fish poacher or large skillet, and cover with water. Add 2 to 4 tablespoons of mild vinegar to the water and bring to a boil. Reduce the heat to a low simmer and poach 10 minutes, or until opaque. Remove from the pan, and take off the skin. Carefully scrape off and discard any gelatinous membrane.

Skate wings come in different sizes. If the wings are larger than ³/₄ pound, cut them in half after poaching, before serving.

1. Remove the skate meat from the cartilage, which will make the meat shred into small pieces. Set aside.
2. Melt 2 tablespoons of the butter in a heavy saucepan. Add the flour and cook over medium heat for 3 to 4 minutes, stirring constantly. Whisk in the milk or cream and cook, stirring, until the sauce starts to thicken. Add the sherry, paprika, salt, and pepper, and stir until the sauce is thick. Add 2 tablespoons of the thickened sauce to the the egg yolk, then stir the egg yolk mixture back into the sauce. Do not let the sauce boil. Mix in the parsley. Set aside to cool.
3. Combine the skate and cooled sauce, mixing until blended. Season to taste.
4. Melt the remaining 2 tablespoons butter. Place the fillo on a clean working surface and cover with a very slightly damp dishtowel. Spread another towel on the counter and place a sheet of fillo on it. Brush the fillo generously with the melted butter and cut it into six lengthwise strips. Place one teaspoon of the filling on one end of each strip. Fold each strip as you would a flag until you end up with a triangle. Place on a cookie sheet and brush the top with melted butter. Repeat until all the fillo and the filling are used. Put plastic wrap or wax paper between the layers of triangles on the cookie sheet.
5. Refrigerate the triangles at least one hour or freeze

them before baking. If frozen, thaw before baking.

6. Bake in a single layer on a cookie sheet in a pre-heated 375-degree oven. Bake 15 minutes, or until golden brown and crisp.

Yield: 3 dozen
Must be prepared in advance

Golden Skate Puffs

If you are unable to find skate, this recipe works equally well with shrimp substituted for the skate. Be sure that the oil is heated to the correct temperature, so that the puffs absorb a minimum of oil.

1 *1-pound loaf of homestyle white bread*
1 *pound prepared skate wings (see directions, page 100)*
$^1/_2$ *pound scallops, rinsed and patted dry*
1 *8-ounce can water chestnuts*
$^1/_4$ *cup minced scallion top*
1 *teaspoon minced gingerroot*
2 *tablespoons medium-dry sherry*
$5^1/_2$ *teaspoons cornstarch*
1 *large egg white, lightly beaten*
1 *teaspoon salt*
White pepper to taste
6 *cups vegetable oil*
Duck sauce (optional)*

*Available in the international food section of a supermarket.

1. Remove the crusts from the bread. Cut the bread into $^1/_4$-inch cubes. Spread them on a baking sheet and let dry in a cool, dry place for 2 hours.
2. In a food processor fitted with the steel knife, process the skate and the scallops into a paste. Transfer to a glass or ceramic bowl.
3. Drain and mince the water chestnuts. Add to the fish paste along with the scallions, gingerroot, sherry, cornstarch, egg white, salt, and pepper. Stir well to combine. Dampen your hands in cold water and form the paste into walnut-size balls. Roll the balls in the bread cubes, pressing the bread lightly into the balls.

If you do not have a deep fryer, a wok is an excellent substitute.

After opening a can of water chestnuts, rinse them and store them in cold water in the refrigerator. They will keep for up to three weeks if the water is changed every few days.

Deep-fat frying, if properly done, produces food that is surprisingly lower in fat than many people think. By heating the oil to the proper temperature and maintaining this temperature throughout, the cooking will sear the outer surface, preventing the penetration of any more oil. The food inside will be cooked and moist.

4. Heat the oil in a deep fryer to 325 degrees. Fry the balls in four batches, turning them, for 1 to 2 minutes or until they are golden. Drain on paper towels.
5. Reheat the oil to 375 degrees and fry all of them at once for 1 minute until they are deep golden. Drain again on paper towels. The puffs can be made up to this point 24 hours in advance and chilled, loosely covered.
6. When ready to serve, preheat oven to 350 degrees.
7. Heat the puffs on baking sheets in the oven for 10 minutes.
8. Transfer the puffs to a serving tray and serve with the duck sauce, if desired.

Variation: Omit the bread cubes and vegetable oil. Pipe the shellfish mixture into snow pea pods that have been opened along one side. This may be done in advance. About $1/2$ hour before serving, place the filled peas in a steamer set over simmering water. Steam 3 or 4 minutes, cool slightly, and arrange on a platter. Serve with duck sauce, if desired.

Yield: 30 puffs
May be partially prepared in advance

"To serve thornback or skate, it should be hung one day at least before it be dressed and may be served either boiled or fried in crumbs, being first dipped in egg."—A *New System of Domestic Cookery*, 1807, author unknown

Chapter 4

Early Fishes: Modern Dishes

The venerable fishes of this chapter trace their ancestry back over hundreds of millions of years. Sturgeon, for instance, are derived from a wave of evolution that crested nearly 250 million years ago. The other fishes in this chapter were probably on the scene by about 70 to 100 million years ago. This conservatism has not stopped them from acquiring new structures or ways of life more suited to a modern world. This is especially true of the catfishes, carps, and their kin. They have become masters at finding their way about in dark, muddy waters with excellent hearing, taste, smell, or even electrical force fields.

Although many of today's early fish families evolved independently, we still group them together because they all lack the spiny fin rays that developed in later fishes. Without these stiffening rays in their fins, early fishes are limited to a more narrow range of lifestyles. For example, among the fishes listed here, only eels have really adjusted to modern coral reefs.

Many early fishes share characteristics that make them easy to catch or raise through aquaculture. Some of them, such as the herrings and cods, are schooling fishes rather than reef fishes, and can be caught in huge numbers by trawlers or purse seiners. Others, like sturgeon, salmon, and trout, swim upstream in spring to spawn, where they are readily captured. Catfish and carp have rugged constitutions that allow them to flourish in fish farms.

Hardly backward, these fishes probably have lasted so long because they started with a sound design. Nonetheless, they have not succeeded in achieving quite the diversity of shapes or habits that appear in the later fishes of Chapter 5.

These early fishes have several common culinary characteristics. Their flesh tends to be firm and flaky when cooked, and it often has small, fine bones. Lots of reliable, old favorite recipes are made with the early fishes, and you will find them here with some new twists. What could be more satisfying on a cold damp night than a steaming bowl of chowder? But, break away from the old routine and add underutilized hake, cusk, or pollock to the broth instead of haddock or cod. In the sizzle of summer, take herring and beet potato salad on a picnic. For an elegant cocktail hour, serve cilantro-cured haddock and cold grill-smoked trout, as well as the familiar smoked salmon. Whether the setting is humble or extraordinary, the early fishes provide cooks with some of their most reliable and flavorful dishes.

First Fishes: Eel and Sturgeon

The ichthyologist coming upon this chapter heading may certainly wonder why we have grouped the sturgeon, one of our most ancient surviving bony fishes, with the American eel, a comparatively recent arrival. The fact is that for a long time many North American and European recipes for long, skinny, snakelike fishes had in mind not the true eel, but quite a different creature called the lamprey, or "lamprey-eel." Lamprey are very primitive jawless fishes—to those who consider them fishes at all—and represent an archaic predecessor of true, jawed fishes as well as all other vertebrates, including humans. However, they are not found very often in supermarkets or restaurants, so we substitute the American eel, and celebrate it in its own right.

AMERICAN EEL

STURGEON

Sturgeon are most remarkable for their odd appearance and the immense size to which some species grow. Their closest relatives were among the first bony fishes to populate the earth over 225 million years ago, so, in many respects, sturgeon are primitive. On the other hand, they have deviated a good deal from the archetypal blueprint of an early fish and hardly qualify for Model-T status. For the record, when scientists call an animal primitive, they do not mean that it is backward or outmoded. They are simply indicating that it still retains many features that characterize forms that evolved early on in life's procession. To these features, animals have added special adaptations of their own that, in most cases, have enabled them to continue to live successfully on this planet. Sturgeon, for example, have added barbels. These are whiskerlike sensory organs that hang from their mouths and are used to feel and taste food.

After hundreds of millions of years of success, ancient fishes are facing strenuous challenges from man; one kind of sturgeon, the short-nose sturgeon, is threatened by dam construction, pollution, and overfishing. Other kinds of sturgeon, however, are common in the West, and occasionally Atlantic sturgeon is seen on menus in New England. Sturgeon aquaculture, recently begun in California, may help augment the supply, as well.

Eel Stew in Red Wine

Eel, when netted, is usually thrown back into the water. However, if you ask a fisherman to keep some for you, you will be delighted with it. This eel stew makes a hearty supper dish. Any firm-fleshed fish, especially those with a rich flavor, will work in this recipe. Try it with mullet, salmon, or even monkfish. All can be successfully stewed in red wine.

2 pound mussels, scrubbed and debearded
1/4 cup water
8 tablespoons butter (1 stick)
1 cup chopped onion
1/2 cup chopped carrot
2 teaspoons minced garlic
1/4 teaspoon dried thyme
6 sprigs parsley
1 1/2 cups dry red wine
2 pounds eel, skinned and cut in 3/4-inch slices
1/2 cup coarsely chopped mushrooms
3 tablespoons flour
2 tablespoons minced fresh parsley
2 tablespoons fresh strained lemon juice
Salt and freshly ground black pepper to taste

1. Place the mussels in a kettle with the water. Bring to a boil, cover, reduce the heat to low, and cook until the mussels have opened. Discard any mussels that do not open. Strain the liquid into a bowl and reserve. Allow the mussels to cool. Discard the shells and reserve the meats.

2. Melt 4 tablespoons of the butter in a large kettle over medium heat. Stir in the onion, carrot, garlic, thyme, and parsley sprigs. Sauté for 4 to 5 minutes until soft, but not browned. Add the wine and the reserved liquid from the mussels to the kettle. Cover and simmer over low to moderate heat for 20 minutes.

3. Add the sliced eel to the kettle and simmer for an additional 10 minutes. While the eel is cooking, sauté the mushrooms in 1 tablespoon of the butter. Add the mushrooms to the kettle.

4. In a small skillet, melt the remaining 3 tablespoons of butter and work in the flour to make a smooth paste. Stir it into the stew to thicken the mixture. Add the minced parsley and reserved mussels, and heat through. Season to taste with the lemon juice, salt, and pepper. Serve immediately with French bread or croutons.

Serves 4

The meat of eels is rich in flavor with a firm texture.

To skin an eel: Hold the head end. Make a slit in the skin and peel it back. If you prefer, your fishmonger can do it for you.

Smoked Eel Pâté

FROM LA TULIPE RESTAURANT, NEW YORK CITY

Sally Darr has graciously shared this pâté recipe from her townhouse restaurant in New York City. This pâté will put to rest any hesitation you may have had of eating eel. The rich flavor of the smoked eel is mellowed by the addition of Bercy Butter and marvelously balanced by the tartness of the Tomato Coulis.

> 2 smoked eels (about 2 1/2–3 pounds)
> 3 anchovy fillets, soaked in water for 30 minutes, rinsed, drained, and halved
> 1 recipe Bercy Butter (see recipe below)
> 1/3 cup fresh Tomato Coulis (see recipe below)
> 1 teaspoon tomato paste
> 1/4 teaspoon freshly ground white pepper
> 1/2 teaspoon fresh strained lemon juice
> Salt to taste

1. Skin and bone the smoked eels. Cut the flesh into 1-inch pieces.
2. Using the metal blade of a food processor, puree the anchovy and eel together.
3. Slowly pour the Bercy Butter, the Tomato Coulis, and the tomato paste through the feed tube while the motor is running. After scraping down the sides of the work bowl, add the white pepper and the lemon juice and pulse twice to combine. Salt to taste.
4. Put the entire mixture through the fine disc of a food mill or through a fine mesh strainer.
5. Pack the pâté into a 1-quart dish; cover and chill until firm, about 2 hours.
6. Serve the pâté with toast points or toasted French bread.

Yield: 3 1/3 cups

Bercy Butter

> 3 tablespoons minced shallots
> 1/2 teaspoon dried thyme
> 1 cup dry white wine
> 1 cup fish stock (see page 277)
> 1 cup unsalted butter, chilled, cut into 16 pieces

1. Combine the shallots, thyme, and wine in a 2-quart saucepan. Cook over medium-high heat until the liquid is reduced to 2 tablespoons.

Smoked eel was a popular Christmas tradition with early settlers in New England. The fish was smoked by hanging it in the fireplace.

As the American eel matures, it goes through color changes. While in fresh water, the eel is a greenish color, which is helpful camouflage. As it travels to the salt water it becomes silvery. This shade acts as protective coloration as the eel can only be seen in rather good light. The silvery color also reflects light, and when many eels are swimming together, they may look like one large fish.

2. Add the fish stock to the reduced wine and continue to cook until this liquid is reduced to ¼ cup.
3. Remove the pan from the heat and whisk the pieces of butter into the mixture one piece at a time. Cool the mixture until it is lukewarm. The recipe makes 1⅓ cups.

Note: Served warm, Bercy Butter will add a touch of panache to simply broiled or baked fish.

Tomato Coulis

1 *tablespoon minced garlic (1 large clove)*
2 *tablespoons chopped onion (¼ small onion)*
3 *large tomatoes (1½ pounds)*
1 *tablespoon vegetable oil*
2 *teaspoons tomato paste*
Salt and pepper to taste

1. Drop the garlic into the feed tube of a food processor while the machine is running, and process with the metal blade until minced. Add the onion and pulse until finely chopped. Remove the onion-garlic mixture and reserve.
2. Peel, quarter, and seed the tomatoes. Place them in the food processor and chop coarsely. Remove and reserve.
3. Put the oil in a 2-quart saucepan over medium heat. When it is hot, add the onion-garlic mixture, and sauté for about 45 seconds. Add the tomatoes and cook over medium-high heat for about 5 minutes. Stir in the tomato paste, reduce heat to medium, and cook for an additional 3 or 4 minutes, stirring constantly. Add salt and pepper to taste.
4. Tomato Coulis may be made ahead and stored, covered, in the refrigerator. The recipe makes 1½ cups. Leftovers may be used as an accompaniment to many fishes. We feel it is particularly good with the richer fishes, such as bluefish, eel, swordfish, and mahi mahi. Just warm it gently before serving.

Yield: 3⅓ cups pâté
Must be prepared in advance

The young eels grow through a larval stage while they glide on the currents of the Gulf Stream back to the Atlantic Coast. When the eels are about 3 inches long, they are called "glass eels" because they resemble adult eels, except they are transparent.

A catadromous fish, such as eel, spends most of its life in fresh water, returning to the ocean to spawn. Both American and European eels spawn in an area of the Atlantic ocean known as the Sargasso Sea. Amazingly, the young eels, known as elvers, arrive back in their respective countries, having coasted on ocean currents such as the Gulf Stream. While the American elvers reach their destination in a year, it takes nearly three years for the European elvers to cover the greater distance.

Coulibiac

This traditional Russian dish, served either hot or cold, makes a spectacular main course for an elegant dinner. Some of the preparation can be done in advance. If you are unable to find sturgeon, monkfish or salmon may be substituted.

> 8 *tablespoons unsalted butter (1 stick)*
> 1 ½ *pounds sturgeon, skinned, boned, and cubed*
> ⅓ *cup raw rice*
> 1 *cup chopped onion*
> ½ *pound chopped mushrooms*
> 3 *hard-boiled eggs, chopped*
> 3 *tablespoons minced fresh parsley*
> ½ *teaspoon salt*
> ¼ *teaspoon freshly ground black pepper*
> 1 *17-ounce package frozen puff pastry, defrosted according to package directions*
> 1 *egg*
> 1 *tablespoon water*
> 1 ½ *cups crème fraîche (optional)*
> ½ *cup minced fresh dill (optional)*

1. Melt 6 tablespoons of the butter. Roll the sturgeon pieces in the butter to coat them. Set aside to cool.
2. Cook the rice according to package directions. Set aside.
3. Melt the remaining 2 tablespoons of butter in a 10-inch skillet over medium-high heat. Add the onion and sauté until soft. Add the mushrooms and cook 3 minutes. Do not allow the mixture to darken. Set it aside to cool.
4. Combine the chopped eggs and parsley in a small bowl. Season with the salt and pepper to taste.
5. Roll out 1 sheet of pastry into a rectangle about 16 inches by 12 inches. Trim any thick edges. Roll out a smaller rectangle, about 12 inches by 8 inches.
6. Place the large rectangle on a buttered baking sheet and spread the sturgeon pieces down the middle. Lightly sprinkle with salt and pepper. Layer the rice on top, then the onion/mushroom mixture, and top with the egg and parsley. Sprinkle evenly with the remaining salt and pepper.
7. Make an egg wash by beating together the egg and water. Brush the smaller pastry with the egg wash and place it on top of the filling, egg side down. Press the sides of the pastries firmly together. With

Sturgeon meat is firm. It is excellent when baked or barbecued. It can be used in many traditional scallopini dishes instead of veal. It is also very tasty when smoked.

Sturgeon is widely available in the Pacific Northwest, but may need to be specially ordered from your fishmonger in other areas of the country.

a sharp knife, trim the excess pastry to about 1 1/4 inches. Fold the border over on itself and crimp the edges with a fork. Brush the top with the egg wash and decorate with fish shapes cut from the pastry trimmings. Coulibiac may be refrigerated for up to 2 hours before baking.

8. When ready to cook, preheat the oven to 400 degrees.

9. Paint the pastry with a final coat of egg wash. Cut a small vent hole in the top of the pastry to allow steam to escape. Bake 30 to 35 minutes.

10. If serving hot, let it rest for 5 minutes. Transfer to a heated serving platter and slice.

11. To serve cold, set aside to cool and then refrigerate. Before serving let sit at room temperature for 20 minutes, then slice. In a small bowl, combine the crème fraîche and the dill for a sauce and serve it on the side.

Serves 6
May be prepared in advance

In the United States, the eighth full moon of the calendar year is called the Sturgeon Moon. This full moon, which occurs in late July or August, coincides with spawning time for sturgeons.

A female sturgeon's eggs may account for as much as one-third of her total weight. The largest of sturgeons may produce as many as 5,000,000 eggs.

Sturgeon grow quickly but mature slowly. A female is not mature until the age of 15 and may easily live for an additional fifty years.

Broiled Sturgeon with Tomato-Basil Sauce

FROM LE GOURMAND RESTAURANT, SEATTLE

Bruce Naftaly and Robin Saunders are the chef/owners of Le Gourmand Restaurant in Seattle, Washington. Their insistence on the best quality in fresh ingredients produces a superior result. For this recipe, they prefer a charcoal fire, rather than broiling in the oven, for the best flavor.

Isinglass is made from the swim bladder of sturgeon. The principal use of isinglass today is in the clarifying of wines and beers.

3 *medium vine-ripened tomatoes, peeled, seeded, and chopped (about 1 cup)*
1 *teaspoon finely minced garlic*
2/3 *cup chopped fresh basil*
2/3 *cup extra-virgin olive oil*
Salt and freshly ground white pepper to taste
4 *8-ounce sturgeon fillets*
Additional olive oil to brush fillets before grilling

1. Combine the tomatoes, garlic, basil, and the olive oil in a bowl. Beat with a wire whisk until a thick sauce forms. Add salt and white pepper to taste. Set aside, covered, in a small stainless steel saucepan. This sauce may be prepared up to 2 hours in advance.

Sturgeon might be referred to as the "knight in shining armor" of the fish world, since its head and body are covered with rows of bony plates.

2. Prepare charcoal grill or preheat broiler. The coals should be glowing with a hint of gray ash before you begin grilling. (Do not place fish on the grill while the fire is still flaming.)
3. Brush the fillets lightly with olive oil. Cook, 3 to 4 inches from heat source, 4 to 5 minutes per side, until just cooked. Arrange on heated serving plates.

Sturgeon fishing will test your skill. And when you catch one, watch out for its powerful tail. In one swipe it can destroy your tackle and inflict wounds.

4. While cooking the fish, uncover the sauce and warm it gently. Do not overcook the sauce or its fresh taste will be lost. Serve over the sturgeon.

Note: If sturgeon is not available, substitute any firm-fleshed fillet, such as tilefish, pollock, or cusk. The Tomato-Basil Sauce also complements steaks such as swordfish, salmon, shark, or halibut.

Serves 4
May be partially prepared in advance

Sturgeon Meunière

The meunière of browned butter is perfectly easy to make and perfectly wonderful with this firm-fleshed fish. If you are not able to find sturgeon, this recipe will work nicely with any other firm-fleshed fish fillet.

1 *cup flour*
$^1/_2$ *teaspoon salt*
$^1/_4$ *teaspoon freshly ground black pepper*
4 *6- to 8-ounce sturgeon fillets*
$^1/_2$ *cup clarified butter (see page 273)*
1 *tablespoon fresh strained lemon juice*
1 *lemon, sliced in thin rounds for garnish*
1 *tablespoon minced fresh parsley for garnish*

1. Combine the flour with the salt and pepper in a shallow plate. Dip the fillets in the flour to coat both sides.
2. Melt the butter in a large heavy skillet over medium-high heat. Sauté the fillets 3 to 4 minutes per side, until the fish is opaque and flakes easily when pierced with the tip of a knife. Remove to a heated serving dish and keep warm.
3. Raise the heat under the skillet and cook until the butter turns brown. Do not let the bits burn.
4. Sprinkle the fillets with the lemon juice, garnish with the lemon rounds, scatter the parsley over the fillets, and top with the brown butter. Serve immediately.

Variation: For a lower-calorie version of this dish, reduce the amount of clarified butter. Use only 1 tablespoon of clarified butter with 3 tablespoons vegetable oil to cook the fish. Serve the fish as soon as it is cooked through, topped with parsley and lemon slices.

Serves 4

A sturgeon swims along the bottom of its feeding ground, detecting food with its whiskerlike barbels. The sensitivity of these fleshy barbels may help to compensate for the sturgeon's very poor eyesight.

Sturgeon fishing in the Caspian Sea goes back hundreds of years. The largest sturgeon of all is the great Russian beluga, *Huso huso*. The world record set by this fish was 27 feet in length and 2860 pounds in weight.

A Haul of Herring: Anchovies, Herring, Sardines, and Shad

ANCHOVIES

HERRING

SARDINE

SHAD

All over the world, people love to eat sardines, anchovies, shad, and herring. But people are not the only predators of these little fishes. Because of their size and abundance, these fishes are an important link in the ocean food chain wherever they flourish, and enormous colonies of seabirds, such as cormorants and terns, depend on them for food.

In addition, a periodic weather change called El Niño threatens sardines, anchovies, and their kin. El Niño, which means "the child" in Spanish, is so named because it usually starts around Christmas. Every ten years or so, this mysterious phenomenon warms the surface of the ocean. During this period, which lasts from three months to a year, the populations of these little fishes are driven away. Although the fishes eventually come back, occurrences of El Niño have brought calamity to the sardine and anchovy fishing industries in those areas.

So the next time you open a can of sardines or blend an anchovy into your Caesar salad, think of what a big effect such a little fish can have.

Mozzarella in Carozza

Just the smell of this sandwich being sautéed is sufficient to convert the most obstinate anchovy hold-out. The combination of bland mozzarella cheese with the salty piquant anchovies works beautifully. The cooked sandwich may be cut into bite-size portions and served as an hors d'oeuvre, rather than as an entree.

2–4 *flat anchovy fillets, drained and finely minced*
8 *slices of bread, crusts trimmed*
4 *slices mozzarella cheese*
Oil *for frying*
2 *eggs, lightly beaten*
2 *tablespoons milk*
1 *cup bread crumbs*

1. Spread the anchovies on 4 slices of bread. Add a slice of cheese, cut slightly smaller than the bread, and top with a second slice of bread. Pinch the edges together to seal.

114

2. Heat a large nonstick skillet and add just enough oil to coat the pan for cooking.
3. Combine the beaten eggs with the milk in a shallow dish. Dip each sandwich in the egg mixture to coat. Dip the sandwich edges in the bread crumbs.
4. Sauté the sandwiches until golden brown on each side. Serve at once on heated plates.

Serves 4

Archie's Herring

Easy. . .good tasting. . .and a snap to prepare ahead for serving as an appetizer or hors d'oeuvre.

1 *pound herring in white wine*
1 *large lemon*
1 *large orange*
1 *large Bermuda onion, thinly sliced*
1 *tablespoon white wine vinegar*
1 *cup sour cream*

1. Drain the herring and place it in a glass or ceramic bowl.
2. Cut off one-quarter of the lemon from one end and reserve. Slice the center portion of the lemon into the thinnest possible slices. Reserve the other end of the lemon. Repeat with the orange.
3. Squeeze the juice from the lemon and orange ends onto the herring.
4. Discard any seeds in the lemon and orange slices. Add these slices and the onion slices to the herring.
5. Combine the vinegar with the sour cream and stir into the herring mixture. Cover and refrigerate for at least 3 hours, or up to several days.
6. Serve on lettuce leaves for an appetizer. To serve as an hors d'oeuvre, serve with crackers or hollow out a large round of pumpernickel. Cut the pieces of bread into thin slices and reserve. Fill the hollow with the herring mixture and serve with the bread slices.

Serves 6
Must be prepared in advance

Anchovies, a close relative of the herring family, are found in many waters of the world. There are ten species of anchovies on the Atlantic Coast and much of the catch is used for bait. However, we can enjoy these fish as much as larger fish do. They are delicious and are served as "whitebait," a term used for lots of very small fish. The anchovy is more commonly known in this country as the tiny fillet that has been salt cured and canned in olive oil.

Atlantic herring inhabit both sides of the North Atlantic Ocean and are found on the east coast of the United States as far south as Virginia. There are many other familiar members of the herring family including the alewife and menhaden. In all, there are 27 species of herrings in North America.

Herring and Beet Salad

You will often find this salad included in a Scandinavian smorgasbord, while in Holland it is considered a New Year's Eve specialty. It makes a delicious appetizer. Salt herring is traditionally used in the salad. It can be ordered at many fish markets as well as some ethnic food stores. German or Scandinavian delicatessens often carry a variety of herring. If salt herring is unavailable, substitute herring packed in white wine and proceed to step 2.

1   *pound salt herring fillets*
1 1/2   *cups diced boiled potatoes*
1 1/2   *cups diced cooked beets*
1   *cup diced tart apple*
1/2   *cup chopped celery*
1/2   *cup chopped mild onion*
1   *teaspoon minced fresh dill*
1   *tablespoon minced dill pickle*
1/4   *cup white wine vinegar*
1   *tablespoon water*
2   *tablespoons sugar*
1/2   *teaspoon freshly ground black pepper*
3/4   *cup sour cream*
Lettuce leaves

1. Rinse the herring, then soak in cold water overnight to "refresh" fish.
2. Drain the fish, remove the skin, and dice.
3. Combine the fish, potatoes, beets, apples, celery, onion, dill, and pickle in a glass or ceramic bowl.
4. Blend the vinegar, water, sugar, and pepper. Stir in the sour cream and pour over the fish mixture. Mix thoroughly, cover, and refrigerate for at least 1 hour, or overnight.
5. Serve on a bed of lettuce.

Serves 4–6
Must be prepared in advance

Herrings and their relatives form one of the world's most important fisheries. They also are a vital part of the marine food chain.

Herring are known as schooling fish; large numbers of similar-size fish swim together, appearing as a dark mass from above, while their silvery sides and bellies flash in the water. Because they swim in these large groups, they are easily harvested with purse seines or in weirs (fish traps).

Deviled Herring

Fresh herring is a spring favorite in New England. This entree is easy to prepare and can be used with a variety of other small fishes such as "snappers" (very young bluefish), smelt, or butterfish.

> 8 *small herring (about 2 pounds), cleaned*
> 2 *tablespoons Dijon-style mustard*
> 3 *drops Tabasco sauce (optional)*
> 1 *cup dry bread crumbs*
> 1/2 *cup butter, melted (1 stick)*
> 1 *lemon, thinly sliced for garnish*

1. Make several diagonal slashes on each side of the fish. Spread a thin coating of mustard (and Tabasco) on the skin of each herring.
2. Roll the fish in the bread crumbs and place on a wire rack for 10 minutes to set the coating.
3. Preheat broiler and broiler pan.
4. Place the fish on the heated pan and broil for 10 minutes about 5 inches from the heat source. Baste the fish with melted butter several times while they cook. Test for doneness with a knife point. The fish should be opaque and flake easily when cooked through.
5. Serve with the lemon slices.

Serves 4

Herring has long played an important role in the economic and gastronomic history of Europe. One of the reasons the Hanseatic League foundered was the shift in abundance of herring from the Baltic to the North Sea, pushing the balance of power to Holland.

Herrings are one of the most plentiful fishes in the Atlantic. There is no great demand for fresh herring, but they are very popular in other forms such as smoked, canned, salted, pickled, or kippered.

Sardine Pâté

For a picnic specialty, serve this pâté with crackers, celery sticks, or cucumber rounds.

6 tablespoons minced onion
1/2 cup fish or chicken stock
2 3 3/4-ounce cans sardines, drained and patted dry
1/2 cup mayonnaise
1 tablespoon chopped sweet pickles
2 tablespoon capers, rinsed and drained
1 hard-boiled egg, chopped
2 tablespoons snipped fresh chives

1. Combine the onion and stock in a small pan. Simmer until the onion is soft and the stock is reduced to about 1 teaspoon. Let cool.
2. Mash the sardines in a bowl. Add the onion and stock mixture, mayonnaise, pickles, capers, egg, and chives. Mix thoroughly and pack into a small crock. Cover and refrigerate at least 1 hour, or up to 24 hours, before serving.

Serves 4
Must be prepared in advance

Sardines are an excellent source of calcium.

If you like sardines, make a Danish Open-Faced Sardine Sandwich. For each sandwich, spread a slice of thin bread, such as Westphalian rye, with mayonnaise and Dijon-style mustard. Place a leaf of Bibb or Boston lettuce on top, then add paper-thin slices of red onion. Top with drained boneless sardines and thinly sliced cucumbers. Delicious!

Sardines in Mustard Sauce

Tired of the same old salad? This tart, lemony dressing combined with sardines is a refreshing and unusual way to usher in almost any entree. Accompany with small slices of dark whole-grain bread, spread lightly with unsalted butter.

1 3³/₄-ounce can of sardines, drained and patted dry
¹/₂ cup fresh strained lemon juice
¹/₄ cup Dijon-style mustard
3 tablespoons olive oil
1 tablespoon white wine vinegar
1 ¹/₂ teaspoons sugar
3 tablespoons minced fresh dill
¹/₄ teaspoon salt
Freshly ground black pepper
Bibb or Boston lettuce
¹/₄ cup sliced radishes

1. Place the sardines in a shallow dish and cover with the lemon juice. Let marinate about 2 hours. Drain and set aside.
2. Spoon the mustard into a small bowl and whisk in the oil gradually. Add the vinegar, sugar, dill, salt, and pepper to taste. Pour this sauce over the sardines. Cover and chill for at least 2 hours, or up to 12 hours.
3. To serve, place the lettuce on 2 plates and divide the sardines and radishes equally between the plates.

Variation: If you are a real sardine fan, you may want to increase the amount of sardines and use this dish as a luncheon entree.

Serves 2
Must be prepared in advance

Young herring, about 4 to 5 inches long, are often called sardines. This name originated from the canning industry that began on the island of Sardinia in the Mediterranean Sea.

"The gentle art of gastronomy is a friendly one. It hurdles the language barrier, makes friends among civilized people, and warms the heart."—Sam Chamberlain

No-Bones Baked Shad

The American shad, the largest member of the herring family, is found from Southern Labrador to mid-Florida. These fish spend their lives in the ocean, migrating to their native river to spawn. The shad is prized more for its roe than its delicious, but very bony, meat.

The Hudson, Connecticut, and Delaware rivers are favorite spawning grounds for the shad, and serious efforts are being made to free these rivers from pollution.

The Shad

I'm sure that Europe never had
A fish as tasty as the shad.
Some people greet the shad
*   with groans,*
Complaining of its countless
*   bones.*
I claim the bones teach table
*   poise*
And separate the men from
*   boys.*
The shad must be dissected
*   subtle-y;*
Besides, the roe is boneless,
*   utterly.*
                    —Ogden Nash

A remarkable method for preparing baked shad. The multitude of small bones dissolve in this slow cooking process, leaving only the sweet and delicate flesh behind.

1 *4-pound shad, cleaned*
Salt and pepper
1/4 *cup fresh strained lemon juice*
3 *celery stalks*
3 *bay leaves*
1 *small onion, peeled and quartered*
3 *cups water*
1 *cup white wine*

1. Preheat oven to 300 degrees.
2. Rinse the shad and pat dry. Sprinkle it inside and out with the lemon juice, salt, and pepper.
3. Place the shad on a rack in a large baking dish or use a fish steamer. Add celery, bay leaves, onion, water, and wine to just touch the bottom of the rack.
4. Cover the dish and steam for 5 hours in the preheated oven.
5. Serve the shad with spring vegetables.

Serves 4

Tasty Touches: Catfish and Carp

Catfishes and carps are members of a large group of fishes distinguished by an excellent sense of touch, as well as superb sense of taste, smell, and hearing. That these faculties are necessary is not surprising to anyone who has tried to see anything in the muddy waters that many such species frequent. Their catlike whiskers, or barbels, help them taste and feel for food along the bottoms of lakes and rivers.

Catfish are raised on fish farms in the United States, primarily in Mississippi, and are now sold in most regions of the country. Carp are farmed extensively in China, but they exist naturally in the United States.

CATFISH

COMMON CARP

Herbed Baked Catfish

This recipe is especially good if fresh herbs are used. Other thin fillets, such as ocean pout, can also be prepared in this manner.

> 1   cup plain dried bread crumbs
> 2   tablespoons minced fresh parsley
> 2   teaspoons lemon zest (use only the yellow part of rind)
> 1   tablespoon minced fresh oregano
> 1/4   teaspoon paprika
> Pinch of cayenne pepper, or more to taste
> 2   pounds catfish fillets, patted dry
> 1   cup buttermilk
> 1   tablespoon olive oil
> Lemon wedges for garnish

1. Preheat oven to 450 degrees.
2. In a shallow bowl, combine the bread crumbs, parsley, lemon zest, oregano, paprika, and cayenne. Mix well.
3. Soak the catfish fillets in the buttermilk for a few minutes.
4. Dip the fillets, one at a time, into the crumb mixture. Coat well and place on a wire rack. Let the fillets "dry" for 10 minutes before baking. This will help the crumbs adhere to the fish.
5. Rub a baking dish with the olive oil and place it in the oven to heat.
6. Place the catfish fillets in the heated baking dish in the oven. Using the Canadian Guideline, bake the

Most catfish have barbels, whiskerlike feelers that extend from each side of the upper jaw. Some catfish also have these barbels on the lower jaw to help the fish locate food.

Catfish farms are a successful aquaculture industry in more than thirty states. This profitable "crop" may yield as much as a ton of fish per acre. The farmed catfish is considered better tasting than those caught in the wild. The cleaner water and regulated diet produce a fish with better texture and flavor.

fish according to its thickness or until it flakes easily when pierced with the tip of a knife.

7. Serve immediately, garnished with lemon wedges.

Serves 4–6

Cajun Catfish

Look out! This recipe uses a hot and spicy seasoning mix for outdoor grilling. The seasoning mix may be made in larger quantities to have on hand all summer for other fish or any-time to "warm up." Try it with skinless ocean perch, ocean pout, hake, cusk, or even flounder fillets.

> 1 1/2 tablespoons sweet Hungarian paprika
> 1/2 teaspoon celery salt
> 1 teaspoon onion powder
> 1 teaspoon garlic powder
> 1 teaspoon cayenne pepper
> 1 teaspoon white pepper
> 1/2 teaspoon black pepper
> 1/2 teaspoon dried thyme
> 1/2 teaspoon dried oregano
> 2 pounds catfish fillets
> 1/2 cup vegetable oil
> Lemon wedges for garnish
> Parsley sprigs for garnish

1. Prepare a charcoal grill.
2. Combine the seasonings.
3. Dip the fillets into the oil, then place them in a wire grilling basket.* Sprinkle approximately 1 teaspoon of seasoning mix on each side of the fish.
4. When the coals are red-hot but not flaming, place the grilling basket on the heated grill. Cook accord-ing to the thickness of the fish, about 3 to 5 minutes on each side.
5. Remove to a heated platter. Serve immediately, gar-nished with lemon wedges and parsley sprigs.

*Note: Using a grilling basket makes it easier to turn the fish during cooking, particularly when using small fish. If such a basket is unavailable, the fish may be placed on heavy aluminium foil on the grill and turned halfway through cooking. Poke several holes in the aluminum foil so that the fish will benefit from charcoal flavor.

Serves 4–6

In Japan, some people say that when a catfish acts nervous, an earthquake may strike.

Pan-fried catfish, a regional specialty of the Deep South, can now be enjoyed in many areas of the country because of the success of catfish farming. For a crisp fried fillet of catfish, follow the directions for Pan-Fried Tilapia or Perch (page 169) (or use another type of breading), adding a pinch of cayenne pepper to the breading. Sauté as directed, in vegetable oil, and serve with Tartar Sauce, or Mustard Mayonnaise, (see Chapter 7).

Gefilte Fish

Gefilte fish is a traditional course at many Jewish holiday dinners. The term "gefilte" fish means filled or stuffed fish. Making gefilte fish in the old-fashioned way is a lengthy, labor-intensive process. Most families now use a good, bottled product, and garnish it with colorful, sweet peppers.

16 *leaves red leaf lettuce*
16 *leaves green leaf lettuce*
2 *24-ounce jars Gefilte fish, made with carp*
1 *large carrot, peeled and cut in matchsticks*
1 *green pepper, cored, seeded, and cut in matchsticks*
1 *yellow pepper, cored, seeded, and cut in matchsticks*
1 *red pepper, cored, seeded, and cut in matchsticks*
4 *hard-boiled eggs, cut in quarters*
3 *tablespoons minced fresh parsley*

1. Arrange one piece of red leaf lettuce and one piece of green leaf lettuce on each serving plate. Place one piece of fish on each plate and garnish with the carrot, different peppers, and an egg quarter. Sprinkle with the parsley and serve.

Serves 16

Carp is one of the important ingredients of many gefilte fish recipes, and carp roe is often made into the favorite Greek dish, Taramosalata.

The Japanese are fond of carp, which represent the qualities of strength and endurance. According to legend, these characteristics may be obtained by eating the carp.

Some of the most beautiful and expensive fish in the world are carp. Koi, which are brilliantly colored and often very valuable Japanese goldfish, are members of the carp family. However, the ones that are usually eaten are rather dark olive green on top, shading to yellow on the belly.

Carp in Aspic with Cognac Mayonnaise

Barbara Rochatka-Riley, food writer and consultant, suggests that although "this recipe may seem involved, try it for a luncheon; it's wonderfully creative and delicious." If you cannot find carp, use another firm white-fleshed fish such as hake. The cognac mayonnaise is simple to make and goes well with a variety of cold dishes.

Some people mistakenly believe that allspice is a combination of spices. Actually it is the dried berry of the Pimento tree, native to the West Indies and Central America. The berry's mingled fragrance of clove, cinnamon, and nutmeg gives rise to its name.

There are three types of Madeira—Sercial, Rainwater, and Malmsey. Sercial is the driest, Rainwater (or Verdelho) is a light but sweeter version, and Malmsey is dark brown in color and the sweetest of the three.

Carp are very hardy fish. They can tolerate either high or low water temperatures for a day or two, and if the oxygen supply in the water becomes low, they are capable of absorbing oxygen from the air.

4 cups chicken broth, preferably homemade
2 pounds skinless carp fillets, cut into 2-inch pieces
7 black peppercorns
2 allspice berries
2 bay leaves
1 tablespoon capers, rinsed and drained
2 sprigs fresh thyme, or 1/8 teaspoon dried thyme
1/4 cup Sercial Madeira
2 teaspoons fresh strained lemon juice
1/2 teaspoon salt
1 1/2 tablespoons unflavored gelatin
3 tablespoons cold water
1/3 cup thin carrot slices, blanched in boiling water for 2 minutes
1 large lemon, thinly sliced and seeded
4 hard-boiled eggs, cut into wedges
1/4 cup small black pitted olives
1/4 cup small parsley sprigs
Spinach leaves, cherry tomatoes, parsley sprigs for garnish
Cognac Mayonnaise (see recipe below)

1. Bring the broth to a boil in a deep skillet. Add the carp, peppercorns, allspice, bay leaves, capers, and thyme. Partially cover the pan, return to a boil, then lower the heat and simmer for 12 to 15 minutes or until the fish is opaque.
2. Remove the fish from the cooking liquid and refrigerate.
3. Line a colander with a double thickness of cheesecloth that has been rinsed in cold water and wrung dry. Pour the cooking liquid through the colander. Combine the strained liquid with Madeira, lemon juice, and salt. Set aside.
4. Dissolve the gelatin in the water in a small bowl. Stir in the reserved liquid and allow it to cool slightly.
5. Pour a thin layer of the cooled liquid into a 3-inch-deep loaf pan or 2-quart mold. Refrigerate. When

the aspic is lightly set, decoratively arrange the carrot and lemon slices, eggs, olives, and parsley sprigs on the surface. Pour another thin layer of liquid over the vegetables and refrigerate.

6. When the aspic is set, arrange the fish pieces on top and gently add the remaining liquid. Cover and refrigerate for several hours or overnight.

7. Unmold the aspic on a bed of spinach leaves and garnish with cherry tomatoes and parsley. Serve with Cognac Mayonnaise.

Cognac Mayonnaise

1 *cup mayonnaise, preferably homemade*
1 *tablespoon tomato paste*
2 *tablespoons cognac*
1 *teaspoon Dijon-style mustard*

1. Whisk the tomato paste, cognac, and mustard into the mayonnaise and refrigerate for 30 minutes to allow the flavors to blend. The recipe makes 1 cup.

Serves 6
Must be prepared in advance

Braised Carp

Braising vegetables along with the fish infuses the fish with hints of thyme, leek, and celery. The bounty of vegetables surrounding the whole fish makes quite a presentation—nothing to carp about! This method of stuffing and braising may be used with any whole cleaned fish.

1 *whole carp, about 5 to 6 pounds, cleaned*
1 *tablespoon fresh strained lemon juice*
3/4 *cup finely diced or shredded carrot*
2 *tablespoons sliced scallions, using white and tender green parts*
2 *tablespoons sliced leek, using white parts only*
1/4 *cup minced celery*
1/4 *cup celery leaves*
1/4 *teaspoon dried thyme or other favorite herb*
3 *cups fish stock (see page 277)*
1 *cup white wine*
4 *tablespoons unsalted butter*
1 *tablespoon minced fresh parsley*
Salt *and pepper to taste*

Native to Asia, the carp has been introduced into many European countries as well as the United States. The common carp was first introduced into the United States by the United States Fish Commission in the late 1870s as a food fish. These imports came from Germany where carp farming was well established.

Izaak Walton referred to carp as "the Queen of the Rivers: a stately, a good, and a very subtle fish. . ."

1. Preheat oven to 400 degrees.
2. Rinse the carp, including the cavity, with the lemon juice. Dry with paper towels.
3. Combine the carrot, scallion, leek, celery, celery leaves, and thyme. Mix well. Fill the fish cavity with this mixture. Sew the sides of the cavity together with a needle and thread, or use skewers and thread in the same manner as trussing a stuffed chicken or turkey. (Unflavored dental floss works extremely well!)
4. Place the fish in a large roasting pan with 1 cup of the fish stock and the wine. Cover the pan loosely with foil and place it in the oven. Cook for about 45 minutes, following the Canadian Guideline of 10 minutes per inch of thickness of the fish. The fish is cooked when it flakes easily when pierced with the tip of a knife. While the fish cooks, baste it frequently with pan juices.
5. Meanwhile, in a small skillet, over high heat, bring the remaining 2 cups of fish stock to a boil. Continue boiling until the stock is reduced to $1/2$ cup. Remove from heat and allow to cool for 10 minutes. Enrich the stock reduction by whisking in the butter, 1 tablespoon at a time. Stir in the parsley and season with salt and pepper to taste. Set aside and keep warm.
6. To serve, remove the skin from the fish, transfer the fish to a heated platter, and open the cavity to serve the vegetable stuffing. The sauce should be served separately.

Serves 4

Carp were a popular food fish during the Middle Ages. Many of the monasteries of that era contain decorative but useful carp pools.

The Chinese have been raising carp in ponds for more than 2000 years. Carp provide an inexpensive source of protein and are used in many Chinese dishes.

Sacred Cods: Cod, Cusk, Haddock, Hake, Pollock, and Whiting

The fishes in this group have several characteristics in common. They are closely related, live and feed near the bottom, swim in large schools, and are dietary staples on both sides of the Atlantic. It was the search for the cod that first brought fishermen from Portugal to the fish-rich waters off the coast of the Massachusetts cape, which was later named for the cod.

The underutilized members of this family (cusk, hake, and pollock) deserve special attention. They are much less expensive than the well-known cod and haddock and have similar firm mild meat. They are excellent in soups and stews and can be used in many baked dishes.

CODFISH

CUSK

HADDOCK

HAKE

POLLOCK

**WHITING
(SILVER HAKE)**

Samuel Adams said, "*The codfish was to Massachusetts what wool was to England or tobacco to Virginia, the great staple which became the basis of power and wealth.*"

127

Brandade

Brandade is a traditional French salt cod preparation that can be made ahead and served as an hors d'oeuvre.

> 1 *pound salt cod, skinned and boned (pre-packaged*
>   *variety)*
> 2 *large garlic cloves, quartered*
> ¹/₄ *cup cooked potato, packed down to measure*
> 1 – 1 ¹/₂ *cups olive oil*
> 1 *tablespoon fresh strained lemon juice*
> *Freshly ground white pepper*

1. Rinse the cod under cold running water. Place it in a large bowl and cover with cold water. Refrigerate 8 to 10 hours, changing the water 4 or 5 times. Place in a saucepan, cover with cold water, and simmer gently 20 minutes over moderate heat. Drain the fish and set aside.
2. Process the garlic until minced in the work bowl of a food processor fitted with the steel knife. Add the cod and process on and off, until smooth. Add the potato and process again. With the machine running, add the oil through the feed tube in a steady stream, scraping the bowl as necessary. Check the consistency after approximately ³/₄ cup of oil has been added; it should resemble mashed potatoes. Keep adding oil until the proper consistency has been achieved. Add the lemon juice and pepper. Taste and correct the seasoning.
3. Cover and refrigerate, if desired. It can be made up to 48 hours in advance. Let it come to room temperature before serving.
4. Serve as a spread with toast points.

Variation: Spread on toast, sprinkle with grated Parmesan cheese, and run under a broiler for 1 minute. Serve hot.

Yield: 3 cups
May be prepared in advance

Codfish Balls

This traditional New England dish has graced many local dinner tables accompanied by Boston baked beans. Whether the fish balls should have a smooth surface or a "whiskery" one, is a typical Bostonian controversy.

Salting cod was one of the earliest methods used to preserve the catch. Canada is a leading producer of salt cod, which is a popular food in many countries. Much of it is consumed in Spain and Portugal where it is known as *bacalao*.

There are two market forms of dried salt cod. Whole dried salt cod, with skin and bone, is usually found only in ethnic markets. Pieces of dried salt cod, skinned and boned, are usually sold in small boxes and available in many supermarkets. The boxed variety needs much less soaking time and is more convenient to use. Although some cooks are adamant about the superior quality of the whole variety, we found the boxed version produces excellent results in our recipes. The length of soaking time depends on the market format, as well as the purity of the salt used in processing, the percent of sodium in the brining solution, and finally, upon one's individual taste. Less soaking time will result in a saltier flavor.

½ pound salt cod, skinned and boned
2 cups cubed potatoes
1 egg, beaten lightly
Freshly ground white pepper
Dash of cayenne pepper
Oil for deep frying

1. Cut the salt cod into small pieces and refresh in cold water for 15 minutes, rinsing several times before draining.
2. Place the salt cod and potatoes in a medium-size saucepan and cover with cold water. Bring to a boil, then reduce heat and simmer for 20 minutes. Drain well and mash thoroughly. Beat in the egg and whip with a hand mixer until the consistency is smooth. Beat in white pepper and cayenne.
3. Using two forks, form the mixture into 16 portions roughly the size of a golf ball. The forks will produce a whiskery surface. If a smoother surface is desired, roll the fish balls around on a dry counter or cutting board. The recipe may be prepared several hours in advance up to this point. Refrigerate the codfish balls, but set them at room temperature about 15 minutes before cooking.
4. Heat oil for deep-fat frying to 375 degrees. A small cube of bread will brown in 30 seconds when the temperature is correct. Place 3 or 4 balls in the hot fat and cook until golden brown. Drain well and place on brown paper to absorb excess oil. Keep them warm while you cook the remaining fish balls. Be certain the oil is at 375 degrees each time you start frying the fish balls.
5. Serve on heated plates accompanied by your favorite baked beans. Cocktail sauce or a good Dijon-style mustard may be served on the side.

Note: These fish balls may be made smaller to serve as an hors d' oeuvre. It is also possible to freeze the smaller size. Fry lightly, drain thoroughly, and place on a cookie sheet in your freezer. When frozen, transfer to plastic freezer bag and seal tightly. To serve: Place the frozen fish balls on a baking sheet and heat for 10 minutes in a preheated 450 degree oven. Turn them over to brown on the other side and heat for an additional 5 minutes. Drain on brown paper and serve at once.

Serves 4 as an entree or yields about 48 hors d'oeuvres
May be partially prepared in advance

The Atlantic Cod is widely distributed in the North Atlantic Ocean and is found along the coast from Cape Hatteras all the way north to Greenland. Thousands of tons of this fish are commercially harvested each year; cod and other members of the cod family are among the most valuable food fishes of the world.

The New England fishing industry began with the settlement in Gloucester, Massachusetts, where fishermen put out in small boats in search of cod and haddock.

The cod was so important to the New England colonies, not only as a source of food but also a wealth, that it was pictured on bank notes and coins; it later became the emblem of Massachusetts. The "sacred cod" that has hung in the hall of the Massachusetts House of Representatives since 1784 is a famous bit of Americana.

Codfish Sauté

In the early seventeenth century, Bartholomew Gosnold, an English navigator, named Cape Cod for the abundance of codfish being harvested in the bay.

The delicate flavor of the firm white meat of cod lends itself to a wide variety of cooking methods. Whole fish may be stuffed and baked, which is sometimes called "Cape Cod Turkey"; steaks and fillets are baked, grilled, steamed, or poached; and small pieces may be deep-fried.

A cod tongue recipe from the late nineteenth century instructs the cook to "Blanch 18 cod tongues and put in a saucepan with ½ gill of the liquor they were blanched in. Serve with a pint of black butter sauce."

"And this is good old Boston,
The home of the bean
        and the cod,
Where the Lowells talk
        only to Cabots
And the Cabots talk
        only to God."—
John Collins Bossidy—
        (a toast given in 1910)

Artichoke hearts turn the common cod into an elegant dinner dish. This recipe adapts to almost any firm-fleshed fish. Try it with monkfish or wolffish, as well as any other fish from the cod family.

> 1 *tablespoon butter*
> 1 *tablespoon oil*
> 1 *pound boiling potatoes, peeled and cut into 1-inch cubes*
> 2 *teaspoons minced garlic*
> ⅓ *cup diced onion*
> *Salt and pepper to taste*
> ½ *cup flour*
> 1½ *pounds cod fillets, cut into 1-inch chunks*
> 1 *10-ounce package frozen artichoke hearts, thawed and drained*
> 1 *cup small tomato wedges*

1. Melt the butter in a deep skillet. Add the oil and increase the heat. When the oil and butter are bubbling, add the potatoes, garlic, and onion. Cover and cook over medium-low heat for 15 minutes, stirring occasionally.
2. Add salt and pepper to the flour. Dust the fish chunks with this flour mixture and add them to the skillet. Stir in the artichoke hearts and tomato wedges and cook for an additional 10 minutes. The fish will appear opaque when it is cooked.
3. Spoon onto a heated serving dish or serve directly from the skillet.

Serves 6

Steamed Scrod and Vegetable Pouch

Make as many pouches as you have diners, selecting a variety of seasonal vegetables. Try using asparagus in the spring or zucchini and eggplant in the summer. The possibilities are almost limitless with vegetables as well as fish. Any firm-fleshed white fish can be used, such as hake, cusk, salmon, flounder, wolffish, and tilefish. Just be certain to adjust the cooking time according to the thickness of the fillet.

1 tablespoon very thin red pepper slices
1/3 cup very thin carrot slices
3 thin onion rings, about 2 inches in diameter
3 snow pea pods, ends trimmed and strings removed
1 6-ounce scrod fillet, at least 1/2-inch thick
1/4 teaspoon minced fresh dill
1 tablespoon butter (optional)
1 tablespoon white wine (optional)

1. Preheat oven to 400 degrees.
2. Blanch the vegetables in boiling salted water for 30 seconds. Drain thoroughly.
3. Place the scrod in the center of a square of heavy-duty aluminum foil. Arrange the vegetables on top of the fish, sprinkle with the dill and add the wine and butter if desired. Fold the foil together, tightly sealing the edges to form a pouch.
4. Place the pouch directly on the oven rack and bake for 15 minutes.
5. Remove the pouch from the oven and poke a small hole in the top to allow steam to escape. Open the pouch and serve with small new potatoes.

Serves 1

It Pays to Advertise

The codfish lays ten thousand
  eggs
The homely hen lays one.
The codfish never cackles
To tell you she's all done.
And so we scorn the codfish,
While the humble hen we prize.
Which only goes to show you,
That it pays to advertise.

Anonymous

Scrod with Mustard Butter

Today, Boston scrod is always young cod or haddock weighing less than 2 pounds. In the olden days "scrod" simply referred to the freshest fish of the cod family, whether it was haddock, cod, pollock, or hake. Use this mustard butter to brown and flavor the fish, whatever kind you use. Any white fish fillet will work in this recipe. Try it with tilapia or freshwater perch.

1/2 cup unsalted butter (1 stick)
2 tablespoons minced onion
2 tablespoons lemon juice
1 1/2 tablespoons Dijon-style mustard
1 teaspoon paprika
2 drops Tabasco sauce
Salt and pepper to taste
2 1/2 pounds scrod fillets

Tomcod is found in relatively shallow water from Labrador to Virginia. Similar in shape to cod, this fish is usually quite small, weighing less than 1 1/2 pounds. It is not commercially harvested, but is considered an excellent eating fish.

1. Preheat broiler.
2. Melt the butter in a skillet over moderate heat. Stir in onion, lemon juice, mustard, paprika, Tabasco, salt, and pepper. Blend well and remove from heat.
3. Dip the fillets in the mustard butter, then place them on a broiler pan. Broil 5 to 10 minutes, depending on the thickness of the fillets. The fish is cooked when it flakes easily when pierced with the tip of a knife. Baste once or twice with the mustard butter while the fillets cook.
4. Transfer the fillets to a heated serving dish and spoon the pan juices over them before serving.

Serves 6

Baked Mustard-Coated Cusk

Many fish are complemented by this mustard-mayonnaise topping. We encourage you to try it with thick fillets, such as bluefish or monkfish, as well as steak cuts, like shark.

    2 tablespoons mayonnaise
    2 teaspoons Dijon-style mustard
    1 teaspoon dried oregano
    2 pounds skinned cusk fillets
    ³/₄ cup toasted bread crumbs
    Lemon wedges for garnish

1. Preheat oven to 350 degrees.
2. Butter a shallow baking dish large enough to contain the cusk in one layer.
3. In a small bowl, combine the mayonnaise, mustard, and oregano. Blend well. Spread the mayonnaise mixture on top of the fillets. Pat the bread crumbs over the mayonnaise and place the fish in the baking dish. Using the Canadian Guideline (10 minutes of cooking for each inch of thickness), bake the fish according to its thickness or until it is opaque and flakes easily when pierced with the tip of a knife. Serve immediately, garnished with lemon wedges.

Serves 4–6

Cusk is a smaller relative of the cod that is found in deep water from the Newfoundland Banks to southern Massachusetts. Chunks of cusk are good in Grandmother's Fish Chowder because cusk does not fall apart as easily as some of the other white-fleshed fish.

"One cannot think well, love well, if one has not dined well."—Virginia Woolf

Pecan-Crusted Cusk

This regal presentation for an economically priced member of the cod family is simple to put together. Hake or any fillet from the cod family that is not more than ³/₄-inch thick may be substituted for the cusk. Ocean perch and sole also would work. Be sure to skin the fillets. Any finely chopped nuts may be substituted for the pecans.

> 3 *tablespoons unsalted butter*
> 1 *tablespoon fresh strained lemon juice*
> ¹/₄ *teaspoon salt*
> ¹/₈ *teaspoon freshly ground black pepper*
> ³/₄ *cup finely chopped unsalted pecans*
> 2 *pounds skinned cusk fillets*
> 2 *tablespoons vegetable oil*
> 6 *tablespoons medium-dry sherry*

1. Preheat oven to 425 degrees.
2. Melt 2 tablespoons of the butter.
3. Combine the melted butter, lemon juice, salt, and pepper in a shallow dish. Spread the pecans in another shallow dish. Dip the fillets first in the butter/lemon juice mixture to cover, then in the nuts to coat both sides. Lay the coated fillets on a wire rack to allow the coating to set for 10 minutes.
4. In a large nonstick skillet, heat the oil over medium-high heat. Arrange the fillets in one layer in the skillet and sauté 3 to 4 minutes. Turn and sauté the other side 2 to 3 minutes. Remove the fillets from the pan and place them in a lightly buttered baking dish large enough to hold all of them in one layer. Bake uncovered for 10 minutes (using the Canadian Guideline), or until the fish is opaque and flakes easily when pierced with the tip of a knife. Transfer the fillets to a heated serving platter and keep warm.
5. Add the sherry to the skillet and bring to a boil over medium-high heat, scraping up the browned bits remaining in the skillet. Reduce the liquid to 3 tablespoons and swirl in the remaining tablespoon of butter. Spoon over the fish and serve immediately.

Serves 4–6

When John Cabot returned from his first voyage to Newfoundland, he reported that the sea was so filled with fishes that they could be caught by lowering weighted baskets into the water and hauling them on board.

It is always a good idea to rinse any fresh fish product in cold water, and then pat dry with paper toweling before proceeding with a recipe.

Cilantro-Cured Haddock

The basic theory of this recipe is to "cure" the fish while adding subtle flavoring with herbs. This makes a fine appetizer when served on a chilled bed of greens accompanied by lightly buttered whole wheat bread, or an hors d'oeuvre presented on small pieces of buttered wheat bread. If you wish, salmon is a good substitute for the haddock, but then substitute fresh dill for the cilantro.

  1 *tablespoon crushed white peppercorns*
  1 *tablespoon coarse salt*
  1 *tablespoon sugar*
  4 *small haddock fillets with skin, 4 to 5 ounces*
    each
  ³/₄ *cup chopped fresh cilantro*

1. Combine the peppercorns, salt, and sugar. Sprinkle the mixture over the flesh side of the haddock, making sure that the mixture adheres to the fillets.
2. Place two fillets, skin side down, in a small shallow glass dish. Cover with the cilantro and place the remaining two fillets on top of the herbs, flesh side down.
3. Cover the dish tightly with plastic wrap and refrigerate for 24 hours. Drain off any accumulated liquid. Reverse the pairs of fillets so that the top becomes the bottom. Recover with plastic and refrigerate for an additional 24 hours.
4. Gently scrape off the cilantro and pat the fillets dry with paper towel. Using a very sharp knife, slice the fillets into thin pieces before serving.

Variation: Use a combination of other herbs such as tarragon or thyme with chives instead of the cilantro.

Serves 4
Must be prepared in advance

Cilantro is the aromatic leaf of the fresh coriander plant and is sometimes called Chinese parsley. This old world herb is now widely used, especially in Spanish and Mexican cooking. Its flavor is markedly different from that of the pungent coriander seed, which is considered a spice. Coriander seed is usually dried and roasted before being used in such dishes as curry.

Grandmother's Fish Chowder

This is an old family recipe for New England fish chowder that's a favorite for Sunday night supper.

> 2 *pounds skinned haddock fillets, cut in 1-inch chunks**
>
> 2 *ounces rindless salt pork, cut in ¹/₄-inch dice (about ¹/₄ cup)*
>
> ²/₃ *cup coarsely chopped onion*
>
> 1 ¹/₂ *pounds boiling potatoes, peeled and cut in ¹/₂-inch dice*
>
> 4 *cups milk*
>
> 1 *cup evaporated milk*
>
> *Salt and pepper to taste*

*Note: Some fish markets sell small chunks of light-fleshed (not oily) fish for chowder. These are often a good value as they are small leftover bits from larger orders. It would be a good idea to remove the skin, but it is not essential.

1. Place the fish in a large pot with 2 cups cold water. Cover and bring to a boil. Remove the pot from the heat and set aside.
2. While the fish is cooking, sauté the diced salt pork. When the pork bits have browned, transfer them to a paper towel to drain and reserve. Stir the onion into the hot pork fat and cook over low heat until soft.
3. Remove the fish from the cooking liquid and reserve. Add the potatoes to the liquid and bring to a boil over moderate heat. Reduce the heat and simmer until the potatoes are tender.
4. Heat the milk with the evaporated milk in a medium saucepan. Do not let it boil. Add the hot milk, on-ions, and reserved fish to the liquid containing the potatoes. Simmer the chowder for 10 minutes. Sea-son to taste. The chowder may be prepared to this point and refrigerated up to 24 hours. Reheat gently; do not let it boil.
5. Serve in bowls and sprinkle the pork bits on top of chowder.

Serves 6
May be prepared in advance

Haddock live in deeper water than cod, ranging from Newfoundland to New England waters. This fish is similar to the cod but has a black patch called the Devil's Thumbprint, just above the pectoral fin, and a black lateral line that extends the length of the fish. Cod has a white lateral line.

Spanish Fish Salad

While this salad calls for cooked haddock, any of the large-flaked fish (cod, hake, or pollock) in the cod family will make up into a fine salad. It will need to be precooked, either by steaming, baking, or microwaving. With fresh basil and ripe olives, this Mediterranean collage of colors and flavors is good for picnics as it can be made ahead and served from the bowl in which it was mixed. It also makes an excellent appetizer serving 10 or 12 people.

3 tablespoons red wine vinegar
1 tablespoon fresh strained lemon juice
1/4 cup tomato/vegetable juice
1/2 teaspoon freshly ground black pepper
Dash of cayenne pepper
1/2 cup olive oil
1 cup chopped tomatoes
1/2 cup chopped cucumber
1/4 cup chopped and seeded green pepper
1/4 cup chopped and seeded sweet red pepper
1 cup chopped celery
1/4 cup finely chopped red or other sweet onion
2 tablespoons minced fresh parsley
1/2 teaspoon minced garlic
2 tablespoons chopped pitted black olives
3 tablespoons snipped fresh basil
Lettuce leaves for garnish
1 1/2 pounds cooked skinless haddock fillet, cut into
   1-inch chunks

1. In a small bowl, combine the vinegar, lemon juice, tomato/vegetable juice, black pepper, and cayenne. Whisk in the olive oil.
2. Place the tomatoes, cucumber, green and red peppers, celery, onion, parsley, garlic, olives, and basil in a large glass salad bowl. Pour the vinaigrette over the vegetables and toss to coat.
3. Add the fish chunks to the salad and mix gently so the fish does not break apart. Cover with plastic wrap and refrigerate for at least 2 hours, but no longer than 6 hours.
4. Before serving, toss the salad once more to redistribute the dressing. Decoratively insert lettuce leaves around the salad bowl and serve.

Serves 8
Must be prepared in advance

Because haddock fillets are relatively higher priced in the market, they are traditionally sold with the skin on, which just adds to the poundage that you are paying for!

"A smell of basil is good for the heart and head, cureth the infirmities of the heart, taketh away sorrowfulness which comes of melancholia and maketh a man merry and glad."—John Gerard, (a contemporary of Shakespeare)

Kedgeree

Kedgeree was a traditional Victorian breakfast dish served under silver from the sideboard. This recipe would make an unusual entree for brunch or an easy Sunday night supper. You may substitute any smoked white fish for the haddock.

1 *pound smoked haddock fillets*
3 *cups water*
1 *cup raw rice*
2 *tablespoons unsalted butter*
1 *cup cooked peas*
3 *tablespoons minced fresh parsley*
Salt and freshly ground black pepper to taste
1/4 *cup heavy cream, warmed (optional)*
2 *hard-boiled eggs, chopped, for garnish*

1. Cover the fish with the water, bring to the boiling point, then reduce heat and simmer for 15 minutes. Drain, reserving the broth. Break the fish into bite-size pieces and set aside.
2. Cook the rice in 2 cups of the reserved broth. The rice will absorb the flavor and unique yellow color from the smoked haddock.
3. Gently stir the butter, peas, parsley, and fish into the hot rice. Season to taste with salt and pepper. Fold in the cream, if desired, and transfer to a serving bowl. Sprinkle top with chopped hard-boiled eggs.

Note: A very simple version can also be made by combining any cooked fish with cooked rice and peas. A good way to use leftovers!

Serves 4

Finnan Haddie is smoked haddock fillets. Developed in the Scottish fishing port of Findon in the nineteenth century, the popular Findon haddock became known as finnan haddie.

Tri-Colored Terrine of Hake

A terrine, with swirls of orange, white and green, is lovely served on individual plates for an elegant luncheon dish any time of year. But on a summer's evening, served with a salad of thinly sliced tomatoes sprinkled with fresh dill, it is a delight. Although the preparation of a terrine is involved, it can be done in stages, and all the cooking can be completed well in advance of the meal. If you wish, try substituting skinless ocean perch or sole fillet for the hake.

1   1-pound skinless hake fillet
$^1/_2$ pound sea scallops, rinsed and dried
2   egg whites
1   teaspoon salt
$^1/_4$ teaspoon white pepper
1   tablespoon fresh strained lemon juice
2   tablespoons thinly sliced scallions, white part only
1 $^1/_2$ cups heavy cream
$^1/_4$ teaspoon mace
$^1/_8$ teaspoon cayenne pepper
$^1/_2$ teaspoon paprika
1   pound carrots, cooked, well drained and pureed
$^1/_2$ cup minced fresh parsley
2   tablespoons minced fresh dill, or 2 teaspoons dried dill
1   10-ounce package frozen spinach, cooked according to package directions, squeezed dry, and pureed
     Roasted Red Pepper Sauce (see page 264) or Red Tomato Salsa (see page 263)

1. Cut the hake into chunks about 1-inch square. Puree briefly in a food processor fitted with the steel knife. Add the scallops and process until well blended. Add the egg whites, $^1/_2$ teaspoon of the salt, pepper, lemon juice, and scallions. Process until well combined. Refrigerate in a large covered bowl until thoroughly chilled, at least 1 hour. At the same time, chill the beaters of a hand mixer.
2. Preheat oven to 350 degrees.
3. Generously butter a $4^1/_2$ x 9-inch glass loaf pan and set aside. Cut a piece of wax paper to fit the top of the pan and butter one side. Set it aside.
4. With the hand mixer and the chilled beaters, beat the heavy cream into the hake/scallop mixture a little at a time, making sure that each addition is fully incorporated before adding more. Set aside.

Hake, both red and white, are members of the large cod family, but do not resemble cod in looks. The two hakes are difficult to distinguish from one another. They are caught in very deep water by trawlers, and sent to the market as just plain hake. The meat has a soft texture and mild flavor and is usually purchased filleted.

Mace and nutmeg are sister spices. The two are similar in flavor, nutmeg being a little sweeter. Mace is actually the husk of the nutmeg seed. Small graters are specially made for grating nutmeg; it always tastes best when freshly ground.

139

5. Add the mace, cayenne, and paprika to the carrot puree and set aside. In a separate bowl combine the parsley, dill, and the remaining $1/2$ teaspoon salt with the spinach puree. Add 6 tablespoons of the fish puree to each of the vegetable purees and mix thoroughly.

6. Pour the remaining fish puree into the loaf pan. Carefully spoon the carrot puree evenly over the fish, repeat with the spinach puree. To create a marbled effect, insert a spatula in the upper lefthand corner of the pan, scoop under to the lower right, and fold over back to the upper left. Repeat in each corner of the pan. Knock the pan on the counter to expel air bubbles. Cover with the wax paper, buttered side down.

7. Set the loaf pan in a large cake pan on the oven rack. Fill the cake pan with boiling water to come two-thirds of the way up the sides of the loaf pan. Bake 1 hour or until the internal temperature reads 125 degrees. Remove from the oven, remove the loaf pan from the cake pan, and cool. When the terrine is cool, refrigerate until completely chilled, at least 4 hours. Unmold and slice $1/4$-inch thick. Serve with either Roasted Red Pepper Sauce or Red Tomato Salsa.

Variation: For a checkerboard effect, spoon the purees into the loaf pan in the following manner. Divide each puree into 3 equal portions. Starting at the left side and moving to the right, spoon $1/3$ of the fish puree, followed by $1/3$ of the spinach puree, and ending with $1/3$ of the carrot puree into the loaf pan to form the first layer. For the next layer, change the order in which the purees are laid down: spinach, carrot, and fish. The third, and final, layer should be in this order: carrot, fish, and spinach. Cover with the buttered wax paper and bake as described above.

Serves 8
Must be prepared in advance

Pollock Fillet Baked in Wine

This recipe comes to us from Malabar Hornblower, author of several cookbooks, who was extremely helpful in editing our recipes for this book. It works with all members of the cod family, as well as with wolffish and monkfish. Adjust the cooking time to match the thickness of the fillet, using the Canadian Guideline.

1 1-pound skinless pollock fillet
¼ cup finely chopped shallots
¼ teaspoon salt
Freshly ground black pepper
½ cup dry white wine
¼ cup heavy cream
¼ cup toasted bread crumbs
2 tablespoons minced fresh parsley
2 tablespoons unsalted butter, melted

1. Preheat oven to 400 degrees.
2. Butter a shallow baking dish just large enough to contain the pollock fillet. Sprinkle the bottom of the pan with 2 tablespoons of the shallots. Place the fillet on top of the shallots and season with the salt and pepper.
3. Combine the wine and cream and pour it over the fish. Cover the surface of the fish with the bread crumbs, the remaining 2 tablespoons shallots, and the parsley. Drizzle the butter over all.
4. Bake 20 minutes, or until the fish is just opaque and flakes easily when pierced with the tip of a knife. Serve immediately.

Serves 2

Many years ago New England fishermen called pollock "Boston Bluefish" to increase its saleability. But the light gray-blue flesh with its mild flavor hardly needs image enhancement. Most retailers today offer the fish under its original name.

Pollock looks like cod but is darker in color and sleeker in appearance. This fish has a gray-blue flesh that turns white with cooking. The meat is flavorful when fresh. It is excellent to use in chowders as the cooked meat holds together well.

Hot and Sour Pollock

Yes, it may seem like Chinese hot and sour pork, but with pieces of pollock and snow peas, this is a spicy variation on an Oriental theme.

1 *large orange*
2 *egg whites*
2 *tablespoons dry sherry*
4 *tablespoons plus 4 cups peanut oil*
3 *tablespoons cornstarch*
1 *teaspoon salt*
1 *pound skinless pollock, cut in chunks about 1-inch square*
1/2 *pound snow peas, ends and strings removed*
1/2 *cup chicken stock, preferably homemade*
3 *tablespoons cider vinegar*
1 *tablespoon sugar*
2 *tablespoons soy sauce*
2 *tablespoons thinly sliced scallions, including 1 inch of green part*
2 *tablespoons minced gingerroot*
2 *teaspoons minced garlic*
1 *red pepper, cored and seeded, cut in 1/4-inch slices*
1 *teaspoon crushed dried hot red pepper flakes*

1. With a swivel-bladed peeler, remove the peel from the orange. Cut the peel into julienne strips about 2 1/2 inches long and 1/8 inch wide. Simmer the strips in boiling water for 5 minutes. Drain on paper towels and reserve. Squeeze the orange and reserve the juice. Measure the juice and add enough orange juice to make 1 cup. Set aside.
2. In a medium-size bowl beat the egg whites lightly until frothy. Fold in the dry sherry, 2 tablespoons of the peanut oil, 2 tablespoons of the cornstarch, and the salt. Mix thoroughly. Add the pollock chunks and toss them to coat with the mixture. Cover the bowl with plastic wrap and chill for 1 hour.
3. Blanch the snow peas in boiling water to cover for 15 seconds. Drain in a colander and refresh under cold water. Drain and reserve.
4. Combine the orange juice, chicken stock, cider vinegar, remaining 1 tablespoon of cornstarch, the sugar, and soy sauce. Blend well. Set aside and reserve.
5. In a wok or deep fryer, heat 4 cups of the peanut oil to 375 degrees. Fry the pollock 2 or 3 minutes, or until the chunks are golden brown. Drain on paper towels.

6. Heat a clean wok or large skillet over high heat until it is very hot. Add the 2 remaining tablespoons of peanut oil and heat again. Add the scallions, ginger-root, and garlic and stir-fry for 30 seconds, or until fragrant. Add the red pepper slices and the crushed pepper and stir-fry for 30 seconds. Stir the orange juice mixture and add it to the wok and cook, stirring constantly, for 3 minutes. Add the reserved pollock and snow peas and simmer for 1 to 2 minutes or until heated through.
7. Transfer the mixture to a heated platter and garnish with the strips of orange peel.

Serves 4
Must be partially prepared in advance

Pollock Vera Cruz

We have adapted this well-known red snapper recipe to pollock. The assertive sauce can be used with any thick fish fillet or steak that has enough taste to stand up to the sauce. Round out the meal with rice and a crisp green salad.

2 *pounds skinless pollock fillets*
$^1/_2$ *teaspoon salt*
$^1/_2$ *cup fresh strained lime juice*
3 *tablespoons vegetable oil*
$^1/_3$ *cup chopped onion*
2 *crushed garlic cloves*
1 $^1/_2$ *cups peeled, seeded, and chopped tomatoes, or*
     1 $^1/_2$ cups drained canned tomatoes
1 *tablespoon tomato paste*
$^1/_2$ *teaspoon dried oregano*
1 *bay leaf*
$^1/_4$ *cup minced fresh cilantro or parsley*
$^1/_2$ *cup green olives, cut in half and pitted*
3 *tablespoons capers, rinsed and drained*
1 *tablespoon minced jalapeño pepper, fresh or canned*
$^1/_4$ *cup fresh strained lemon juice*

1. Arrange the fillets in a glass or china baking dish large enough to hold them in a single layer. Pierce the fillets in several places. Combine the salt and lime juice and pour over the fish. Marinate in the refrigerator, covered, at least 3 hours or up to 5 hours, turning several times.
2. Heat the oil in a large skillet. Add the onion, and sauté 3 to 4 minutes over moderate heat until softened. Add the garlic and cook 2 minutes. Add all the remaining ingredients. Cook, uncovered, stirring frequently, until most of the liquid has evaporated, about 8 to 10 minutes. The sauce may be prepared up to 5 hours in advance.
3. When you are ready to finish the preparation, preheat the oven to 325 degrees.
4. Drain off all but 2 tablespoons of the lime juice marinade from the fillets. Top the fillets with the sauce. Bake, uncovered, for 20 minutes or until the fish flakes easily when pierced with the tip of a knife. Serve immediately.

Serves 6
May be partially prepared in advance

"Woe to the cook whose sauce has no sting."—Chaucer

Chilled Whiting Fillets with Ginger Sauce

Grated ginger in a yogurt-cream sauce is a summery accompaniment to chilled poached whiting. The dish is a delicious entree on a hot day. Served in smaller portions, it makes an excellent appetizer.

2 *pounds whiting fillets*
6 *cups fish stock (see page 277)*
1 *cup white wine*
12 *black peppercorns*
Lettuce leaves
Parsley sprigs for garnish
1 *recipe Ginger Sauce (see recipe below)*

1. Place the fillets in a large saucepan and cover with the fish stock. Add the wine and peppercorns and bring to the boiling point over moderate heat.
2. Remove the pan from heat and allow the fish to cool in the stock for 30 minutes. Then remove the fillets from the stock and refrigerate at least 1 hour, or up to 24 hours. Strain and reserve the stock for future use. Remove the skin from the fillets before serving, if desired.
3. Serve the whiting on a bed of lettuce, topped with the Ginger Sauce and garnished with a parsley sprig.

Ginger Sauce

3/4 *cup plain yogurt*
1 *tablespoon lemon zest (use only the yellow part of rind)*
2 *teaspoons grated fresh ginger**
1/4 *teaspoon white pepper*
1/4 *cup heavy cream, whipped*

*Note: For a slightly sweet flavor, substitute 1 teaspoon of finely minced preserved (candied) ginger for 1 teaspoon of the grated ginger.

1. Combine the yogurt, lemon zest, grated ginger, and white pepper in a small bowl. Fold into the whipped cream and refrigerate for 1 hour before serving. The sauce will yield about 1 1/3 cups.

Serves 4–6
Must be prepared in advance

When using a wine in cooking, only use one that is fit to drink.

Silver hake, or whiting, live in very deep waters off the New England coast. They are much smaller than other members of the cod family. This fish has mild white meat and, because of its size and texture, is a good fish to poach. Most of the fish is processed and frozen for sale as basic white fish fillets. In the Mediterranean, hake is called *merluza*.

River Runners: Salmon, Trout, Whitefish, and Pike

ATLANTIC SALMON

FRESHWATER TROUT

FRESHWATER WHITEFISH

PIKE

In numbers of species, this is a small group. But its influence in the kitchen is enormous. The firm, rich, oily flesh of salmon, trout, and whitefish delights the eye as well as the palate.

Trout and whitefish live mostly in freshwater streams and lakes, although some species can be found at sea. Like the closely related salmon, trout are nest makers, scooping out depressions in sand or gravel stream bottoms in which to lay their eggs. The elusive ways of the trout are the obsession of many a "compleat angler."

The salmon is famous for its peripatetic life style. As the story goes, adult salmon leave the ocean to swim up rivers and streams in search of the spot where they were hatched. Finally, they arrive exhausted at their goal where they spawn just before dying. In fact, this is only a true description of the several species of Pacific salmon. Atlantic salmon return to the sea after spawning, and over the course of time, make many spawning trips upstream.

Whitefish have a kind of double nature. On the outside they are a drab, dull silvery-white that belies their close relationship with the colorful salmon and trout. On the inside, however, they are filled with rich, flavorful flesh that lends itself to a variety of recipes and especially to smoking. All whitefish live in cold Northern Hemisphere lakes and streams and often are caught commercially with nets rather than hooks.

Only five species of pike survive in the fresh waters of Europe and North America. All specialize as "lunge" predators. A pike lies in wait among the reeds with its toothy mouth agape, and then darts after unwary fishes with a flick of its powerful tail.

Salmon and their kin are very adaptable in the kitchen. All are delicious when smoked.

Salmon Tartare

With wonderful farmed salmon so readily available, it is possible to serve fresh salmon year round. This recipe is a variation of steak tartare, using fresh fish instead of beef. We found this appetizer a delicious change of pace.

3/4 *pound skinless salmon fillet*
1 *teaspoon fresh strained lemon juice*
1 *teaspoon Worcestershire sauce*
1 *tablespoon olive oil*
1 *tablespoon minced fresh parsley*
2 *teaspoons minced sweet onion, such as a Vidalia onion*
1/4 *teaspoon freshly ground black pepper or to taste*
Capers, rinsed and drained, for garnish
Lemon wedges for garnish

1. Mince the salmon very finely. This can be done in a food processor if you are careful not to overprocess.
2. Combine the lemon juice, Worcestershire sauce, and olive oil in a glass bowl. And the minced salmon and mix well. Stir in the parsley, onion, and black pepper. Cover and chill for 30 minutes, or for no more than 2 hours.
3. Spoon the tartare onto chilled plates, garnish with capers and lemon wedges, and serve with buttered toast points.

Serves 4
Must be prepared in advance

Salmon aquaculture has been very successful; as a result, salmon is available year-round. The care and controlled diet of farmed salmon produce consistent quality that is difficult to match in the wild. Salmon belong to the trout family, *Salmonidae*, and are delicious raw or cooked.

Salmo salar is found in coastal waters of the North Atlantic, freshwater streams, and lakes. In the New England area, it is often referred to as "Eastern" salmon. Salmon are anadromous (they go upstream to reproduce), but unlike Pacific salmon, Atlantic salmon do not die after spawning.

To prepare attractive seedless lemon wedges, first cut a thin slice from the stem end of the lemon so that it can stand upright. Then make a cut straight down just to the right of center. Repeat slicing around the center, leaving a squarish core full of seeds. The core may be squeezed for juice. The resulting lemon "wedges" may be made smaller if desired.

Salmon Butter

This is a good spread or dip for melba toast, cucumber slices, and celery sticks.

Salmon is among the most ancient of gourmet foods. Its bones have been discovered in midden heaps dating back to the Stone Age.

$^1/_2$ cup butter (1 stick)
1 $^1/_2$ cups skinned and boned cooked salmon
1 teaspoon grated onion
1 tablespoon fresh strained lemon juice
$^1/_2$ teaspoon salt
$^1/_8$ teaspoon cayenne pepper
3 tablespoons snipped chives

1. Place all the ingredients in the work bowl of a food processor fitted with the steel knife. Pulse on and off until well combined, but not perfectly smooth. Chill for at least 30 minutes, or as long as 24 hours. Serve in a pretty bowl.

Smoked Salmon

Smoked salmon, no matter how it is served, is always elegant. Whether it is small bits on buttered rye bread for hors d'oeuvres, a whole side neatly sliced for an appetizer, or individual portions with favorite garnishes accompanied by a bottle of champagne for a quiet celebration, smoked salmon is a delight to the palate.

Before the actual smoking process begins, the fish is "cured" either with dry salt or in a 70 to 80 percent saline brine. This important step firms up the flesh and preserves the fish. Curing takes from 1 to 24 hours, depending on the size of the fish and the particular recipe. When the curing is finished, the fish is rinsed in fresh water and allowed to air-dry for several hours before being placed in the smokehouse.

Variation: This salmon butter may be piped into cherry tomatoes or snow pea pods. For small cherry tomatoes, remove stem, slice off top, and reserve. Hollow out the cherry tomato and turn upside down on a paper towel to drain. Fill hollow with salmon butter and replace top. To fill snow pea pods, first remove the ends and strings.

Yield: 2 cups
Must be prepared in advance

Smoked Salmon Appetizer

Slices of smoked Scotch salmon served on glass plates, garnished with lemon slices and parsley, make an elegant appetizer. Other types of salmon such as hot smoked salmon, which has a smokier flavor, and Nova salmon may also be served in this manner. Allow 1 1/2 to 2 ounces per person.

1   *side of smoked Scotch salmon (about 1 1/2 to 2 pounds), with skin*
2–3 *lemons, sliced*
Parsley for garnish
Mild olive oil
Freshly ground black pepper
1   *large sweet onion (such as Vidalia), thinly sliced*
3/4 *cup capers, rinsed and drained*
24 *thin slices of whole wheat bread, crusts removed, cut in half*
Unsalted butter at room temperature

1. Place the side of salmon, skin side down, on a large carving board. Use a very sharp, flexible knife. Holding the knife at a 45-degree angle toward the fish's tail, cut very thin slices, starting at the tail end and working toward the head.
2. To serve, arrange several slices on a plate along with lemon slices and a parsley sprig. Drizzle a few drops of oil and grind the pepper mill once over the slices.
3. Place the onion slices and capers in separate bowls as optional accompaniments. A small cruet of olive oil and a sturdy pepper grinder should be available for those who want more.
4. Lightly butter the bread slices to serve with the salmon.

Serves 10–12

The two basic smoking methods, "cold smoking" or "hot smoking," determine the consistency and flavor of the finished product. The slower "cold smoking" process does not actually cook the salmon, but dries it out and lends flavor to the fish, particularly if aromatic woods are used. The smokehouse temperature is maintained between 75 and 90 degrees Fahrenheit, and the fish is smoked from 36 to 72 hours. The resulting "cold smoked" salmon is slightly moist, delicately flavored, and easy to slice.

In the "hot smoking" process, smokehouse temperatures range between 160 and 180 degrees Fahrenheit, and the fish actually cooks. The smoking is accomplished in several hours and results in a finished product that is drier and flakes more easily than cold-smoked salmon.

Danish, Irish, Norwegian, and Scotch smoked salmon are usually products of the "cold smoked" method using the Atlantic salmon.

Pacific or Alaskan smoked salmon is generally available using either the "hot smoked" or the "cold smoked" method.

Fourth of July Salmon Salad

In New England, it is traditional to serve salmon and peas on July 4. You needn't wait for the 4th to enjoy this recipe, however, as it is good year-round. If you like, you may use this salad in pita bread sandwiches.

> 1 tablespoon fresh strained lemon juice
> 1 tablespoon Balsamic vinegar or red wine vinegar
> 1 teaspoon Dijon-style mustard
> 1/2 teaspoon salt
> 1/4 teaspoon freshly ground black pepper
> 1 hard-boiled egg yolk, mashed to a paste
> 4 tablespoons olive oil
> 2 cups skinned and boned cooked salmon, dark portions removed, or canned salmon, rinsed and drained
> 1/2 cup fennel bulb or celery cut in matchsticks
> 1/3 cup red radish, in small dice
> 5 tablespoons minced fresh dill
> 2 tablespoons thinly sliced scallions
> 1/2 cup peas, preferably fresh, cooked until barely tender, cooled
> Lettuce leaves

1. In a small bowl, whisk the lemon juice, vinegar, mustard, salt, and pepper until well blended. Add the egg yolk and whisk until smooth. Add the oil by tablespoons, whisking to incorporate the oil before adding more. Refrigerate this dressing until needed.
2. Break the salmon into bite-size chunks in a large bowl. Add the fennel, radish, dill, and scallions, mixing lightly until blended. Add the dressing and toss lightly. Gently fold in the peas.
3. To serve, arrange on lettuce in a salad bowl or on individual serving plates.

Serves 6
May be partially prepared in advance

Both fresh and canned salmon make wonderful salads. When using canned salmon, rinse with cold water and remove bits of skin. Do not remove the bones, as they are a wonderful source of calcium and are edible after the canning process.

Alaska Pink salmon, *Oncorhynchus gorbascha*, is the smallest Pacific salmon, weighing an average of 4 to 5 pounds. Sometimes this fish is called the humpback, as spawning males develop a pronounced hump on their backs. Pink salmon is low in oil content and is generally canned.

Whole Poached Salmon

A whole poached salmon served hot or cold is a masterpiece of culinary presentation. The garnishes alone provide the cook with a wide latitude for artistic skills, yet even the novice will enjoy producing a perfectly poached fish for a special meal. Two things are important to the success of this recipe: a very fresh whole salmon and a pot large enough to hold the fish. Although a fish poacher (a long oval pan designed for this purpose) is ideal, it is not essential. A deep roasting pan may be substituted as long as the cooking liquid will cover the fish. Any large whole fish, such as striped bass or red snapper, may be poached in this fashion.

1 *8- to 10-pound whole salmon, cleaned, head and tail left on*
4 *quarts Vinegar Court Bouillon (see page 279)*
1 *cup parsley, dill, or watercress sprigs*
2 *cups of sauce: either a flavored mayonnaise for cold salmon, or Hollandaise or a variation for hot poached fish (see Chapter 7)*

1. Wrap the fish in cheesecloth. Knot the cheesecloth at each end. Measure the depth of fish at the thickest part to determine the cooking time, allowing about 10 minutes per inch of thickness.
2. Bring the court bouillon to a boil in the pan selected for cooking the fish. Remove the pan from the heat. Carefully lower the fish into the hot liquid, cover the pan, and return to medium heat. The court bouillon should be just barely simmering to cook the fish. Poach the fish the required amount of time, then remove the pan from the heat. Allow the fish to cool slightly before removing it from the liquid.
3. Place the fish on a large serving platter, discard the cheesecloth, and carefully remove the skin.
4. If the fish is to be served hot, decorate the platter with parsley, dill or watercress sprigs, or perhaps all three, and serve with a sauce.
5. To serve the fish cold, chill for several hours. Remove the salmon from the refrigerator. Cover its eye with an olive or grape half. If desired, trim away the dark-colored meat that lies along the median line. The fish may be coated with aspic (see page 278), or served plain, or decorated in any manner. Place a line of parsley, dill, or watercress sprigs along the median line before serving. Accompany with a choice of sauce.

Variation: This recipe can be made with a smaller portion of salmon, such as the tail, for a smaller group of people.

Serves 8–10
May be prepared in advance

Chinook salmon, *Oncorhynchus tschawytscha*, or king salmon is the largest of the Pacific salmons. While the average size of chinook is 12 to 26 pounds, 126 is the record. The chinook salmon of the Yukon River journey some 2000 miles to spawn. Since Pacific salmon do not feed once they have entered a freshwater river, their stored fat provides energy for the long swim.

Chum salmon, *Oncorhynchus keta*, averages about 9 pounds and is not as highly prized as coho, sockeye, or chinook salmons due to its coarse texture. However, it is tasty salmon, just the same.

Sautéed Salmon Scallops

Salmon scallops cook quickly, sealing in the flavor. Watching calories? Sauté them in a nonstick skillet, using less butter. Served with steamed new potatoes and a green vegetable, this salmon recipe is hard to beat.

2 1-pound skinless salmon fillets
4 tablespoons butter
Freshly ground black pepper
Parsley sprigs for garnish
Lemon slices for garnish

1. Using a sharp knife, held at a 45-degree angle, slice each fillet into 3 or more thin scallops, not more than ¼ inch thick. If you'd prefer, your fishmonger do it for you.
2. Melt the butter in a large skillet, over medium-high heat. Sauté the salmon pieces in the hot butter for about 3 minutes. Because the salmon scallops are so thin, they cook through easily without turning. They are done when the tops become opaque.
3. Place the salmon scallops on a heated serving platter and garnish with freshly ground pepper, lemon slices, and parsley sprigs.

Variation: To enhance salmon scallops, serve with any number of sauces, such as Orange-Saffron Beurre Blanc (see page 274), Caper Butter (see page 270), or any other favorite.

Serves 6

Coho salmon, *Oncorhynchus kisutch*, is also called silver salmon because of its silvery color. Like all Pacific salmon, after spawning has occurred, cohos die.

Lox and Nova refer to cold-smoked salmon that have a mild flavor and in general a lower salt content. They are popular delicatessen items.

Baked Marinated Salmon Scallops

This potent marinade imparts a zing to salmon scallops. The recipe is easy to prepare, and the marinade can be made 24 hours ahead.

2 1-pound skinless salmon fillets
¼ cup olive oil
¼ cup fresh strained lemon juice
1 garlic clove, smashed
2 teaspoons minced gingerroot
1 teaspoon dried red pepper flakes

1. Using a sharp knife, held at a 45-degree angle, slice each fillet into 3 or more thin scallops, not more than ¼-inch thick. If you'd prefer, have your fishmonger do it for you.
2. Combine the olive oil, lemon juice, garlic, gingerroot, and red pepper flakes in a plastic bag. Add the salmon scallops, making sure that all surfaces are covered. Seal the bag tightly and refrigerate, allowing the fish to marinate for 30 minutes.
3. Preheat oven to 400 degrees. Place a baking dish in the oven to heat for 10 minutes.
4. Drain the salmon scallops. Place the fish on the heated baking dish in the oven. Close the oven door and turn off the heat. The scallops will become opaque in about 10 minutes. Serve immediately.

Serves 4
Must be partially prepared in advance

Charcoal-Grilled Salmon Steaks

This recipe is an adaptation of a native Alaskan "Salmon Bake." Native Alaskans grill literally tons of salmon for visitors each summer.

> 4 6- to 8-ounce salmon steaks
> 2 tablespoons fresh strained lemon juice
> ½ cup butter, melted
> ½ cup brown sugar
> ½ cup dry rosé wine

1. Prepare grill. The fire is ready when the coals are glowing, not flaming. A fire that is too hot will burn fish.
2. Mix together the lemon juice, melted butter, brown sugar, and wine. Brush the steaks with this marinade before placing them on the grill.
3. Measure the thickness of the salmon steaks to determine the cooking time, using the Canadian Guideline. Place the steaks on the grill rack about 5 inches from the coals. Baste the steaks with the marinade while cooking. Turn the steaks over halfway through cooking. Serve at once.

Serves 4

Sockeye salmon, *Oncorhynchus nerka*, is also called red salmon because of its ruby-red flesh. The rich, oily meat is primarily marketed in cans.

"I have laid aside business and gone a-fishing."—*The Compleat Angler*, by Izaak Walton

Le Saumon Roti À la Graine de Moutarde, Beurre de Cerfeuil

FROM DOMAINE CHANDON, YOUNTVILLE, CALIFORNIA

Philippe Jeanty, chef de cuisine of Domaine Chandon, suggests serving this with homemade potato chips and a watercress salad with a vinaigrette dressing.

- ¹/₄ cup whole-grain mustard
- ¹/₂ cup Dijon-style mustard
- ¹/₄ cup plus 2 tablespoons vegetable oil
- 6 6-ounce skinned salmon fillets
- 4 tablespoons Chervil Butter (see recipe below)

1. Mix the two mustards together in a small bowl. Whisk in the ¹/₄ cup oil. Brush the mustard mixture on the salmon fillets and let rest at least 20 minutes before cooking.
2. Heat the remaining 2 tablespoons of oil in a cast-iron skillet over moderately high heat. Cook the salmon 2 to 3 minutes on each side until golden brown and a crust has formed, but be careful not to overcook.
3. To serve, place the salmon on a heated serving platter, with slices of Chervil Butter on top. Warm in the oven for 30 seconds to start melting the butter. Serve immediately.

Chervil Butter

- 3 tablespoons minced fresh chervil (about ¹/₂ ounce)
- 1 teaspoon fresh strained lemon juice
- 1 tablespoon minced garlic
- ¹/₂ teaspoon salt
- 1 teaspoon Dijon-style mustard
- ¹/₂ cup unsalted butter (1 stick)

1. Place the chervil, lemon juice, garlic, salt, and mustard in the work bowl of a food processor fitted with the steel blade. Process until well mixed. Add the butter in pieces and process until smooth. Roll into a log, wrap in plastic, and refrigerate. The chervil butter may be kept for several weeks in the coldest part of the refrigerator. It makes ³/₄ cup.

Serves 6
May be partially prepared in advance

Chervil has a subtle flavor reminiscent of anise and pepper. It should always be added at the end of cooking, as heat destroys its flavor.

A salmon may leap distances several times its length in its quest to travel upstream to spawn. The Latin name given to the Atlantic salmon is *Salmo salar*. According to the dictionary, the Latin root of the word *salmo*, *salmonis*, is probably derived from *salire*, to leap. *Salar* is from the Latin *salarius*, pertaining to salt.

Salmon with Sorrel Sauce

FROM CHÂTEAU-PYRENEES, ENGLEWOOD, COLORADO

Chef Georges Mavro at the Château-Pyrenees sends us this unusual recipe for salmon garnished with chanterelles and a sauce of sorrel and ginger. The chanterelle mushrooms are complemented by the lemony flavor of the sorrel. Although this recipe was created for coho salmon, it works very well with salmon fillets too. If you do use salmon fillets, plan on about 6 to 8 ounces of fillet per person.

4 *coho salmon, about 12 ounces each*
1 *cup dry white wine*
3 *teaspoons minced shallots*
2 *ounces gingerroot, peeled and sliced in thin*
   julienne
¹/₄ *cup fresh sorrel (about 2 ounces)*
¹/₂ *cup chicken stock*
11 *tablespoons unsalted butter*
¹/₂ *teaspoon salt*
Freshly ground black pepper to taste
1 *teaspoon minced garlic*
10 *ounces chanterelle mushrooms*
2 *tablespoons olive oil*

1. Fillet the salmon, leaving the skin intact. Set aside.
2. Bring the white wine, 2 teaspoons of shallots, and the gingerroot to a rolling boil in a medium-size saucepan, then reduce the liquid to 3 tablespoons.
3. Puree the sorrel with the chicken stock in a blender and add to the reduction. Add 10 tablespoons of the butter, one at a time, stirring to incorporate each tablespoon before adding the next. Taste and correct seasoning. Set the sauce aside and keep warm.
4. Melt the remaining tablespoon of butter in a small skillet, over medium heat. Add the remaining teaspoon of shallot and the garlic. Sauté for 2 minutes. Add the chanterelles and cook for an additional 2 minutes. Season to taste. Set aside.
5. Season the salmon with the salt and pepper. Heat the olive oil in a preheated nonstick skillet over medium-high heat. Add the fillets and sauté about 2 or 3 minutes on each side or until just cooked.
6. To serve, spoon the sauce onto 4 heated dinner plates, place the salmon on the sauce, and top with the chanterelle mixture.

Serves 4

Young salmon are called smolts when they are old enough to start their journey downstream to the open ocean.

Salmon, trout, and whitefish all belong to the salmonidae family. These fishes are found in fresh and/or salt water of the Northern Hemisphere. There are 39 species of salmonids in North America alone.

Mushroom addicts need no longer stalk wild mushrooms in the woods. Today chanterelles, shiitakes, and oyster mushrooms are cultivated and frequently available in the produce section of the supermarket. They may be costly, but their flavor, texture, and aroma are priceless.

Salmon Papillion with Apple-Curry Sauce

FROM CHEZ THOA RESTAURANT, DENVER

Chef Mark Schiffler deftly combines an apple-curry sauce with a fillo-encased salmon fillet. The resulting combination of rich flavors and textures is complemented by a simple steamed vegetable. The recipe can be doubled easily to serve 4.

4 tablespoons unsalted butter
1 6- to 8-ounce Red Delicious apple, cored, peeled, and chopped (about 1/2 cup)
1/4 cup coarsely chopped onion
2 2/3 cups chicken stock
2 teaspoons curry powder
1/2 cup heavy cream
2 ounces fresh spinach, trimmed and shredded
Nutmeg to taste
Salt and pepper to taste
1 12-ounce skinless salmon fillet
6 sheets of fillo dough, defrosted according to package instructions
3/4 cup light cream
2 tablespoons minced fresh parsley for garnish

1. Melt 2 *teaspoons* of the butter in a medium-size saucepan. Add the apple and onion and sauté until the onion is lightly browned.
2. Add the chicken stock and bring to a boil over high heat. Reduce heat and simmer for 20 minutes. Remove from heat and allow to cool slightly before pureeing in a blender or food processor. Strain through a fine sieve, pressing out the solids. Discard the solids. Stir the curry powder into the strained stock and reduce over medium-high heat to 1 1/3 cup. Set aside. This curry base may be made up to 48 hours in advance and refrigerated.
3. Bring the heavy cream to a boil in a small saucepan. Reduce heat and continue to boil gently until the cream is reduced by half. Place the shredded spinach on top of the hot cream, cover the pan, and remove from heat. Allow to rest for 5 minutes, then stir the spinach into the cream, mashing it slightly. Season with nutmeg, salt, and pepper to taste. The sauce may be prepared up to 6 hours in advance.
4. Preheat oven to 375 degrees.

5. Cut the salmon fillet into 4 equal rectangular pieces. Spread 1 tablespoon of the spinach mixture on top of a piece of salmon and cover with a second piece to make a "sandwich." Repeat with the remaining 2 pieces of salmon.

6. Melt the remaining 3 1/3 tablespoons of butter in a small saucepan. Lightly butter an 8-inch-square baking dish and set aside. Thoroughly butter a small pie plate. Keep the fillo dough tightly covered to prevent its drying out until you are ready to use it. Lay 3 sheets of fillo dough on top of each other across the pie plate, and place one of the salmon sandwiches on top. Butter the exposed portion of the top sheet of dough. Working quickly, fold the top side down toward the center and the bottom side up toward the center. Next fold the left side toward the right and the right side toward the left to completely enclose the salmon. Immediately butter the exposed portion of the second sheet of dough and fold as described above. Repeat with the third sheet.

7. Place salmon packets in baking dish, seam side down. Bake for 15 minutes or until the fillo is lightly browned.

8. While the papillions are cooking, place 6 tablespoons of the curry base in a small saucepan with the light cream. Over moderate heat reduce the mixture by half. Keep warm.

9. To serve, place a salmon papillion on a warm serving plate and ribbon the sauce over the middle. Sprinkle with parsley.

Serves 2
May be partially prepared in advance

Salmon, herring, and some species of trout are anadromous fishes. This means they start their lives in freshwater rivers and streams and then swim with the current to the sea. When they mature and are ready to spawn, they leave the ocean and fight their way back upstream in their native river.

157

Smoke-Cooked Trout with Herb Butter

You can have smoked fish without a smoker. Use a grill with a cover to smoke trout for a special treat.

4 *whole trout, cleaned, boned, and butterflied*
$^1/_2$ *cup coarse salt*
4 *quarts water*
1 *tablespoon minced fresh dill*
1 *tablespoon freshly grated horseradish, or bottled horse radish, newly opened and drained*
2 *tablespoons minced fresh parsley*
$^1/_4$ *cup unsalted butter, at room temperature*

1. Rinse the trout and set aside. Pour the water into a large glass or ceramic bowl and stir in the salt. When the salt is completely dissolved, add the trout, making sure that the fish are covered by water. Cover and refrigerate for 24 hours.
2. Soak hickory chips in water for 30 minutes.
3. Place a drip pan (either use a pan from your kitchen or form one out of heavy-duty aluminum foil) on one side of the bottom of the grill and charcoal on the other. Light the charcoal. When the coals have turned slightly gray cover them with some wet hickory chips. Cover the grill. Wait about 10 or 15 minutes for smoke to build up inside the grill.
4. Drain the fish and rinse in cold water. Pat dry. Place the trout on the grill over the drip pan, skin side down. Cover the grill and smoke-cook the fish for 30 minutes. While the fish cooks, check that smoke is coming out of the grill. Add more wet chips to the coals whenever you think more smoke is needed.
5. While the trout is cooking, prepare the herb butter. Combine the dill, horseradish, and parsley with the slightly softened butter.
6. Remove the fish from the grill and serve. Place a generous spoonful of herb butter on each trout.

Note: Smoke-cooked trout may also be served cold. When the fish has finished cooking, remove from grill and wrap in foil. Refrigerate. It is particularly good served with Lemon Mayonnaise (see page 252).

Serves 4
Must be partially prepared in advance

Campfire Trout

Clean and scale four fresh brook or lake trout. Rinse well and dry. Dredge the trout in 1 cup of flour (or $^1/_2$ cup flour and $^1/_2$ cup cornmeal) and shake off the excess. Melt bacon grease or butter in a cast-iron skillet. When it's hot, add the trout and cook about 5 to 6 minutes per side, basting with the pan juices. When the fish flakes easily, it's ready to eat.

If you use an aluminum skillet for your campfire cooking, coat the outside of the bottom of the pan with liquid detergent before using. It will make washing up a lot easier.

Trout with Caper Vinaigrette

This is an easy do-ahead luncheon dish, as both the fish and the vinaigrette may be prepared the night before. Also try the vinaigrette with cold poached salmon fillets.

2 tablespoons fresh strained lemon juice
2 tablespoons white wine vinegar
$^1/_2$ teaspoon salt
$^1/_4$ teaspoon freshly ground black pepper
1 teaspoon Dijon-style mustard
$^1/_2$ cup olive oil
2 teaspoons thinly sliced scallions, white part only
2 tablespoons minced fresh parsley or dill
2 tablespoons capers, rinsed, drained, and lightly mashed with a fork
3 cold poached trout
Lettuce leaves for garnish
1 hard-boiled egg, chopped, for garnish

1. In a small bowl, combine the lemon juice, vinegar, salt, pepper, and mustard. Gradually whisk in the olive oil until emulsified. Whisk in the scallions, parsley or dill, and capers. Refrigerate until needed.
2. Remove the skin and backbone from the trout and cut each in half along the back to make 6 fillets. Refrigerate, covered, until needed.
3. When ready to serve, arrange lettuce on serving plates and center a trout fillet on each. Spoon on the vinaigrette and sprinkle with the egg.

Serves 6
May be prepared in advance

The first fish hatchery in the United States was established in 1864 in New York for the production of trout.

Because the developing eggs of trout and salmon are easily shipped, these fish have been widely distributed around the world. The present distribution of any particular species may be quite different from its original range.

Trout prefer to spawn on a gravel bottom. The small pieces of stone help to hold the eggs in place.

Sautéed Rocky Mountain Trout with Pignolia Nuts

FROM SNOWMASS CLUB, SNOWMASS VILLAGE, COLORADO

Hubert Senac, executive chef of the Snowmass Club, created this recipe, which is a variation of the classic trout amandine, in which almonds are used. Try the recipe with tilapia or freshwater perch.

2 10- to 12-ounce trout, boned
Salt and white pepper to taste
1/4 cup flour
1/4 cup unsalted butter (1/2 stick)
2 teaspoons fresh strained lemon juice
2 teaspoons toasted pignolia (pine nuts)
1/4 teaspoon Worcestershire sauce
1 tablespoon minced fresh parsley
1 tablespoon dry vermouth

1. Season the trout with salt and pepper. Dip into the flour, coating both sides.
2. Melt the butter in a large cast-iron skillet over medium-high heat. Carefully add the fish and cook quickly on both sides, about 2 1/2 minutes per side, until golden brown. Remove to a heated platter and keep warm.
3. Add pignolia nuts, lemon juice, Worcestershire sauce, parsley, and vermouth and cook over high heat for 1 minute. Arrange the trout on serving plates and cover with the sauce. Serve at once.

Serves 2

Cast iron retains heat evenly. It is indispensable in creating a golden brown crust on a sautéed fillet.

The sale of all wild trout, except steelhead, is prohibited. Steelhead are seagoing rainbow trout.

Trout fishing is a very popular sport, and we've all heard about "the ones that got away." However, record catches of rainbow and brown trout actually have bettered 35 pounds!

An average brook trout weighs about a pound, is 8 to 12 inches long, and is just right for the frying pan.

Raw Salmon and Whitefish Terrine

FROM RITZ HOTEL, CHICAGO

A terrine is an elegant addition to a holiday buffet. This unusual terrine, with a gingerroot sauce, comes to us from the Ritz Hotel in Chicago.

1 1/2 *pounds skinned salmon fillet*
1 1/2 *pounds skinned whitefish fillet*
2 *tablespoons sugar*
2 *tablespoons salt*
1 *cup fresh strained lemon juice*
1/4 *cup dry white wine*
3 *ounces gingerroot, peeled and chopped*
2 1/4 *cups vegetable oil*
2 *tablespoons minced fresh chervil*
2 *tablespoons minced fresh parsley*
2 *tablespoons minced fresh chives*

1. Slice the salmon and whitefish fillets on a 45-degree angle as thinly as possible.
2. Line a 6-cup terrine or glass loaf pan with wax paper. Combine the sugar and salt in a small bowl. Mix 1/4 cup of the lemon juice with the wine in a measuring cup. Alternate layers of salmon with layers of whitefish in the terrine, sprinkling each layer with the sugar/salt mixture and lemon juice/white wine mixture until the mold is full. Cover the top with wax paper. Tip the mold to drain off any excess liquid. Weight the top with a large juice or vegetable can and marinate in the refrigerator for 3 days.
3. Combine the gingerroot, vegetable oil, and the remaining 3/4 cup lemon juice in a glass jar. Close and shake well. Refrigerate for 3 days.
4. Just before serving, place the dressing in a blender and blend for 3 seconds. Add the chervil, parsley, and chives and blend for 2 seconds. Do not process too much or the dressing will turn white.
5. Invert the terrine onto a platter and slice into individual servings. An electric knife is a great help in producing neat slices. Serve on chilled plates, accompanied by the dressing.

Variation: Place very thinly sliced lemon rounds on the bottom of the terrine. Proceed as directed in step 1. After unmolding, press parsley or mint leaves in an attractive design around the lemon slices.

Serves 8
Must be prepared in advance

"In the hands of an able cook, fish can become an inexhaustible source of perpetual delight."
—Brillat-Savarin

Whitefish has many of the same characteristics as trout and salmon but is nonmigratory, living in large, deep lakes. This fish is good eating and has a relatively low sodium content.

Broiled Whitefish

This is a simple, light treatment that allows the flavor of a delicate fish to shine through. It is excellent with all kinds of broiled fish, whether they are steaks or skinless fillets. If using steaks or very thick fillets, we suggest you turn the fish midway through the broiling.

1 1/2 *pounds fresh whitefish fillets*
2 *tablespoons butter*
1/4 *cup dry vermouth*
1/2 *teaspoon paprika*
Salt and pepper
1/2 *cup minced fresh parsley for garnish*
Lemon wedges for garnish

1. Preheat broiler.
2. Generously butter an ovenproof pan. Arrange the fillets in the pan.
3. Dot the fish with the butter. Sprinkle the vermouth over the fillets to moisten them. Dust with the paprika and salt and pepper to taste.
4. Place the pan under the broiler and cook until the fish is opaque, about 10 minutes depending on the intensity of your broiler and the thickness of the fillets (or use the Canadian Guideline for timing).
5. Garnish the fish with parsley and serve with lemon wedges.

Serves 4–6

"Let not the sauce be better than the fish."—Old French proberb

Whitefish spawn in the shallows near lake edges. Their roe is made into "golden caviar," named for its pale yellow color. In the past, these eggs were dyed black to emulate true caviar, which is made exclusively from sturgeon eggs.

Pike with Sauce Nantua

Pike is a lean and mild flavored fish that lends itself to poaching. After being cooked in a simple court bouillon, it can be served hot or cold. This recipe, using the traditional Sauce Nantua that usually accompanies pike quenelles, is simpler to make and retains more of the original flavor of the fish. Sauce Nantua is usually made with small crayfish; however, it is equally successful made with a small lobster.

> 8 *cups water*
> 1 ½ *teaspoons salt*
> 6 *black peppercorns*
> 1 *leafy celery stalk*
> 1 *4- to 5-pound whole pike, cleaned, or 2 pounds pike fillets with skin*
> *Parsley sprigs for garnish*
> *Sauce Nantua (see recipe below)*

1. Combine the water, salt, peppercorns, and celery in a pan large enough to hold the fish. Bring to a boil, then reduce the heat so that the court bouillon is just simmering.
2. Measure the thickness of the fish to determine the cooking time—about 10 minutes per inch of thickness. Carefully lower the fish into the simmering liquid and poach until done.
3. Transfer the fish to a heated platter. Cover with Sauce Nantua and a garnish of parsley sprigs.

Note: If you serve the pike chilled, Lemon Mayonnaise (see page 252) goes extremely well with it.

Sauce Nantua

> 1 *pound cooked crayfish or lobster, in the shell*
> 6 *tablespoons unsalted butter*
> 2 *cups milk*
> 2 *tablespoons flour*
> *Dash of cayenne pepper*
> *Salt and freshly ground pepper to taste*

1. Remove the tail meat from the crayfish or lobster. Leave the crayfish tails whole, or cut the lobster tail into small pieces. Set aside or refrigerate.
2. Crush the bodies, including the shells, in a mortar or with a rolling pin.
3. Melt 3 tablespoons of the butter in a small saucepan. Add the crushed crayfish or lobster bodies and the milk. Heat to the boiling point over medium

The classic French preparation, *Quenelles de Brochet*, is made with pike.

The northern pike is a large voracious fish found in lakes and streams of North America, Europe, and Asia. This fish is thought to be the most widely distributed freshwater fish in the world. It may reach a length of over 4 feet and is considered an excellent catch for the sports fisherman. The meat of this fish is sweet, white, firm, and delicious in a number of preparations.

163

heat, lower the heat, and simmer for 5 minutes. Strain through a fine sieve; discard the solids. The recipe may be prepared to this point and refrigerated for up to 24 hours.

4. Melt the remaining 3 tablespoons of butter in another small saucepan, over moderate heat. Blend in the flour and allow to cook for a minute, stirring constantly. Using a wire whisk, beat in the strained warm milk. Stir constantly as the sauce begins to thicken to avoid lumps. Season to taste. Add the crayfish tails or the lobster meat. The recipe makes 2 cups of sauce.

5. Serve the sauce over the poached pike.

Serves 4
May be partially prepared in advance

The largest North American member of the pike family is called the muskellunge and may weigh as much as 30 pounds. Nicknamed the "musky," the name is thought to come from the Native American Ojibway dialect. In their language *mas* means ugly and *kinononge* refers to fish. The French-Canadians interpreted this name as masquallongee.

The smaller chain pickerel inhabits clean lakes, ponds, and deep-stream pools in the eastern part of the United States. It is considered a popular sports fish as well as a tasty dinner.

Chapter 5

Latest Arrivals: An Abundance of Riches

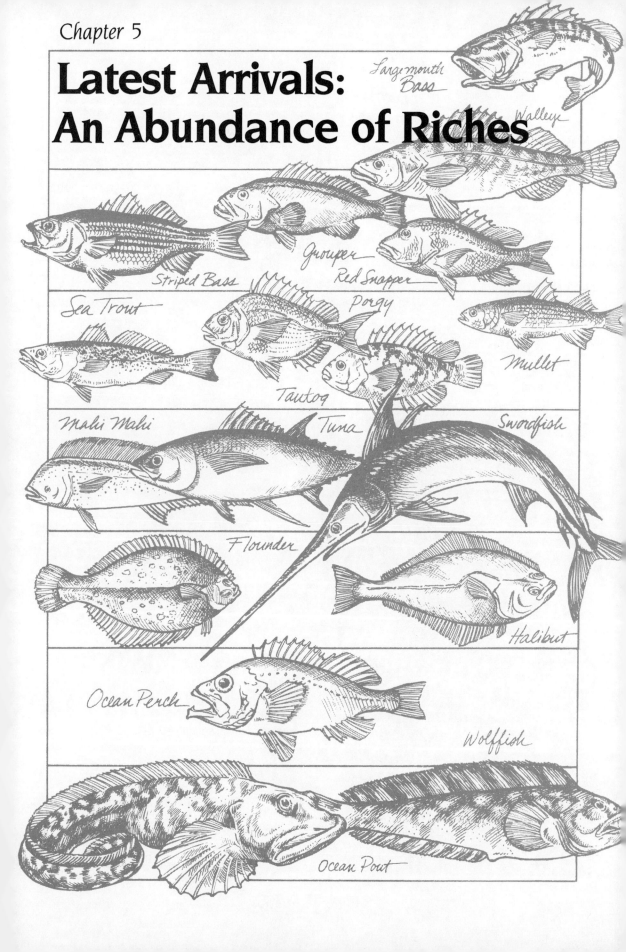

Largemouth Bass

Walleye

Grouper

Red Snapper

Striped Bass

Sea Trout

Porgy

Mullet

Tautog

Mahi Mahi

Tuna

Swordfish

Flounder

Halibut

Ocean Perch

Wolffish

Ocean Pout

Small improvements sometimes cause dramatic changes. The differences between the early fishes and the later arrivals seem, at first glance, relatively minor. But these slight differences resulted in one of the most impressive evolutionary explosions in the history of life on Earth. Today, this group represents 90 percent of all the world's fishes and 95 percent of all fishes commercially available.

Unlike the early fishes, the later spiny-rayed fishes come in every imaginable shape and live in every conceivable watery habitat. We find among them the fastest fishes in the sea: tuna, marlin, and sailfish. We also find huge groupers that spend most of their lives resting on the bottom. The "flying" fish launch themselves into the air to glide long distances on winglike fins. Puffers can be as round as basketballs and flounders are as flat as pancakes. Pup-fish live in hot desert springs. And some, like seahorses, don't even look like fish at all.

This symphony of diversity was made possible by a few anatomical changes. The swim bladder that served as a kind of lung to augment the gills of early fishes has become sealed off from the outside world and keeps the later fish weightless in the water. The fins, freed from the need to keep the fish from sinking, have developed into devices for propelling, steering, walking, gliding, and feeling. The stiff, spiny fin rays have also contributed to new variations. They support the "wings" of flying fishes, become poisonous needles in lionfishes, and have even evolved into the fishing rod of angler fishes.

It is no surprise that the diversity of the spiny-rayed fishes is reflected in a wide variety of flavors and textures. The basslike fishes (seabass, grouper, snook, and striped bass) are all big and meaty. Perches are small, sweet, and full of bones. Sleek, fast-swimming fishes, such as bluefish, jacks, mackerel, tuna, and mahi mahi, are rich and oily.

Flatfish, like flounder, turbot, halibut, and sole, have firm-textured, delicate flesh. Some of the most delicious fishes from this chapter are porgies and tilefish, which live on shellfish and have a rich lobsterlike flavor.

If the early fishes of chapter 4 are reliable kitchen mainstays, then the spiny-rayed fishes of this chapter are the high-tech fun fishes. They are fun to catch, fun to cook, and full of flavorful nourishment, whether they are baked, broiled, steamed, or grilled. With their great variety of tastes and textures, they present an incredible array of possibilities to the cook. Many of the fish from this chapter are particularly well suited to grilling and are ideal for spontaneous entertaining. A simply

The amateur fisherman is probably the best source of supply for most of the freshwater fishes of this chapter. The fishes are often small enough to cook whole. If the fish are filleted, the skin is usually not removed, as it is helpful in keeping the flesh from falling apart during the cooking.

grilled tuna steak or filet of tautog or snapper needs only a wedge of lemon and a grind of pepper, and it's ready to serve. Refreshing light meals that may be made in advance and cooked in an instant are always welcome in our busy life-styles; they appear frequently in this chapter. Although simple straightforward recipes prevail, it is easy to add a touch of panache by using a sauce or special garnish from Chapter 7. The Latest Arrivals will provide you with many opportunities for easy enjoyable entertaining and eating. Have fun!

FRESHWATER PERCH

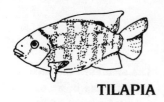

TILAPIA

FRESHWATER BASS

WALLEYE PIKE

Freshwater Perchlike Fishes: Freshwater Perch, Tilapia, Freshwater Bass, and Walleye Pike

Members of the huge perch family inhabit fresh waters of all the continents. Tilapia is found in the sea of Galilee and in African lakes. It is fast becoming an important source of protein throughout the Third World. Very easily farmed by inexpensive methods in the southeastern United States, the tilapia grows rapidly and provides a delicious, high-quality meal. It will soon begin appearing in our fish markets and can be cooked in the same way as freshwater perch.

All perches have small bones and a full flavor. They have been called the raspberries of the fish world—very sweet, but with prickles.

Pan-Fried Tilapia or Perch

If you're lucky enough to catch freshwater perch, cook them as soon as possible. If you don't catch any, try tilapia, a species farmed in this country. It is a white-meated fish, which is excellent in simple preparations such as this. Freshwater bass, porgy, walleye pike, and grunt can be prepared in this way.

8 *perch fillets (about 2 pounds)*
1 *egg, lightly beaten*
²/₃ *cup milk*
³/₄ *cup finely crushed soda crackers*
Salt and freshly ground black pepper to taste
3 *tablespoons unsalted butter*
2 *tablespoons vegetable oil*
4 *lemon wedges for garnish*
Tartar Sauce (see page 269), optional

1. Measure the fillets at their thickest point.
2. Combine the egg and milk in a shallow dish. Place the crumbs on a large piece of wax paper. Dip the fillets into the egg and milk, and then into the cracker crumbs, coating each side. Place the breaded fillets on a rack for about 10 minutes to dry and set the coating.
3. Heat the butter and oil in a large skillet over medium-high heat. When it begins to foam, add the fillets, skin side up, and cook according to the Canadian Guideline, turning once. This will be about 2 minutes per side, as perch fillets are usually small.
4. Serve immediately, accompanied by lemon wedges and Tartar Sauce.

Variation: The tilapia or perch may also be cooked whole, adjusting the cooking time accordingly. Be careful of the bones.

Serves 4–6

If you are blessed with a plethora of perch, try grilling them, using the recipe for Grilled Bluefish Fillets (page 193).

Tilapia are one of a species called "mouth-breeders". For the first seven to ten days of life, the mother protects them inside her mouth, releasing them only for feeding.

Freshwater perch live in lakes, ponds, and quieter parts of streams. They spend the day in deeper water, and at night move to the shore to feed. They are carnivorous.

One tilapia enthusiast describes the fillets as "meatier than bass, and tastier than snapper." The market form is the fillet.

Pan-Fried Bass

Anyone who questions fish for breakfast has never been treated to freshly caught pan-fried bass. This recipe is a must for any freshwater fisherman. Although you may coat the fillets with any combination of cornmeal and flour, we think the cornmeal crunch is particularly well suited to bass. Try this recipe also with tilapia, freshwater perch, porgy, grunt, and walleye pike.

The largemouth bass has lean, white flesh. Pan-frying is an excellent method of cooking this fish.

Largemouth bass is a designated game fish and is not sold in retail stores. However, it is a relatively common fish and fun to catch yourself.

Largemouth bass have a black to greenish color, while smallmouth bass are bronze. The largemouth are two to three times as big as the small and have a longer upper lip, extending back beyond the eye. Both species are stocked in every state except Alaska. Largemouth bass prefer warmer water, such as lakes and ponds, while smallmouth are more likely to be found in cooler, moving water.

³/₄ cup cornmeal
Salt and freshly ground black pepper to taste
4 whole bass, cleaned, heads removed (about 1
*   pound each)*
¹/₄ cup bacon fat or vegetable oil
Lemon wedges for garnish
Tartar Sauce (see page 269), optional

1. Combine the cornmeal with the salt and pepper in a shallow dish. Dip the fish into the cornmeal. Set aside.
2. Heat the bacon fat in a large cast-iron skillet over medium-high heat. Cook two fish, about 4 to 5 minutes per side, turning once. Check to be sure that the fish is not sticking. Remove and keep warm while cooking the remaining fish. Serve immediately with the lemon wedges. If this is a lunch or dinner entree, you might want to pass Tartar Sauce on the side.

Serves 4–6

Turban of Walleye Pike

FROM DELMONICO'S AT THE WESTIN, CINCINNATI, OHIO

This elegant appetizer comes to us from Chef de Cuisine Robert Sturm. An impressive way to begin a meal, it is very rich, so you may want to follow it with a simply prepared entree. Freshwater trout may be substituted for the walleye pike.

1 pound walleye pike fillets, skinned, cut into
  1/2-inch pieces
1 egg
1 cup heavy cream
1/2 teaspoon salt
1/4 teaspoon freshly ground white pepper
1 recipe Pureed Spinach (see recipe below)
1 cup cooked crabmeat, heated
1 recipe White Wine Sauce (see recipe below)

1. Preheat over to 350 degrees.
2. In a chilled food processor fitted with a chilled steel knife, puree the pike for 1 minute. Add the egg while the machine is running and process for 15 seconds. Slowly pour in the cream while the machine is running. Add the salt and pepper. Pour the mixture into 4 buttered 1/2-cup custard cups. Place the cups in an 8-inch square cake pan and add boilingwater to the pan to come halfway up the sides of the cups. Bake for 15 minutes.
3. To serve, divide the pureed spinach among 4 serving plates, and unmold the turbans into the middle of the spinach. Top the turbans with 2 tablespoons of hot crab and nap with the white wine sauce.

Pureed Spinach

1 tablespoon unsalted butter
4 cups packed spinach, tough stems cut off and
  discarded
Salt and freshly ground black pepper to taste
1/4 cup white wine

1. Melt the butter over medium heat. Add the spinach, cover, and steam for 3 minutes, stirring occasionally. Season to taste with salt and pepper.
2. Transfer the spinach to a food processor fitted with a steel knife, or a blender. Add the wine and process until pureed. Set aside and keep warm.

> *"Plain cooking cannot be entrusted to plain cooks."*
> —Countess Morphy

Walleye pike is not really a pike; it's a perch, and the largest member of the perch family, at that.

A freshwater fish from central United States, the walleye pike acquired its name from the flat glasslike appearance of its eyes when the fish is out of water.

White Wine Sauce

2 *cups dry white wine*
1 *cup heavy cream*
Salt and freshly ground black pepper to taste

1. Bring the white wine to a boil in a small saucepan and reduce to ¼ cup. Add the cream and reduce by half. Season to taste with salt and pepper. Keep warm.

Serves 4

GROUPER

RED SNAPPER

SEA BASS

STRIPED BASS

Basslike Fishes: Grouper, Red Snapper, Sea Bass, and Striped Bass

This is a large, marine group of meaty fishes, closely related to the perches. They can be easily identified by their round midsection, large mouths and eyes, and double dorsal fins. Most of them are daytime predators of the rich fish communities near the shore. Some of the most popular of the game fishes, such as the famous striped bass or "striper," belong to this group. In fact, striped bass is so much in demand, it is often overfished. Why not try some of the underutilized sportfishes, such as the ubiquitous bluefish, instead?

172

Grilled Grouper with Ginger-Lime Butter

When the grilling mood strikes, make this very simple, very good recipe. A touch of fresh ginger and lime juice is all that is needed to accent the fish. You may want to add some sweet red or yellow peppers and zucchini to the grill too, and round out the meal with a rice salad and a bottle of cold white wine. Use this recipe with any thick firm-fleshed fillet, such as mahi mahi, red snapper, or bluefish.

$^1/_2$ cup unsalted butter (1 stick)
2 teaspoons minced gingerroot
2 tablespoons fresh strained lime juice
1 teaspoon grated lime peel (zest)
4 6- to 8-ounce grouper fillets

1. Prepare a charcoal grill or preheat the broiler.
2. In a shallow pan just large enough for one fillet, melt the butter over medium heat. Add the gingerroot, lime juice, and lime peel and cook 2 minutes. Remove from heat and dip each fillet in the butter mixture to coat on both sides.
3. Place the fish 4 inches below the broiler or on a rack 4 inches above the red-hot, but not flaming coals, and grill about 2 minutes. Turn, and cook another 2 minutes, or until the fillets flake easily. Serve immediately.

Variation: Fish steaks instead of fillets are also excellent in this recipe. Steaks should be at least 1 inch thick and be cooked 4 minutes on each side.

Serves 4

Several species of grouper are found along our Atlantic coast, in the Caribbean, and South America. They vary in size from 2 to 5 feet and may weigh hundreds of pounds. However, the average size of this fish in the market is considerably smaller.

Groupers have mottled skin patterns and are able to change the intensity of their color quite rapidly . . . a definite asset for attracting the opposite sex or escaping a predator!

Groupers are sought after by anglers because they are both delicious and a challenge to catch. Groupers are bottom fish; they grab the bait and zip back into a coral patch. If the angler can't keep a grouper away from his hiding hole, the grouper will snag the line on a piece of coral, leaving the angler with no hook, bait, or dinner.

Baked Snapper in Parchment

FROM COBBLESTONE RESTAURANT, TEQUESTA, FLORIDA

Chef Frank Encalitto's menu frequently features red snapper. This recipe, with its bounty of fresh vegetables, is easy to prepare and great fun to serve. Each diner receives a puffy golden-brown parchment packet that contains both entree and vegetables and a delicious fragrant herbal broth. You may want to pass a basket of hot bread as an accompaniment. The recipe can also be used with grouper.

Red snapper is the best known of the snapper family. It generally weighs about 4 pounds, but specimens of up to 30 pounds and 2½ feet in length have been found. They are in season all year.

Parchment paper for baking is sold in food stores and in kitchen supply stores. If you cannot find it, aluminum foil may be used instead. The parchment paper is more attractive, but the taste will be equally good with either.

4 red snapper fillets, 6 to 8 ounces each, skinned
4 tablespoons unsalted butter, melted
Salt and pepper
½ cup thinly sliced leek, white part only
¼ cup sliced red onion
½ red pepper, cored, seeded, and cut in thin strips
½ yellow pepper, cored, seeded, and cut in thin strips
4 large mushrooms, thinly sliced
1 medium tomato, peeled, seeded, and chopped
8 medium shrimp, shelled and deveined
16 thin asparagus spears, tips only, about 4 inches long
¼ cup fresh bread crumbs
4 tablespoons finely chopped fresh herbs, such as parsley, dill, basil, or thyme
¼ cup fresh strained lemon juice
¼ cup dry white wine

1. Cut 4 pieces of parchment paper into 10 x 15-inch rectangles. Fold each piece of parchment in half crosswise. Cut each piece into a heart shape. Brush the inside of each heart to within one inch of the edge with ½ tablespoon of the melted butter.
2. Position one fillet on one side of a heart, close to the fold. Sprinkle with salt and pepper. Divide the leek, onion, peppers, mushrooms, and tomato evenly and place, in that order, on top of each fillet. Next place 2 shrimp and 4 asparagus spears on top of the vegetables. Evenly distribute the bread crumbs and herbs between the fillets. Drizzle the lemon juice and wine over the surfaces. Spoon ½ tablespoon of the remaining butter over each fillet.
3. Fold the top half of the parchment paper heart over on top of itself. Then make narrow overlapping folds along the edge to tightly seal the packet. The heart

may be prepared 1 or 2 hours in advance and kept refrigerated until 15 or 20 minute before baking; then let them warm up to room temperature.

4. When you are ready to cook, preheat oven to 375 degrees.

5. Transfer the parchment packets to a rimmed baking sheet and bake for 10 minutes. The packet will puff up and become slightly brown.

6. To serve, place a packet on each serving plate and cut open with scissors or knife in front of each guest. Carefully slide the paper out from underneath the fish.

Serves 4
May be prepared in advance

Steamed Pink Snapper with Grenadine and "Confetis"

FROM L'AUBERGE DE FRANCE RESTAURANT,
PALM BEACH, FLORIDA

The demand for red snapper often exceeds the supply, which explains the high asking price on restaurant menus. Several other members of the snapper family, including gray snapper and yellowtail snapper, are similar in consistency and taste.

Chef Michel Huchet's snapper with grenadine and diced vegetables is pure food fantasy. Bright tropical colors of red, purple, and green vegetables create a dramatic backdrop for the pale pink snapper. The unexpected flavors of raspberries and hazelnuts are subtly combined to make the dish taste as exceptional as it looks. For a finishing touch, grenadine is ribboned over the arrangement. This is the dish for a special occasion and special people. The ingredients are expensive and may involve visiting a gourmet grocer, but the results are certainly worth the effort.

1 *red bell pepper, cored, seeded, and finely chopped (about 1 cup)*
1 *yellow bell pepper, cored, seeded, and finely chopped (about 1 cup)*
¹/₄ *cup finely chopped chives*
1 *medium zucchini (about ¹/₂ pound), cut in small dice*
1³/₄ *cups extra-virgin olive oil*
1 *tablespoon hazelnut oil*
2 *tablespoons raspberry vinegar*
¹/₂ *pound red radishes, ends trimmed, sliced thin*
2 *leaves blue or purple savory cabbage*

175

4 pink or red snapper fillets, 6 to 8 ounces each,
  without skin
Salt and freshly ground black pepper to taste
2 tablespoons grenadine

1. Combine the red and yellow peppers, the chives,
   and zucchini in a bowl. Toss to mix. (This is the "confetis.")
2. Mix the olive oil, hazelnut oil, and vinegar in a medium-size saucepan; warm over moderately low
   heat. Add the "confetis" and simmer 2 to 3 minutes.
   Set aside.
3. In another pan, boil the cabbage leaves for 2 minutes to soften. Drain and set aside.
4. Meanwhile, arrange the snapper fillets on the rack of
   a steamer. Divide the radishes equally over the surface of the fillets. Sprinkle with salt and pepper to
   taste. Steam over boiling water for 6 minutes.
5. Position the cabbage leaves on a warmed serving
   dish. Place a fillet and its radishes on each leaf. Pour
   the "confetis" sauce over the fish. As a final touch,
   drizzle the grenadine over the sauce in an attractive
   pattern.

**Snapper flesh is juicy and
white, with a delicate flavor.
Many consider it one of the
greatest delicacies our
oceans offer.**

Serves 4

Grilled Snapper with Fennel

The mild anise flavor of the fennel stuffing complements any small whole fish. Be sure to clean, scale, and bone the fish before stuffing.

> 2 tablespoons unsalted butter
> $^1/_4$ cup chopped onion (1 small onion)
> 2$^1/_2$ cups chopped fennel (if fresh fennel is not available, substitute celery and add 1 teaspoon dried ground fennel)
> 1 tablespoon thinly sliced scallions or chopped chives
> 2 tablespoons minced fresh parsley
> 1$^1/_2$ teaspoons Pernod
> $^1/_2$ teaspoon freshly ground black pepper
> 2 whole red snappers, about 1$^1/_4$ pounds each, cleaned and boned

1. Preheat the broiler or prepare a charcoal grill.
2. Melt the butter in a large skillet over medium heat. Add the onion. Cook 2 minutes, stirring occasionally, then add the fennel and scallions. Cover and cook 5 minutes. Remove from heat and stir in the parsley, Pernod, and pepper. Cool.
3. Generously butter 2 10x12-inch sheets of aluminum foil. Center one fish on each. Spoon the fennel mixture into the cavities of both fish. Seal the foil tightly.
4. When the coals are red-hot but not flaming, place the packets on the grill 4 inches above the coals. Or you may use the broiler. Cook according to the Canadian Guideline of 10 minutes per inch of thickness of the fish, turning once. Open the packets and slide the fish onto a heated serving platter. Spoon the juices from the packets on top of the fish and serve immediately.

Serves 4

Extra-virgin olive oil, from the first pressing of the olives, has a marvelous fruity flavor.

Red snapper lives at depths up to 200 feet and is a mainstay of Gulf Coast fisheries as well as a popular sporting fish.

The skin of red snapper is mottled rosy red with a silvery sheen, while the fins and eyes are bright red.

Steamed Whole Sea Bass

Sea bass and black sea
bass range from Cape Cod
south into the Florida Keys.
Since they feed on
crustaceans and mollusks, it
is no wonder that the sea
bass is considered such
excellent eating.

In this classic Chinese dish, the whole fish is presented—
head to tail. Though these Chinese ingredients are traditionally reserved for sea bass, any whole fish may be prepared
in this manner. For a change of pace, try the black bean
sauce from page 23, with the steamed bass.

> 2 *whole sea bass, about 1¹/₄ pounds each, cleaned*
>   *and scaled, head and tail left intact*
> 1 *tablespoon dry sherry*
> 2 *tablespoons soy sauce*
> ¹/₈ *teaspoon pepper*
> 2 *teaspoons minced gingerroot*
> 2 *whole scallions cut into julienne strips, for garnish*

1. Rinse the fish and place on a flameproof nonmetallic
   dish that is able to fit into your steamer.
2. Combine the sherry, soy sauce, pepper, and ginger.
   Pour a small amount in each fish's cavity, then pour
   the rest over the two fish.
3. Steam over simmering water about 15 minutes or
   until the fish is opaque throughout and flakes when
   prodded with the tip of a knife.
4. Serve each person one side of a fish garnished with
   the julienned scallion.

Serves 4

To avoid the black sea
bass's spiny fins, ask your
fishmonger to prepare it
whole (for baking or
steaming) or to cut it into
fillets. Your fishmonger
usually scales the fish
before selling it, but if you
shop in Oriental markets,
you may have to request
that the fish be scaled.

**How to Make Your Own
Steamer**
Select a glass or enamel pie
plate large enough to hold
the fish in a single layer,
and a large, wide pan (such
as a roaster or a wok) with
a lid, in which the pie plate
will fit. Place an empty tuna
fish can, top and bottom
removed, in the bottom of
the large pan, and add an
inch of boiling water. Insert
the pie plate containing the
fish, and cover with the lid.
The water should not touch
the pie plate. Steam
according to directions.

Lime Fish

The flavors of lime, cayenne pepper, and mint interact to produce a refreshing, lively taste. Steaming in a foil packet assures moistness, and a bounty of citrus-flavored juice will accumulate that can be served with the fish. If you wish, the packet may be made up to 2 hours in advance.

> 1 *4-pound whole fish (striped bass, sea trout, sea bass, or red snapper), cleaned and scaled, but with head and tail intact*
> 4 *tablespoons unsalted butter (¹/₂ stick)*
> ¹/₂ *teaspoon cayenne pepper*
> 1 *teaspoon salt*
> 4 *limes, sliced crosswise in rounds*
> 12 *fresh mint leaves*
> *Extra mint leaves and lime rounds for garnish*

1. Preheat the broiler or prepare a charcoal grill.
2. Make a cut along the backbone of the fish, as deep as possible. Mix the butter, cayenne, and salt in a small bowl. Spread half the butter inside the cut and insert as many lime slices as you can. Spread the remaining butter on both sides of the fish and top one side with the mint leaves and remaining lime slices. Wrap the fish in a packet made of heavy-duty aluminum foil, sealing it tightly.
3. Place the foil packet under the preheated broiler or 4 inches above red-hot coals. Cook about 15 minutes each side, depending upon the Canadian Guideline of 10 minutes per inch of thickness.
4. Serve the fish garnished with additional mint leaves and lime slices.

Serves 6
May be partially prepared in advance

Poached Striped Bass

This recipe makes an absolutely superb buffet dish. It is easy and can be done in advance, yet it never fails to delight and impress guests. The zippy tomato vinaigrette adds a welcome flavor boost to the mild poached fish.

2 quarts water
1 cup dry white wine
¹/₄ cup white wine vinegar
1 large onion, peeled and sliced
2 carrots, peeled and sliced
8–10 black peppercorns
1 bay leaf
6 parsley sprigs, leaves removed
1 celery stalk with leaves
1 3- to 4-pound striped bass, cleaned and scaled, head and tail intact
6 lettuce leaves, washed and dried
Parsley sprigs for garnish
Tomato wedges for garnish
Tomato Vinaigrette (see page 256)

(see page 256)

1. In a large kettle, combine the water, wine, vinegar, onion, carrots, peppercorns, bay leaf, parsley sprigs, and celery. Bring to a boil, then remove from heat and let cool.
2. Pour the court bouillon into a fish poacher. Measure the bass at its thickest point and place it on the rack of the poacher. Cover the fish with the lettuce leaves, and carefully lower it into the bouillon. Cover and bring to a boil, then reduce the heat and simmer gently until the fish is cooked, following the Canadian Guideline. The fish should be opaque throughout and should flake away from the bone when prodded with the tip of a knife. Turn off the heat and let the fish remain in the pan, undisturbed, for 10 more minutes.
3. Transfer the fish to a heated serving platter. Discard the lettuce leaves and carefully peel off the skin. Garnish with additional parsley sprigs and tomato wedges. Serve accompanied by Tomato Vinaigrette.

Serves 4–6

Striped bass is native to the Atlantic Ocean, ranging along the East Coast from the St. Lawrence River south into the Gulf of Mexico. Successfully transplanted to the Pacific Coast in the late 1800s, this anadromous fish has also adapted well to life in landlocked freshwater lakes.

Stripers are a favorite with sport fishermen, as the fish put up a good fight when hooked with rod and reel. Recorded catches of these fish have bettered 100 pounds, but fish of this size are rare today due to their declining numbers.

Nantucket Striped Bass

The soy-based marinade with its crunch of sesame seeds is a snap to prepare. The marinade is especially suitable to stripers or another rich-flavored fish steak, such as shark, mahi mahi, or swordfish.

> 6 *striped bass steaks, about 1-inch thick*
> 1 *recipe Soy Marinade (see page 249).*
> 1/4 *cup cognac*
> 6 *tablespoons sesame seeds*

1. Preheat the broiler or prepare a charcoal fire.
2. Place the steaks in one layer in a shallow glass or ceramic dish. Pour the marinade and cognac over them. Turn the steaks to coat completely. Cover and let stand at room temperature for 30 minutes. Turn the steaks over once while they marinate.
3. Arrange the steaks in a broiler pan and place 4 inches below the broiler element. Or place them on an oiled rack 4 inches above red-hot but not flaming coals. Cook the steaks 8 to 10 minutes, turning once and basting with the remaining marinade.
4. Sprinkle the steaks with the sesame seeds and serve immediately.

Variation: The fish may also be baked in a lightly oiled shallow glass or ceramic dish in a preheated 375 degree oven for 20 minutes. Turn them over once while they cook.

Serves 6
Must be partially prepared in advance

The firm, white flesh of striped bass has good flavor and can be prepared in a variety of ways. If you are presented with a whole striped bass, stuff it with chopped celery and herbs, then bake it whole, using the Canadian Guideline for timing.

Striped bass is named for its dark stripes running the length of the fish. Because of declining stocks, commercial fishing for stripers has been limited in many East Coast states.

PORGY

GRUNT

TILEFISH

MULLET

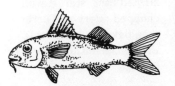

RED MULLET

TAUTOG

**SEA TROUT
(WEAKFISH)**

In the 1800s there was such an abundance of scup that they were often used as fertilizer. The Narraganset Indians knew that these fish were good fertilizer and called them mishcuppauog. Later this word was shortened to "scup" or "porgy."

The Epicureans: Porgy, Grunt, Tilefish, Mullet, Tautog, and Sea Trout

It may not always be true that you are what you eat, but you often taste like what you eat. All of the fishes in this group forage on the bottom of the ocean for shellfish and seaweed, and as a result, they have a distinct, rich flavor. They are frequently referred to in the fishery industry as ground fish.

This is a very noisy group. The grunt grunts and the male sea trout makes a loud tapping sound. Other members of the group (not included in this book) act out their names: the drum drums and the croaker croaks. Besides their vocalizing, many of these fishes have interesting teeth. Some are sharp like incisors for clipping off seaweed, while others are broad anvils for crushing the shellfish they enjoy in their diet.

Although closely related, the diverse fishes in this group look quite different, as they come in a wide variety of shapes and colors. Once you have tasted their sweet flesh, however, you will agree that they have one striking similarity. They are all uncommonly delicious.

Steamed Porgy

The spicy taste of Chinese black bean sauce combined with the porgy makes this a favorite. Try this recipe with tautog fillets as well. The black bean sauce also works nicely with whole steamed freshwater trout, red snapper, whiting, or sea bass.

    4 small porgies (10 to 12 ounces), cleaned and
        scaled, head and tail intact
    3 tablespoons dry sherry
    3 tablespoons light soy sauce
    2 tablespoons oriental sesame oil*
    1/2 teaspoon freshly ground black pepper
    4 scallions, trimmed to 3 inches and cut into thin
        slivers
    1 tablespoon fermented Chinese black beans*
    2 teaspoons minced garlic
    1 teaspoon minced gingerroot

2 small zucchinis, cut into 2-inch lengths and
   julienned
1 large carrot, cut into 2-inch lengths and julienned
1/2 cup fish stock (see page 277)
1 tablespoon cornstarch
1 1/2 tablespoons cold water
1 tablespoon vegetable oil

*Available in oriental markets or in specialty section of
   your supermarket.

1. Slash each fish 3 or 4 times diagonally on both sides.
2. Stir together the sherry, soy sauce, sesame oil, and
   1/8 teaspoon pepper. Rub this mixture into the
   slashes in each fish.
3. Press half of the slivered scallions into the slashes.
   Set the fish aside.
4. Rinse the black beans under running water and then
   soak them for 10 to 15 minutes in 1/2 cup water.
   Drain, then mash and mix with the garlic and ginger.
   Set aside.
5. Measure the porgies at their thickest point. Place
   them on a steamer rack over boiling water. Cover.
   Reduce the heat to simmer and steam the fish for 10
   minutes per inch of thickness, according to the Canadian Guideline.
6. Meanwhile, heat the vegetable oil in a heavy pan.
   Stir in the black bean/garlic/ginger mixture and cook
   for 10 seconds. Add the remaining scallions, the zucchini, and carrots, and stir. Cook for another 10 seconds. Add the fish stock and bring to a simmer.
7. Mix the cornstarch with the water and stir it into the
   simmering sauce. When the sauce begins to thicken
   remove it from heat and keep warm.
8. Place the porgies on a warm platter and spoon the
   sauce over the fish. Serve at once.

Serves 4

Porgy and scup are similar, and one can almost always be substituted for the other.

There are more than a dozen species of porgy found in the Atlantic; outside of America, porgy are known as sea bream.

Scup (*Stenotomus chrysops*), our local porgy, is found from New England south to the Carolinas. The average adult scup is 12 to 15 inches in length, weighing between 1 and 2 pounds. These fish have silvery skin flecked with large, blue scales, which are well embedded.

Scup or porgy are commercially harvested by trawlers with large nets, but they are fun to catch with rod and reel as well. These fish are excellent when pan-fried and especially good for oriental steaming.

Pan-fried porgies are delicious cooked with a breading (see suggestions for perch and tilapia on page 169). Before you coat the porgies, score the fish by cutting 3 or 4 slits diagonally across each side. This will allow for more even and rapid cooking. If you use a marinade, scoring increases the rate at which the marinade is absorbed.

Fried Grunts Bahamian Style

Bahamians traditionally serve fried grunts with a portion of hot grits.

> 2 *small grunts, cleaned and scaled, head and tail intact, about ¹/₂ to ³/₄ pound each*
> 4 *tablespoons fresh strained lime juice*
> 1 *teaspoon minced hot pepper*
> 6–8 *tablespoons oil*
> ¹/₂ *cup flour*
> ¹/₂ *teaspoon salt*
> ¹/₂ *teaspoon freshly ground black pepper*
> *Lime wedges for garnish*

1. Slash each fish 3 or 4 times diagonally on both sides.
2. Rub the lime juice onto each side of the fish, then rub the peppers against the skin. Set aside and let rest for 30 minutes.
3. On a piece of paper toweling, combine the flour, salt, and pepper. Dredge each fish lightly on both sides in the flour mixture and shake off the excess.
4. Heat 4 tablespoons of oil in a heavy skillet. When it is smoking, carefully fry the fish about 3 to 5 minutes on each side or until golden and crisp. Be careful that you do not get splattered by the hot oil when you turn over the fish. Add the remaining oil, if necessary.
5. Serve the fish with lime wedges.

Serves 2
Must be partially prepared in advance

There are 20 species of grunts in North America, and most are found south of the Chesapeake Bay. They are well named as they can make a grunting noise when removed from the water. One species grunts so loudly that it is called pigfish; another is called porkfish.

In general, grunts are relatively small fish, seldom larger than 2 pounds.

Baked Stuffed Tilefish

FROM OFFICE OF THE ROMAGNOLI'S TABLE, BOSTON

This recipe was created by the Office of the Romagnoli's Table for their restaurants in Boston and Salem, Massachusetts. Tilefish is lean and sweet. It responds best to a recipe using subtle aromatic ingredients that will not mask its lovely delicate taste. We would serve it with baked or boiled rice, preferably Italian Arborio, and a cold crisp Italian white wine.

> 1 *whole tilefish (5 to 6 pounds), cleaned and scaled, head and tail intact*
> 1 *teaspoon salt*
> 4 *tablespoons olive oil*
> $^1/_4$ to $^1/_2$ *pound mushrooms, sliced*
> 4 *stalks celery, sliced*
> 4 *slices day-old Italian bread, crustless, cut in $^1/_2$-inch cubes*
> *Freshly ground black pepper*
> 2 *tablespoons minced fresh Italian parsley*
> 5 *sprigs parsley*
> 3 *tablespoons fresh strained lemon juice*
> 2 *lemons, cut in wedges, for garnish*

1. Preheat oven to 425 degrees.
2. With a very sharp knife and working from the inside of the fish, cut the flesh away from the spines on both sides of the backbone. Sever the bone just under the head and lift the bone out. This should remove most of the bones, but probably not all. Be careful not to pierce the skin. Open up the fish and sprinkle it with $^1/_2$ teaspoon salt.
3. In a sauté pan, heat the olive oil over medium heat and brown the bread cubes, tossing frequently. Add the mushrooms and celery, and sauté until the mushrooms give up their natural juices. Sprinkle with the remaining $^1/_2$ teaspoon salt and freshly ground pepper. Remove from the heat. Add the minced parsley. Taste and correct the seasoning, adding more salt if desired.
4. Mound the stuffing on one side of the fish and fold the other half over it. Secure with small skewers. Sew the fish closed with thread (unwaxed dental floss works well). Remove the skewers.
5. Place a piece of aluminum foil in the bottom of a baking dish just large enough to hold the fish. Place the parsley sprigs on the foil and center the fish on top of the parsley.

Tilefish is sometimes called Golden Sea Bass.

Tilefish is violet tinged with yellow tilelike spots. It is found in very deep water off the New England coast.

For a long time, it was speculated that tilefish were extinct, and scientists thought that a drop in ocean temperature was responsible. Fortunately, they have returned to the Atlantic coast and are back in good supply.

An average tilefish weighs 5–6 pounds, and its flesh is dense, sweet, and firm—similar to that of lobster.

6. Bake 25 to 30 minutes (or about 6 to 8 minutes per pound of total fish). Using two spatulas, remove the fish from the baking dish and place on a heated serving platter. Remove the thread. Drizzle with the lemon juice. Garnish with the lemon wedges and serve.

Serves 8

Smoke-Flavored Grilled Mullet

The rich nutty flavor of striped mullet takes little more than grilling to be at its best. Our favorite preparation utilizes a charcoal or gas grill and a variety of aromatic woods. Sweet fruit woods such as cherry and apple, wood from nut-bearing trees like oak and walnut, or the time-tested favorites of hickory and mesquite will lend subtle flavor during cooking.

> 4 8- to 10-ounce mullet fillets, with skin
> 4 tablespoons unsalted butter (¹/₂ stick), softened
> 2 tablespoons minced fresh chives
> Freshly ground black pepper to taste
> Lemon wedges for garnish

1. Prepare a charcoal or gas grill.
2. Soak 2 cups of aromatic wood chips in water to cover for 15 or 20 minutes.
3. When the coals are red-hot but not flaming, drain the wood chips and scatter them on top of the hot coals.
4. Place the mullet fillets on the grill rack, skin side down. Cover the grill to retain as much smoke as possible. The fillets will take 10 to 15 minutes to cook, or use the Canadian Guideline to determine the cooking time.
5. While the fish is cooking, whisk the chives into the softened butter, and transfer to a small serving bowl to accompany the fish.
6. When the fillets are cooked, transfer them to a heated serving platter, grind some pepper over them, and garnish the platter with lemon wedges.

Serves 4

The striped mullet ranges from Massachusetts south into the Gulf of Mexico, the Caribbean, and the West Indies. It is one of the six species of mullet found in North America, and is the only one that inhabits New England waters.

Fillet of Mullet with Red Butter and Crayfish

FROM RESTAURANT LE BATEAU IVRE, COURCHEVAL, FRANCE

Chef Jean-Pierre Jacob, from this fine restaurant located in Hotel Pomme de Pin, creates a glorious combination using an assertively flavored fish with red wine. The presentation is striking; a pool of deep red sauce is topped with emerald green, barely cooked spinach and adorned with pink shrimp. If your fishmonger does not have red mullet, substitute sea bass or tautog.

> Fish prepared in this manner needs a red wine to accompany it. Good choices would be a Beaujolais Village, a light Côtes du Rhône, or one of the lighter California Zinfandels.

- 4 *red mullets, about ¹/₂ pound each, head and tails intact*
- 1 *bottle (750 milliliters) full-bodied red wine, such as a Côtes du Rhône*
- 2 *tablespoons minced shallots*
- ¹/₄ *teaspoon dried thyme*
- 1 *bay leaf*
- 9 *tablespoons unsalted butter (1 stick plus 1 tablespoon)*
- *Salt and freshly ground black pepper to taste*
- 2 *pounds fresh spinach, washed and dried, tough stems removed*
- 12 *crayfish, prawns, or jumbo shrimp, shelled and deveined*
- 3 *tablespoons olive oil*

> The mullet is a popular food fish with light, mild-flavored, firm-textured meat. Smoked mullet is delicious and makes a good pâté.

1. Remove the bones, heads, and tails from the fish. Discard the tails, but reserve the heads and bones. Cut each fillet in half lengthwise, leaving the skin on each piece. You will have 16 pieces.
2. Place the bones and heads in a medium-size enameled saucepan. Add the wine, shallots, thyme, and bay leaf. Bring to a boil and lower the heat to medium. Reduce until 4 to 6 tablespoons of liquid remain. Over low heat, whisk in 8 tablespoons of butter, one tablespoon at a time, until the butter is fully incorporated. Strain the sauce and add salt and pepper to taste. Keep warm over hot (145-degree), not boiling water.
3. Melt the remaining tablespoon of butter in a large saucepan. Add the spinach, tossing to coat with the butter. Cook over medium heat until barely cooked. The spinach should remain relatively crisp to keep its flavor and bright green color. Set aside and keep warm.

> The silver or gray mullet is very similar to striped mullet and may be used in any recipe calling for mullet. These fish feed on small algae and are known to frequent estuaries in search for food.

4. Bring water to a boil in a medium-size saucepan. Add the crayfish, prawns, or shrimp, and cook until they just turn pink, about 3 to 5 minutes. Drain and keep warm.

5. Heat the olive oil in a large nonstick skillet, over medium-high heat. Add the fish fillets, skin side down, in one layer and cook for 3 to 4 minutes. Turn carefully and cook the other side for 1 minute. Set aside, keeping them warm.

6. To serve, divide the sauce among 4 warmed plates. Place the spinach neatly in the center, and top decoratively with 4 pieces of fish per plate. Intersperse the fish with the crayfish or shrimp and serve immediately.

Serves 4

"**The discovery of a new dish does more for human happiness than the discovery of a new star.**"**—Brillat-Savarin**

Grilled Tautog

Remarkably easy to prepare, grilled tautog makes an ideal meal for a summer evening. The sweet meat of the fish is enlivened with a zippy avocado salsa. Almost any grilled fish tastes great with Salsa Cruda with Avocado. Try this recipe with grouper. Add a leafy green salad, steamed corn or potatoes, and a frosty mug of ice-cold beer for a complete feast.

> 6 *tautog fillets, about 6 to 8 ounces each*
> 1 *recipe Herbal Wine Marinade (see page* 250)
> 1 *recipe Salsa Cruda with Avocado (see page* 265)

1. Place the fillets, skin side down, in a ceramic dish. (If you have fewer but larger fillets, divide them into 6 equal pieces.) Drizzle the marinade over the fish. Cover with plastic wrap and marinate 20 minutes at room temperature or one hour in the refrigerator.
2. Prepare a charcoal fire. The coals should be red-hot but not flaming. Place a greased rack about 6 inches above the coals and grill the fillets, skin side down, 4 to 5 minutes. Carefully turn the fillets over and grill an additional 3 to 4 minutes.
3. Serve with Salsa Cruda or another sauce of your choice.

Serves 6
Must be partially prepared in advance

Tautog, also known as blackfish, are found commercially in the Atlantic from Nova Scotia to South Carolina. They prefer a rocky bottom and are a common sport fish. They average 2 to 4 pounds in size.

Fishermen's Rules
When the wind is in the East,
Then the fishes bite the least.
When the wind is in the West,
Then the fishes bite the best.
When the wind is in the North,
Then the fishes do come forth.
When the wind is in the South,
It blows the bait into the
*   fishes' mouth.*

Mediterranean Baked Sea Trout

This gusty dish abounds with Mediterranean nuances of rosemary, garlic, olive oil, and tomatoes. Serve the sea trout on a winter evening with crusty hot bread, salad dressed with our Vinaigrette (see page 256), and red wine. Any thick fillet that is flavorful enough to stand up to these ingredients may be substituted.

2 pounds sea trout fillets
2 tablespoons olive oil
1/4 cup chopped red onion (about 1 small)
2 teaspoons minced garlic
2 tablespoons fresh parsley
2 tablespoons fresh basil, or 2 teaspoons dried
2 tablespoons fresh oregano, or 2 teaspoons dried
1 teaspoon fresh rosemary, or 1/4 teaspoon dried
1 14-ounce can Italian plum tomatoes, drained and chopped
1 cup halved cherry tomatoes
1/4 teaspoon pepper
2 tablespoons Pernod
2 tablespoons fresh strained lemon juice
1/4 cup crumbled feta cheese

1. Wash fish and remove any small bones. Cut into 4 equal-size portions.
2. Heat the oil in a nonstick skillet. Add the onion and sauté over medium heat until softened, about 5 minutes. Stir in the garlic, parsley, basil, oregano, rosemary, plum and cherry tomatoes, and pepper. Bring to a boil, then lower heat and simmer about 10 minutes, stirring frequently. Set aside. The recipe may be prepared to this point up to 4 hours in advance. Refrigerate the tomato-herb mixture, covered.
3. When you are ready to complete the preparation, preheat oven to 375 degrees.
4. Lightly oil a dish large enough to hold all the fillets in a single layer. Arrange the fish in the dish, skin side down, and cover with the tomato-herb mixture. Sprinkle the Pernod and lemon juice over the tomatoes. Cover the dish tightly with foil.
5. Bake for 15 minutes, remove the foil, and raise the oven temperature to 425 degrees. Sprinkle the feta cheese on the surface and spoon some of the juices over everything. Bake 5 minutes more, uncovered.
6. Place each fillet on a warmed plate and spoon sauce on top.
Serves 4
May be partially prepared in advance

Sea trout (Cynoscion regalis) are not members of the trout family. They are found from Massachusetts to Florida and have olive green backs and silvery undersides. These fish are often referred to as weakfish because they have delicate mouths that are frequently torn by fishhooks. This weakness frustrates many a fisherman as the sea trout pulls away from the hook.

Sea trout fillets grilled over a charcoal fire are excellent. Serve them with an herbal butter such as Tarragon Butter (page 271).

Sleek Open-Water Fishes: Bluefish, Mackerel, Mahi Mahi, Swordfish, Tuna, and Marlin

These are fishes from several different families with some important things in common. To the cook, they are flavorful and rich in healthful oils. To the sport fisherman, they are prizes. And to the scientist, they are all streamlined and swift predators of the near shore and open ocean.

There is also a food chain to be found within this group. They seem to find each other just as delicious as we find all of them. During the summer fishermen can witness schools of mackerel leaping from the water to escape a hungry school of bluefish. And one is also apt to see bluefish leaping to evade a huge bluefin tuna.

For those attracted to a fish diet for health reasons, look no further. The fish in this section are rich sources of the oils recommended to help lower blood serum cholesterol.

BLUEFISH

ATLANTIC MACKEREL

MAHI MAHI

SWORDFISH

TUNA

MARLIN

Bluefish Couscous Salad

Couscous, or Moroccan pasta, is an alternative to rice in the North African diet. Its strong wheaty flavor combines well with anything from cooked chicken to cooked fish. Wolffish, tilefish, sea trout, and salmon, as well as shrimp or squid, would all be delicious in this recipe. Thick fillets or steak cuts are recommended, as they will not fall apart during the tossing and mixing.

1 cup quick-cooking couscous
1 1/4 cups chicken stock, heated to the boiling point
3 tablespoons olive oil
3 tablespoons fresh strained lemon juice
1/2 cup thinly sliced scallions, white part only
2 teaspoons Dijon-style mustard
1 tablespoon grated lemon rind (zest)
1/4 teaspoon freshly ground black pepper
Salt to taste
1 tablespoon minced fresh parsley
2 tablespoons finely chopped fresh basil
2 tablespoons snipped fresh dillweed
1/2 cup chopped fresh mint
1/2 cucumber, seeded and cut in 1/4-inch dice
1 cup halved cherry tomatoes
1 cup assorted diced fresh vegetables: green peppers, green beans, zucchini
1 pound bluefish, cooked, skinned, and cut in small pieces
Lettuce leaves
Black olives, pitted, for garnish

1. Place the couscous in a large bowl and add the boiling stock. Cover and let stand for 15 minutes, or until all the stock has been absorbed. Fluff with a fork.
2. Immediately pour the olive oil over the couscous and toss. Set scallions aside to cool.
3. In another bowl, combine the lemon juice, mustard, lemon rind, and pepper. Mix well. When the couscous has cooled to room temperature, stir in this lemon-mustard mixture. The recipe can be prepared to this point up to 8 hours before serving.
4. Just before serving, or no more than 2 hours before serving, add the parsley, basil, dillweed, mint, cucumber, cherry tomatoes, and assorted vegetables to the couscous and toss vigorously to distribute thoroughly. Refrigerate, if preparing ahead, and then let it sit at room temperature for 20 minutes prior to serving.

5. Immediately before serving, mix in the bluefish. Arrange beds of lettuce on salad plates. Divide the salad equally between them and garnish with the black olives.

Serves 6
May be prepared in advance

Grilled Bluefish Fillets

This simple method for grilled bluefish produces moist and delicious results. The addition of favorite herbs will impart different flavors. Almost any combination of herbs and spices may be used.

 1   *1-pound bluefish fillet with skin*
 1   *tablespoon fresh strained lemon juice*
 2   *teaspoons mayonnaise*
 1   *tablespoon snipped fresh dill*
     Freshly ground black pepper to taste

1. Prepare charcoal fire.
2. Rinse the fillet with lemon juice and pat dry. Spread a very thin layer of mayonnaise on the flesh side of the fillet. Sprinkle the dill and pepper on top of the mayonnaise.
3. When the coals are red-hot, but not flaming, place the rack 4 to 6 inches above the fire. Place the fillet directly on the rack, skin side down. The skin acts as the cooking pan in the recipe. Cook the fish using the Canadian Guideline, for about 10 minutes. If a slightly smoky flavor is desired, cover the grill while cooking.
4. To serve, carefully transfer the fish to a heated plate, leaving the skin on the grill. Discard the skin.

Serves 2

Some people prefer skinning blues before cooking, as they think the skin gives the fish a strong flavor. To grill without the skin, remove the skin as directed below. Place fish, skinned side down, on a double thickness of lightly oiled heavy-duty aluminum foil. The foil will prevent the skinned fillets from sticking to the grill.

How to Skin Fillets
Lay the fillets, skin side down, on a flat, smooth surface (if only a wood surface is available, cover with a few sheets of waxed paper).
Hold the tail of one fillet in your hand. About $1/2$ inch from the tail, cut down through the flesh to the skin at a 45-degree angle. Do not cut through the skin. With the knife almost parallel to the cutting surface, move it in a back and forth motion toward the midsection of the fillet. At the same time, hold the skin tightly. Continue moving the knife in the same way until the skin is completely separated from the fillet. The sharper the knife, the easier the job.

Grilled Mackerel Fillets

Mackerel fillets are readily available during the summer months in New England. Very fresh mackerel is delicate and delicious, especially when cooked on a charcoal grill. This recipe can also be used for broiling mackerel, with the fillets 4 to 5 inches from the broiler element.

2 *tablespoons soy sauce*
1 *tablespoon fresh strained lime juice*
2 *tablespoons fresh strained orange juice*
2 *drops Tabasco sauce*
1 *teaspoon minced garlic*
1 *teaspoon freshly ground black pepper*
1 *pound mackerel fillets, with skin*

1. Prepare charcoal grill.
2. Combine the soy sauce, lime and orange juices, Tabasco, garlic, and pepper. Mix thoroughly.
3. Remove the strip of dark red flesh containing the fine bones that runs along the midline of the mackerel fillets. To do this, place a fillet on a cutting board, flesh side up, and using a sharp knife, make an angled cut down the length of the fillet at the edge of the dark flesh. Make a similar cut on the other edge of the dark flesh, forming a long wedge. Grasp one end of the strip of flesh and pull it away from the skin. It separates quite easily, leaving the more delicate pale flesh, which is now completely boneless. Repeat with the other fillets. Rinse the fillets and pat dry.
4. When the coals are red-hot but not flaming, place the rack about 4 inches above the fire. Brush the fillets with the soy mixture and place them on the grill, skin side down. The skin is rich in oil and will burn very quickly if the fire is too hot. Baste several times during grilling. Because the fillets are usually quite small, they will cook very quickly without being turned.
5. Remove from the fire and serve at once. The crispy skin is very good to eat if it has not been burned.

Note: Grilling the fillets in a wire basket makes the grilling process much easier.

Serves 2

The mackerel family (*Scombridae*) includes some of the most popular game fishes in North America. In addition to Atlantic mackerel (*Scomber scombrus*), some other members of the family are wahoo, tunas, bonito, and king mackerel.

The Atlantic mackerel travels in huge schools in the open ocean from Newfoundland south to Cape Hatteras. Commercial fishermen may net thousands of pounds when they find a big school.

Some fishermen think that the choicest mackerel are caught in the fall when they are the fattest. These fish are particularly tasty when cooked on the grill. The rich meat is soft textured and delicious.

King Mackerel

FROM RISTORANTE TOSCANO, BOSTON

This simple recipe, which was created by Chef Vinicio Paoli, with its pine-fresh accent of rosemary and dash of garlic, permits the flavor of the mackerel to stand out. Broiled tomatoes and eggplant, along with a loaf of chewy Italian bread, would be compatible with the mackerel. Chef Paoli uses king mackerel, but Atlantic, Spanish, or painted mackered can also be used.

1 pound king mackerel fillets
2–3 fresh rosemary sprigs
1 teaspoon minced garlic
2 tablespoons extra-virgin olive oil
Salt and freshly ground black pepper to taste

1. Preheat oven to 400 degrees.
2. Place the fillets in a lightly buttered baking dish just large enough to hold them in one layer. Lay the rosemary on top and sprinkle the garlic, salt, and pepper over the fillets. Drizzle with the olive oil.
3. Measure the thickness of the fillets. Following the Canadian Guideline, allow about 10 minutes of cooking time per inch. Bake accordingly, until the fish flakes easily. Serve immediately with the pan juices.

Serves 2

The mackerel has a sleek body, a pointed head, and forked tail. The skin appears iridescent, shiny dark blue green to blue black, and the scales are tiny.

King mackerel (*Scomberomorus cavalla*) is a large member of the mackerel family weighing as much as 90 pounds, but averaging 15 to 20 pounds. An open ocean fish, the king mackerel is generally found south of New England and as far south as Brazil.

Rosemary is an intensely flavored herb that combines well with strong flavored oil-rich fishes such as mackerel and bluefish.

Mahi Mahi with Mole Verde

FROM RATTLESNAKE CLUB, DENVER

Using flavors of the Southwest, Jimmy Schmidt has created a sauce containing rich, spicy overtones of peppers along with the cool piquancy of greens. If you live outside the West or Southwest, don't be deterred by the ingredients. Many specialty green grocers and Hispanic markets carry the poblano chile peppers and achiote paste.

5 fresh tomatillos, mashed, or 5 canned
1 garlic clove
1 medium onion, quartered
1/2 cup chopped spinach, tough stems removed
1/2 cup chopped romaine lettuce
1 poblano chile pepper, roasted, peeled, seeded, diced
1 tablespoon minced fresh mint
1/4 cup chopped sorrel
1/4 cup chopped arugula
2 tablespoons walnut oil
3 tablespoons pignolia (pine nuts), roasted
Salt to taste
1/4 cup achiote paste
1/4 cup olive oil
8 escalopes of Mahi Mahi, 3 ounces each, cut no thicker than 3/8 inch
4 sprigs of cilantro for garnish

1. To make the Mole Verde: In a food processor fitted with a steel blade, combine tomatillos, garlic, and onion. While the machine is running, add the spinach, romaine, pepper, mint, sorrel, and arugula until coarsely chopped and combined. Do not overprocess. Add oil and pine nuts and whirl again briefly. Adjust seasoning and set aside. It can be made 3 or 4 hours in advance.
2. Preheat broiler or prepare charcoal grill.
3. Combine the achiote paste and oil in a small bowl. Immerse the fish in the mixture.
4. When the coals are red-hot but not flaming, place the fish on the grill rack, 4 inches from the flame. (If you are using the broiler, place the fish 4 inches from the broiler element.) Cook until browned, about 2 minutes. Turn over and cook 2 minutes more until done.
5. Meanwhile, warm the reserved Mole Verde in a small saucepan over medium heat.

Mahi mahi is also known as dolphinfish, though it is related to the mammal of the same name. It is readily available in the warm waters of Hawaii, Florida, and the Caribbean.

Mahi mahi is also known as dorado or dourade and makes excellent chowder.

Poblano chile peppers are dark green and similar in shape to bell peppers. They are a mild chile, which develop a rich aromatic flavor when roasted.

You are probably familiar with scallops (escalopes) of veal, which are boneless slices of the meat cut 1/4 to 3/8 inch thick. While veal scallops usually are pounded to reduce their thickness, fish scallops are ordinarily not pounded.

6. Ladle a spoonful of sauce on each plate. Position 2 escalopes on top of the sauce, slightly overlapping. Garnish with cilantro and serve.

Serves 4

A tomatillo, or Mexican green tomato, is one species in a group known as Chinese lantern plants because the fruits are enclosed in papery calyxes that cover them like oriental shades. Cooked, the tomatillos have a lemony-herbal flavor. They can be used raw if a sharp acid flavor is desired.

Achiote paste is made from the red pulp that surrounds the annatto seed. It is a plant native to Central and South America and is frequently used in Mexican cuisine. Its primary purpose in cooking is to add a deep golden red hue. Look for it in Hispanic markets, or substitute saffron.

Swordfish Steaks with Avocado Butter

Rich, firm-fleshed swordfish willingly accepts this highly flavored lemon-soy-mustard marinade. An unexpected dollop of avocado butter adds a colorful finishing touch. Mako shark steaks are a good substitute.

¹/₃ cup soy sauce
1 teaspoon grated lemon rind (zest)
8 tablespoons fresh strained lemon juice
1 teaspoon minced garlic
3 teaspoons Dijon-style mustard
¹/₂ cup vegetable oil
4 pounds small swordfish steaks, about 1 inch thick
¹/₂ cup unsalted butter (1 stick), at room
* temperature*
¹/₂ cup mashed ripe avocado
2 tablespoons snipped fresh dill
1 ¹/₂ teaspoons Worcestershire sauce
Lemon wedges for garnish
Dill sprigs for garnish

1. Combine the soy sauce, lemon zest, 4 tablespoons lemon juice, garlic, mustard, and oil in a small bowl. Blend well. Place the swordfish steaks in a shallow baking dish large enough to contain them in one layer. Pour the marinade over the fish, pricking its flesh so that the marinade penetrates it well. Turn the fish several times and marinate 2 hours in the refrigerator.
2. Preheat the broiler. Arrange the fish on a broiler pan and place about 4 inches from the heating element. Broil 5 to 6 minutes on each side. (The fish may also be barbecued on a grill, using the same timing as in the broiler.)
3. Meanwhile, whip the butter until soft and creamy. Beat in the mashed avocado, the remaining 4 tablespoons lemon juice, dill, and Worcestershire sauce. Blend thoroughly. Brush the warm swordfish steaks generously with the mixture and serve with dill sprigs on top and lemon wedges on the side.

Serves 8
Must be partially prepared in advance

A perfectly grilled or broiled swordfish steak needs little in the way of embellishment. For variety and added flavor, we suggest a brief marinade in one of the marinades from Chapter 7. Another easy method of adding flavor is the addition of a slice of compound butter or a teaspoon of melted herbal butter. You will find recipes for these in Chapter 7.

Swordfish Tonnato

The famous Italian dish, "Vitello Tonnato," is the inspiration for this delicious swordfish rendition. It is an excellent choice for a summertime lunch or supper, and benefits from advance preparation.

1 *2¹/₂-pound swordfish steak, about 1 inch thick*
1 *7-ounce can tuna, packed in oil, drained*
1 *2-ounce can flat anchovy fillets*
3 *tablespoons capers, rinsed and drained*
3 *tablespoons fresh strained lemon juice*
¹/₂–³/₄ cup olive oil
1 *recipe Mayonnaise, (see page 252)*
Pitted black olives for garnish

1. Poach the swordfish. Let the fish cool while proceeding with the rest of the recipe. When the fish is cool, remove the skin.
2. In a food processor fitted with the steel knife, or in a blender, process the tuna, 6 anchovy fillets, capers, lemon juice, and ¹/₂ cup olive oil until pureed. Add the additional ¹/₄ cup olive oil as needed. Transfer the puree to a bowl and carefully fold it into the mayonnaise, making sure it is thoroughly combined. Taste and add salt, if necessary.
3. Ladle several spoonfuls of the tuna sauce over the bottom of a serving platter. Place the swordfish on top of the sauce and ladle the remaining sauce over the fish. Decorate with the remaining anchovies and the olives. If you wish, you may also use lemon slices and capers as a garnish.
4. Tightly cover the platter with plastic wrap. Refrigerate at least 24 hours in advance, or up to 48 hours. Remove the platter from the refrigerator 30 minutes prior to serving so that the food is cool, not cold.

Serves 6
Must be prepared in advance

Swordfish, whose name is derived from its long, swordlike beak, is rich in flavor with a solid, meatlike flesh that retains its firm texture even when cooked. The most popular cooking method for swordfish is broiling, but it should also be tried barbecued, baked, or fried. Elaborate sauces are unnecessary because they tend to mask its delicate flavor.

Tuna Salad Niçoise

Traditionally, Salad Niçoise is made from canned imported oil-packed tuna. We prefer using fresh tuna to reduce the fat content.

3 *tablespoons olive oil*

2 *teaspoons minced garlic*

1 1/2 *teaspoons fresh thyme leaves, or* 1/4 *teaspoon dried*

1 1/2 *pounds tuna, about 1 inch thick*

3/4 *pound fresh green beans, ends trimmed*

6 *small red potatoes, quartered*

3/4 *cup Vinaigrette, made with wine vinegar (see page 256)*

8 *flat anchovy fillets, thinly sliced crosswise*

Red lettuce leaves

6 *small fresh tomatoes, or 1 pint of cherry tomatoes*

1 *small red onion, thinly sliced (about 1/2 cup)*

24 *black, oil-cured olives, preferably "niçoise"*

3 *tablespoons minced fresh parsley*

1. Combine the olive oil, garlic, and thyme in a flat-bottomed glass or ceramic dish large enough to hold the tuna in one layer. Add the tuna, turning to coat both sides. Cover with aluminum foil and marinate at room temperature for 30 minutes.
2. Preheat over to 375 degrees.
3. Drain the tuna and discard the marinade. Bake the tuna in the oven, tightly covered, for 10 to 15 minutes, depending upon thickness (use Canadian Guideline). The tuna may be slightly pink in the center, but it will continue to cook as it cools; it should remain moist, not overcooked and dry. (The tuna may be prepared a day ahead and refrigerated.)
4. Fill a two-quart pan three-quarters full with salted water and bring to a boil. Add the green beans and cook until tender-crisp. Drain and refresh in cold water. Cook the potatoes in the same manner, until tender, about 10 minutes. Drain and cool.
5. Whisk the vinaigrette and anchovies together. Break the cooled tuna into bite-size chunks. Marinate the fish in half of the vinaigrette for 1 hour.
6. To assemble the salad, arrange beds of lettuce leaves on 6 luncheon plates. Mound portions of tuna in the center of each bed and surround the fish with green beans, potatoes, and tomatoes. Distribute the onions decoratively between the vegetables. (This may be done up to 1 hour before serving; keep the plates covered with plastic wrap in the refrigerator.) Drizzle the remaining vinaigrette over the vegetables

"Let the salad maker be. . . . a diplomat with salt and a madman with mixing."—Spanish proverb

Tuna salad has been a part of lunch boxes and picnics for as long as most of us can remember. Here are some suggestions for updating the traditional tuna salad:
*Save calories by using half low-fat yogurt and half mayonnaise for the binder.
*Use fresh tuna, poached according to instructions in Chapter 1.
*Toss in a handful of alfalfa or radish sprouts.
*Add toasted slivered almonds and seedless red grapes.

and place 4 olives on each salad. Sprinkle each salad with parsley.

Serves 6
Must be prepared in advance

Tuna Tostados

FROM REBECCA'S RESTAURANT, VENICE, CALIFORNIA

The zesty flavors of Southwest cuisine combine nicely with the rich, dark meat of tuna. Chef William Hufferd prepares this recipe with homemade arbol chile salsa. Arbol chiles are not available in the Northeast, so we used a commercially prepared salsa verde. Prepared fresh salsas can be found in the produce sections of most supermarkets. Homemade refried beans are an especially nice touch, but you may also use a commercial variety.

> ³/₄ cup refried black or pinto beans, preferably
>   homemade
> 4 tortillas, 8 to 10 inches
> Vegetable oil or lard for frying
> Kosher salt to taste
> 1 teaspoon fresh strained lime juice
> ¹/₂ pound fresh tuna, ¹/₄ inch thick, cut in 4 pieces
>   of equal size, about 2¹/₂ inches square
> ¹/₂ small head of cabbage, shredded
> ¹/₂ cup sour cream
> 4 teaspoons grated Queso Anejo, or other hard
>   cheese such as Parmesan or Romano
> 4 teaspoons hot chile salsa
> 4 slices tomato, cut in half to make 8 pieces

1. Preheat broiler.
2. Warm the refried beans in a small saucepan over low heat while preparing the remainder of the recipe.
3. Place the oil or lard in a large frying pan, to a depth of ¹/₄ inch, and heat until nearly smoking. Fry the tortillas, one at a time, until golden brown, turning once. Remove them from the pan, drain on brown paper, and sprinkle with the salt and lime juice. Set aside.
4. Place the pieces of tuna on a lightly oiled broiler pan and broil, 4 inches from the heating element, about 1¹/₂ minutes. Turn and broil the other side 1 minute. Remove the tuna from the oven.
5. To serve, spread each tortilla with the beans, top with a piece of tuna, and then a fourth of the cabbage, sour cream, cheese, salsa, and tomato slices.

Serves 4

Most of the bluefin tuna caught off the east coast of the United States is sold to Japan, where it is prized and commands a high price. The tuna found in U.S. markets is mostly yellowfin or albacore tuna. They are delicious raw or cooked. The meat of these species is lighter in color than bluefin, with albacore the lightest of the three.

Six-to eight-ounce tuna steaks are delicious when grilled and served with our Tapenade (see page 267), garnished with black olives. They should first be rubbed with olive oil. Arrange them on the grill rack about 4 to 6 inches from the coals and cook about 4 to 6 minutes per side.

Le Thon aux Tomates, Citron Verts, Basilic, et Huile D'Olive

FROM JEAN-LOUIS AT WATERGATE, WASHINGTON, D.C.

Jean-Louis Palladin highlights the sweet juicy qualities of tuna by combining it with only the simplest and freshest of ingredients. Everything must be of superb quality, as there is nowhere for even a bruised basil leaf to hide.

3 1/2–4 *pounds center-cut tuna, sliced into escalopes about 1/3-inch thick*
1 1/4 *cup extra-virgin olive oil*
Salt and freshly ground black pepper to taste
1/2 *cup fresh strained lime juice*
5–7 *large ripe tomatoes, peeled, seeded, and cut in 1/2-inch dice (about 3 cups)*
10 *basil leaves, washed and dried, sliced thin*
8–10 *additional basil leaves, washed and dried, for garnish*

1. Preheat broiler. Preheat a heatproof pan large enough to hold all or half the escalopes in one layer.
2. Combine 2/3 cup of the olive oil, the lime juice and salt and pepper to taste, and rub on the tuna. Let rest 5 minutes.
3. Place 1/3 cup of the olive oil in a medium-size skillet and bring it to the smoking point. Add the tomatoes, season with salt and pepper, and stir constantly for about 30 seconds. Add the sliced basil and cook another 30 seconds. Remove from heat and set aside.
4. Place all (or half) the escalopes in the heated pan. Broil 3 inches from the broiler element for about 15 seconds, turn and cook another 15 seconds. The center of the fish should remain red. (Repeat if doing the fish in two batches.)
5. Remove the tomatoes from the skillet with a slotted spoon. Divide them among 8 serving plates and top with the tuna. Add the remaining 1/4 cup olive oil to the skillet with the tomato juices and heat until just warm. Spoon over the tuna and garnish with the basil leaves.

Serves 8

Tuna rare? Many people are reluctant to eat it that way, but tuna is a very "beeflike" fish. Its flesh is firm and closely grained, and its rich hearty flavor is often likened to that of tenderloin. Sushi bars, long a tradition in Japan, and currently the rage in this country, serve tuna raw, not rare. It is their belief that tuna's juicy, tender qualities are too good to be altered by cooking.

Marlin Niçoise

We found that marlin, swordfish, and shark are all excellent in this recipe. The full-flavored sauce complements these ocean game fish.

> ¹/₂ cup unsalted butter (1 stick)
> ¹/₄ cup fresh strained lemon juice
> 1 or 2 teaspoons minced garlic
> 4 anchovies, mashed with a fork
> ¹/₄ cup plus 4 teaspoons minced fresh parsley
> 1 tablespoon green peppercorns, crushed
> ¹/₂ cup black olives, pitted and chopped
> 3 large tomatoes, peeled, seeded, and chopped (about 2 cups)
> 2–3 pounds marlin (or swordfish or shark) steaks, about 1 inch thick
> 4 lemon wedges for garnish

1. Prepare a charcoal fire.
2. To make the Niçoise Sauce: Melt the butter in a small saucepan. Add the lemon juice, garlic, anchovies, ¹/₄ cup parsley, and pepper. Cook over low heat, stirring occasionally, for 10 minutes. Hold over very low heat until ready to use.
3. When the coals are red-hot but not flaming, grill the fish steaks 4 inches from the coals for about 5 or 6 minutes per side. Transfer to a heated serving platter.
4. Add the olives and tomatoes to the Niçoise Sauce and pour over the fish steaks. Sprinkle with the remaining 4 teaspoons of parsley and serve with lemon wedges.

Serves 4

Due to concern about the number of marlin that have been taken in recent years, some states have banned their commercial sale. For the fisherman who wants to try marlin, this is a good recipe.

While many sportfishermen practice conservation by returning marlin to the sea after a thrilling fight, other anglers wish to keep their first marlin and have it mounted. Those torn between the desire for a trophy and the wish to release this fish alive, however, can now have it both ways. Taxidermists no longer make skin mounts from the species; the mount is a model made from a mold of the fish. Therefore, if an angler takes the standard measurements of the catch, the fish can be accurately modeled and returned to the sea as well.

Marlin is a large game fish. White marlin average 50 to 70 pounds in weight. Blue marlin average about 100 pounds in weight, but blue marlin weighing as much as 1500 pounds have been caught.

"In cooking, as in all arts, simplicity is the sign of perfection." —Curnovsky

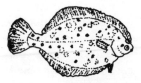

FLOUNDER

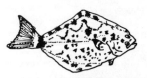

HALIBUT

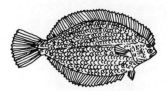

SOLE

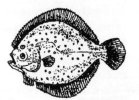

TURBOT

Although the terms flounder and sole are used rather interchangably in the United States, there is a difference in the body shape of these fishes. While both fishes are flatfishes, flounder are rounder (*it rhymes nicely*) and sole are more elliptical in shape. To complicate matters further, the winter flounder is so named when this fish is less than 3½ pounds; when it weighs more than 3½ pounds, it is called lemon sole!

Flatfishes: Flounder, Halibut, Sole, and Turbot

This closely related family contains some of the most peculiar looking fishes in the sea. All of them begin life looking like many other baby fishes. But as they grow, striking changes occur in their shapes and their way of life. Gradually they lose the air-filled swim bladder that most fishes use to keep afloat. As a result, they sink to the bottom. At the same time, one of their eyes begins to migrate from one side of the head to the other, and the body becomes extremely flat and thin. The adult flatfish lies on its side with both eyes on the "top." By changing the colors and patterns of its skin, it can blend in with the ocean bottom and escape predators.

The flesh of flatfishes is firm, yet pliable. Thus, it is an excellent choice for rolling around fillings and stuffings.

Willie Troup's Pan-Fried Flounder

Willie Troup is a committed sport fisherman who has caught a lot of flounder in his day. He evolved this recipe out of necessity but we feel it is a fine showcase for freshly caught flounder. Freshwater bass also is good in this recipe.

>1 cup white cornmeal
>½ teaspoon salt
>¼ teaspoon freshly ground black pepper
>1 tablespoon Old Bay Seasoning
>6–8 flounder fillets, about 2½ to 3 pounds
>¾–1 cup vegetable oil
>Parsley sprigs for garnish
>Lemon wedges for garnish
>Tartar Sauce (see page 269)

1. Combine the cornmeal, salt, pepper, and Old Bay Seasoning in a paper bag. Shake the fillets in the bag, one at a time, to coat with the cornmeal mixture.
2. Warm the oil until hot in a large cast-iron skillet over medium-high heat. Sauté the fillets, turning once, until golden brown, about 4 minutes per side. The trick is to brown the coating before overcooking the fish.
3. Serve on a heated platter, garnished with parsley sprigs and lemon wedges. Pass the Tartar Sauce separately.

Variation: Instead of the Tartar Sauce, serve with Red Tomato Salsa (page 263).
Serves 6

Carrot-Stuffed Flounder Rolls

This recipe can be multiplied easily for a party and it can be prepared in advance. The stuffing is worth the fuss. Use the stuffing with ocean pout or sole instead of flounder.

½ cup unsalted butter (1 stick)
1 cup finely chopped onion
½ cup minced pimientos
2 tablespoons minced fresh parsley
1 cup fresh bread crumbs
¾ cup finely shredded carrots
1 egg, slightly beaten
½ cup dry white wine
¼ cup freshly grated Parmesan cheese
1 teaspoon celery seed
4 large or 8 small flounder fillets (about 1 ½
* pounds total)*
Lemon slices for garnish
Parsley sprigs for garnish

1. Melt the butter in a large skillet over moderately low heat. Remove 1 tablespoon of butter and reserve. Add the onions, pimientos, and parsley and sauté for 3 minutes. Remove the skillet from the heat and add the bread crumbs, carrots, egg, wine, cheese, and celery seed. Mix well.
2. Spread the carrot mixture on the surface of each fillet. Roll up from the thin end, secure with toothpicks, and place in a shallow baking dish seam side down. Brush the tops with the reserved melted butter. The fish rolls may be prepared up to 4 hours in advance and kept covered with plastic wrap in the refrigerator. Remove them from the refrigerator ½ hour prior to baking.
3. Preheat oven to 350 degrees.
4. Bake the fish rolls for 25 to 35 minutes until the fish flakes easily with a fork.
5. Transfer to a heated serving platter and garnish with lemon slices and parsley sprigs.

Serves 4
May be prepared in advance

Winter flounder usually range from Newfoundland south to the Chesapeake Bay. Their ability to change their skin color patterning helps to protect them from predators, as they can effectively imitate a patch of bottom sand or gravel.

Summer flounder, four spot flounder, and windowpane flounder are all left-eyed flatfish that are available in the New England markets.

Grilled Halibut with Spiced Pepper Purees and Mushrooms

FROM RARITIES, CAMBRIDGE, MASSACHUSETTS

Chef Walter Zuromski uses pungent red and yellow pepper purees, which add a wonderful texture and flavor to the halibut. This recipe does require last minute preparation, but the pepper purees may be made in advance and gently reheated before assembling the entree. If you have a problem finding halibut fillets, we think any white-fleshed fillet of fish would look and taste great reposing on these flavorful pools of red and yellow.

1 Recipe Roasted Red Pepper Sauce (see page 264)
1 Recipe Yellow Pepper Puree (see page 268)
2 teaspoons minced fresh marjoram, or ¹/₂ teaspoon dried
2 tablespoons minced fresh basil, or 1 teaspoon dried
2 teaspoons minced fresh oregano, or ¹/₂ teaspoon dried
3 tablespoons butter
1 tablespoon olive oil
1 ounce shiitake mushrooms, thinly sliced
12 thin slices of turnip
6 very small new potatoes, peeled, steamed until tender
4 6- to 8-ounce halibut fillets

1. Prepare a charcoal fire or preheat broiler.
2. Place each of the pepper purees in a small saucepan and stir 1 teaspoon marjoram, 1 tablespoon basil, and 1 teaspoon oregano into each.
3. Melt 1¹/₂ tablespoons of butter in a nonstick skillet over medium heat. Sauté the mushrooms for 4 to 5 minutes, or until soft. Set aside and keep warm.
4. Wipe out the skillet and melt the remaining 1¹/₂ tablespoons butter in it. Sauté the turnip and potatoes until they are tender throughout and beginning to brown. Set aside and keep warm.
5. Lightly brush the fillets with the olive oil. Grill the fillets 4 inches from glowing but not flaming coals for 6 to 10 minutes, or until they flake easily. If using the broiler, broil the fillets about 5 inches from the heat for 6 to 10 minutes, or until they flake easily.
6. While the fillets are cooking, gently warm the pepper sauces.

Atlantic halibut is a member of the "right-eyed" flounder family, having both eyes on the right or top side. All flatfishes start out in life with an eye on either side of their compressed body. As they grow and develop, one of the eyes migrates to pair up with the other eye on either the left or right side of the body—which side depends on the species.

The right side, which becomes the top side of this halibut, is a mottled dark brown, while the underside is almost white.

These bottom-swimming fish have delicately flavored, firm, white meat. Because of the size of the fish, it is most often sold as steaks. If the halibut is small enough, it may be filleted.

7. To serve. Ladle a spoonful of each of the pepper sauces on warm plates. Place the grilled fish over the sauces. Garnish with the mushrooms, turnips, and potatoes.

Serves 4

Halibut and Prawn Brochettes

FROM TARANTINO'S RESTAURANT, SAN FRANCISCO

From Chef Jack Louie comes this Worcestershire-spiked marinade with halibut and shrimp. We think the marinade would also complement most of the fishes from this chapter. Try it with tuna, swordfish, marlin, or mahi mahi. In summer, serve this dish with a cold rice or grain salad speckled with lots of fresh herbs, and broiled tomatoes. In winter, substitute baked rice, risotto, or pasta for the rice salad.

¹/₄ cup dry white wine
¹/₄ cup Worcestershire sauce
¹/₂ cup olive oil
¹/₂ teaspoon minced garlic
¹/₄ teaspoon freshly ground white pepper
¹/₄ teaspoon salt
1 lemon, thinly sliced
1 ¹/₄ pounds halibut steak, 1 inch thick, skin removed
12 prawns or jumbo shrimp, shelled and deveined

Atlantic halibut is the largest of the flat fishes, weighing as much as 600 pounds. However, the average catch today is usually in the 50 to 100 pound range. These fish live in very deep water from Labrador south to New Jersey and are commercially harvested by trawlers.

1. Combine the wine, Worcestershire sauce, olive oil, garlic, pepper, and salt and stir to blend. The marinade may be prepared up to 48 hours in advance.
2. Cut the halibut into 12 pieces of equal size. Place these pieces and the shrimp in a glass or ceramic dish and pour the marinade over them. Turn the fish and shrimp over to coat them on all sides. Cover with plastic wrap and refrigerate. Marinate up to 1 hour, turning the fish and shrimp once or twice.
3. Preheat broiler or prepare a charcoal fire.
4. Thread the seafood onto 4 skewers, alternating the halibut and shrimp. Broil or grill, 4 to 6 inches from the heat, about 4 to 5 minutes. Turn and cook an additional 4 to 5 minutes, until the fish flakes easily.

Serves 4
Must be partially prepared in advance

Oven-Poached Halibut Steaks with Warm Vinaigrette

Using a warm vinaigrette to enhance the flavor of poached fish is not a new idea. The French have been using this technique for years. We think this unique dressing, which combines champagne vinegar and walnut oil, is outstanding on poached halibut. The dish is attractive and quite simple to prepare.

1 *quart White Wine Court Bouillon (see page 279)*
6 *6- to 8-ounce halibut steaks, about 1 inch thick*
1 *recipe Walnut Oil Vinaigrette, made with champagne vinegar* (see page 256)*
1 *tablespoon thinly sliced scallions*
2 *tablespoons minced fresh parsley*
1 *tablespoon minced fresh tarragon, or ¹/₂ teaspoon dried*
1 *bunch arugula, watercress, or other bitter green, trimmed, washed, and dried*

*Note: If champagne vinegar is not available, try raspberry or tarragon vinegar.

1. Preheat oven to 350 degrees.
2. Bring the court bouillon to a boil in a kettle.
3. Place the halibut steaks in a glass baking pan large enough to hold them in one layer. Cut a piece of wax paper to fit the pan and butter one side. Pour the hot court bouillon over the fish. Top with the piece of buttered wax paper, buttered side down. Cover tightly with aluminum foil and bake for 12 minutes, or until the fish flakes easily.
4. While the fish is cooking, prepare the warm vinaigrette: Place the vinaigrette and scallions in a small saucepan, and gently warm over low heat. Add the parsley and tarragon and remove from heat.
5. Arrange a bed of arugula on each of 6 serving plates.
6. To serve, carefully remove the skin. Place the steaks on top of the arugula. Ladle 2 or 3 spoonfuls of the warm vinaigrette on top of each steak and drizzle some over the greens.

Serves 6

208

Sole Kokonda

This recipe is an adaptation of an appetizer served in the South Pacific. The sweetness of the coconut complements the sharpness of the lime-marinated fish. Try this recipe with ocean pout or flounder.

³/₄ *cup fresh strained lime juice*
¹/₄ *cup white wine vinegar*
1 *tablespoon minced jalapeño pepper*
1 *teaspoon minced garlic*
¹/₈ *teaspoon salt*
¹/₈ *teaspoon freshly ground black pepper*
2 *pounds sole fillets, cut into 1-inch squares*
1 *cup coconut milk (see recipe below)*
Lettuce leaves

1. In a large glass bowl, combine the lime juice, vinegar, jalapeño pepper, garlic, salt, and pepper. Stir to mix well. Add the sole, making sure that the marinade covers all of the pieces. Cover the bowl with plastic wrap and refrigerate for 4 hours.
2. About 15 minutes before serving, combine the coconut milk with the marinated sole. Leave the bowl at room temperature.
3. To serve, make a bed of lettuce on each of 8 plates. Divide the fish among the plates, topping with a spoonful of the marinade.

Coconut Milk

1 *coconut*
1 ¹/₂ *cups hot water*
1 ¹/₂ *cups hot milk*

1. Insert coconut in a heavy plastic or brown paper bag and crack the shell into several pieces with a hammer. Discard the liquid. The shell should be in 4 or 5 pieces.
2. Place each piece over a stove burner turned to medium-low, shell side down, for about 1 minute. Using a towel or oven mitt to protect your hands, separate the white flesh from the shell. Discard the shell. Using a swivel-bladed vegetable peeler, cut off the dark interior skin. Cut the coconut meat into small cubes. There should be about 3 cups.
3. Place half the cubes in a food processor fitted with a steel knife. Add the hot water and process, off and on, until the coconut is finely minced. Pour into a

(There is no true sole in the U.S.) All the fish sold as sole in New England are varieties of flounder.

Gray sole (*Glyptocephalus cynoglossus*) are right-eyed flatfish and are often called witch flounder. They are relatively small, 1 to 2 pounds, and range from Newfoundland to North Carolina.

Coconut milk is made from steeping grated coconut in milk, or a combination of milk and water, and then pressing the liquid from the solids. For our purposes, it is not the liquid inside the coconut, although people often refer to that as coconut milk. Both sweetened and unsweetened varieties can be found in Asian grocery stores.

bowl. Repeat with the rest of the coconut and the hot milk. Combine the two batches and let rest 15 minutes.

4. Pour the mixture through a fine sieve into another bowl, pressing on the solids to extract as much liquid as possible. Discard the solids. The milk can be stored in a jar for 1 week, or frozen for a couple of months. The recipe makes about 2 cups; use 1 cup now in this recipe and freeze the rest for a future use.

Serves 8
Must be prepared in advance

Deviled Turbot Fillets

A crunchy topping and a delicate fish base offer contrasting textures in a simple dish. The topping is amenable to almost any fillet. If a thicker fillet is used, adjust the cooking time accordingly and cover with an aluminum foil tent if the bread crumbs begin to burn.

2 *pounds turbot fillets*
3 *tablespoons unsalted butter*
1/4 *green pepper, chopped (about 1/4 cup)*
1/4 *cup chopped onion*
1 *tablespoon Dijon-style mustard*
1 *teaspoon Worcestershire sauce*
1 *dash Tabasco sauce*
3 *tablespoons fresh strained lemon juice*
Salt and freshly ground black pepper to taste
1 *cup fresh bread crumbs, toasted*
2 *tablespoons freshly grated Parmesan cheese*
Lemon wedges for garnish

1. Preheat broiler.
2. Cut fillets into 6 portions and place in a buttered baking dish large enough to hold them in one layer.
3. Melt the butter in a saucepan. Over moderately low heat, sauté the green pepper and onion in the butter until the onion is just soft. Stir in the mustard, Worcestershire sauce, Tabasco, and lemon juice. Taste and correct seasoning. Add salt and pepper if needed. Spread the mixture over the fish.
4. Combine the bread crumbs and cheese in a small bowl.
5. Position the baking dish on a rack 4 inches below the heating element. Broil 5 minutes. Turn the fillets over and top with the bread crumb mixture. Broil 5 minutes longer, making sure that the crumbs do not scorch.
6. Serve immediately, accompanied by lemon wedges.

Serves 6

The meat of the turbot is white and firm and is widely marketed as "generic" frozen white ocean fish fillets in this country.

Turbot with a Fricassee of Wild Mushrooms and Pearl Onions

FROM ERNIE'S RESTAURANT, SAN FRANCISCO

Chef Bruno Tison uses a rich chicken stock to add flavor to his delicate rendition of turbot. Chef Tison urges you to make your own rich stock by browning three chicken carcasses in the oven along with aromatic vegetables before adding the other ingredients that your favorite recipe for chicken stock requires. This initial browning step will create a flavorful brown chicken stock. If time does not allow, a good-quality canned chicken stock will also produce admirable results. Hot crusty bread is essential to absorb the flavorful juices of this dish.

The name turbot is sometimes given erroneously to other flat fish. The true turbot does not come from New England waters. It is a flat fish primarily found in the Mediterranean or off the coast of England.

1 *quart rich chicken stock, preferably homemade*
1 *medium carrot, chopped (optional)*
1 *stalk celery, chopped (optional)*
1/2 *medium onion, chopped (optional)*
1 *bouquet garni, composed of 3 sprigs of parsley, 1 teaspoon thyme, and 1 bay leaf in a cheesecloth bag*
2 *cloves garlic, smashed*
10–11 *tablespoons unsalted butter*
4 *ounces pearl onions, peeled*
6 *ounces wild mushrooms, such as chanterelles or shiitakes, sliced 1/8-inch thick*
3 *tablespoons dry white wine*
1 *red pepper (about 1/2 pound), cored, seeded, and cut into julienne*
4 *8-ounce turbot fillets*
1/4 *cup minced fresh chervil or parsley for garnish*

1. Heat the chicken stock to the boiling point in a large saucepan. (If you are not using homemade stock, add the optional carrot, celery, and onion.) Add the bouquet garni and garlic to the boiling stock. Continue to boil the stock over high heat until it is reduced to 1 cup. Strain. The stock may be prepared up to 24 hours in advance. Store, covered tightly, in the refrigerator. Reheat to a boil before proceeding.
2. Melt 2 tablespoons butter in a large skillet over medium heat. Add the chopped onion and brown, stirring frequently. Add the mushrooms and 1 more tablespoon butter if necessary. Toss to coat and

cook 5 minutes, stirring often. Pour in the wine and simmer until the wine evaporates. Set aside.

3. In a small saucepan, steam the red peppers over simmering water, covered, just until they lose their crispness, about 5 minutes. Remove from heat and set aside.

4. Meanwhile, bring the chicken stock to a simmer and whisk in the remaining 8 tablespoons of butter, one tablespoon at a time. Add the onions and mushrooms and taste for flavoring. Season with salt and pepper if necessary. Set aside and keep warm.

5. Find a skillet large enough to hold the fillets in one layer (they will be folded in half lengthwise). Add water, enough to cover the turbot. Bring the water to a boil. Lightly salt and pepper the fillets and fold them back on each other, skin side in, to create a rectangular shape of double thickness. Slip each into the boiling water and reduce the heat to a simmer. Cover and poach until the fillets are opaque and springy to the touch, about 7 to 8 minutes. Immediately remove from the heat.

6. Place the fillets on rimmed plates or in shallow soup bowls. Ladle the mushroom stock over the fillets and decorate them with the bell peppers. Sprinkle with the chervil or parsley and serve immediately.

Serves 4
May be partially prepared in advance

Well-Armed Fishes: Ocean Perch, Sculpin, and Sea Robin

OCEAN PERCH

SCULPIN

Ocean perch, sculpin, and sea robin are scorpion-fishes, members of a large order of fishes that are fully armed in several senses. Sometimes referred to as "mail-cheeked fishes," they have heavy, bony heads complete with spikes and shields fit to deter all but the most determined predator. Should this not suffice, many species also have venomous spines. Most sculpin are too small to eat, but the cabezon, found mainly on the west coast of the United States, is an underutilized but delicious fish. Be advised that sculpin roe cannot be eaten, as they are extremely toxic.

Sea robins are more literally "armed" than ocean perch and sculpin. They have long, armlike pectoral fins that they use for walking along the soft bottom and stirring up sediment in search of shrimps, crabs, clams, and worms. When threatened, they use their "arms" to burrow into the bottom and leave only their eyes showing. A classic example of an underutilized species, the sea robin's mild white meat is very tasty but inexpensive because of low demand.

Ocean perch is easier to find at fish markets than either sculpin or sea robin.

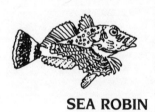

SEA ROBIN

Sesame Perch

The Cape Cod Cooperative Extension in Barnstable, Massachusetts, sent us this recipe for ocean perch. Try it also with sculpin, sea robin, and whiting.

1 *tablespoon vegetable oil*
4 *ocean perch fillets, 6 to 8 ounces each, skinned*
1 *tablespoon sesame seeds*
3 *tablespoons fresh strained lemon juice*
1 *teaspoon dried basil leaves*
2 *tablespoons minced fresh parsley for garnish*

1. Heat the oil in a 10-inch skillet over medium heat until hot. Place the fillets in the pan and cook about 5 minutes or until lightly browned; turn over carefully and cook about 5 more minutes.
2. Remove the fillets from the skillet and keep them warm.
3. Pour the sesame seeds into the same skillet and cook over medium heat until golden brown, about 5 minutes. Remove from heat. Dribble the lemon juice over the sesame seeds and stir in the basil. Spoon the mixture over the fish. Sprinkle with parsley and serve.

Serves 4

The ocean perch is bright red to pinky orange with large black eyes. Although a close relative of the Pacific rockfish, it lives in the Atlantic, preferring the deep, cold water from southern New England to Labrador.

Paprika Ocean Perch

While not usually associated with fish, sweet Hungarian paprika, when fresh, adds a pungent flavor to this dish. The sour cream–paprika combination, a familiar one, is special when served with fish. Try this also with ocean pout or whiting, adjusting the timing accordingly.

$^1/_2$ cup minced onion
1 tablespoon vegetable oil
1 tablespoon sweet Hungarian paprika
2 tablespoons water
$^1/_2$ green pepper, cored, seeded, and chopped (about $^1/_2$ cup)
$^1/_4$ cup chopped, peeled, drained, and seeded Italian plum tomatoes, plus 2 tablespoon juice
1 medium tomato, peeled, seeded, and chopped (about $^1/_4$ cup)
2 pounds ocean perch fillets, skinned
1 teaspoon flour
3 tablespoons sour cream or plain yogurt
Salt and pepper to taste
Thin slices of any available sweet pepper for garnish

1. Heat the oil in a large skillet over moderate heat. Sauté the onion until soft. Remove from heat and stir in the paprika and water.
2. Add the green pepper, tomato, and tomato juice and bring to a boil over moderate heat. Then reduce the heat, cover, and cook for 8 to 10 minutes until soft.
3. Lay the perch fillets on top of the vegetable mix, cover, and cook over medium heat for 8 to 10 minutes. When the fish is cooked through, it will appear opaque.
4. Transfer the fillets to a heated platter. Stir the flour into the vegetable mix and cook for 1 or 2 minutes longer. Remove the skillet from the heat and stir in the sour cream. Adjust seasonings to taste. Pour the sauce over the fillets and garnish with very thin slices of colorful peppers. Serve immediately.

Serves 4–6

The meat of ocean perch is firm and flavorful as a result of its diet of crustaceans and mollusks. It lends itself to a variety of preparations and is often considered to be the perfect "generic" fish. The fish in fish sandwiches served at fast-food restaurants is often ocean perch.

Paprika is the national spice of Hungary. There are several varieties that range from sweet and mellow to spicy hot. As with most spices and dried herbs, paprika goes stale very rapidly once the can has been opened. For the best flavor, store it in the refrigerator and use within several weeks of opening.

Chinese Perch with Snow Peas

This simple Chinese stir-fry brings out the best in ocean perch. It is just firm enough to hold together during the cooking process, yet tender enough to melt in your mouth.

2 teaspoons peanut oil
1 teaspoon Oriental sesame oil
4 teaspoons minced garlic
2 teaspoons grated gingerroot
1 large carrot, julienned (about ³/₄ cup)
¹/₂ cup sliced scallions, using white and green parts
1 ¹/₄ cups fish stock (see page 277) or chicken stock
2 tablespoons sherry
1 tablespoon soy sauce
2 pounds ocean perch fillets, skinned, cut into
    1-inch pieces
1 cup fresh snow peas, strings removed and ends
    trimmed
1 tablespoon cornstarch dissolved in 1 ¹/₂ tablespoons
    cold water

1. Heat the peanut and sesame oils in a large skillet or wok. Stir in the garlic and ginger. Sauté, stirring constantly, for 1 minute over medium heat. Add the carrot and scallions and cook for an additional 30 seconds.
2. Pour in the fish stock, sherry, and soy sauce and bring to a boil. Reduce heat. Add the perch pieces, and snow peas and simmer, covered, for 1 minute.
3. Add the cornstarch mixture and bring to a boil, stirring constantly, until the sauce becomes slightly thickened.
4. Transfer to a heated platter and serve immediately over beds of steamed rice or noodles.

Serves 4–6

The skin of ocean perch is very tough and should be removed before the fish is cooked.

Bouillabaisse

The wonderful fact about bouillabaisse is that you can improvise with available fresh fish! The bigger the crowd, the more variety and amount of fish you can combine. The tail of a scorpionfish or a sea robin is considered by many to be the only major requirement of a true bouillabaisse. In fact, catching one might be the occasion to prepare this famous dish. Prepare the soup base a day ahead, if possible, then see what the fishmonger has to offer and complete the stew as your guests arrive. A good bread, salad, Beaujolais or Côtes du Rhône, and company complement the bounty.

3/4 cup olive oil
1 cup chopped onion (about 3 medium)
1 cup chopped leeks white parts only (about 5 medium)
4 teaspoons minced garlic
4 cups peeled, seeded, and chopped tomatoes, or drained canned tomatoes *NO MORE*
4 cups fish stock (see page 277)
2 cups clam juice or water
2 cups dry white wine
2 teaspoons crushed fennel seeds *? find*
1 teaspoon dried thyme
1 bunch of parsley
1 bay leaf
1 teaspoon salt
4 whole peppercorns
1/4 teaspoon saffron threads
6 pounds assorted fish, using a combination of firm fish, such as sea robin, sculpin, monkfish, wolffish, or halibut; tender fish, such as flounder, sole, or tautog, cut in chunks; and shellfish, such as lobster, hard-shell clams, scallops, shrimp, and mussels
1 recipe Rouille (see page 251)

1. In a large nonreactive (such as enamel) kettle, heat the olive oil over medium heat. Add the onions and leeks and cook for 5 minutes, stirring. Add the garlic and tomatoes and cook 5 minutes more.
2. Add the fish stock, clam juice, wine, fennel, thyme, parsley, bay leaf, salt, peppercorns, and saffron. Simmer, uncovered, 30 minutes. If you like a clear stock, strain through a fine sieve. Store, tightly covered, in the refrigerator for up to 24 hours. You can even freeze the soup base for up to 2 months.

3. Just before serving, bring the prepared soup base to a boil. Drop in the lobster and firm fish, and simmer 5 minutes. Lower the heat and add the tender fish and other shellfish. Cover the pot and barely simmer 5 minutes. The tender fish should disintegrate as it cooks to add body to the soup.

4. To serve in the traditional manner, the fish is removed from the soup with a slotted spoon and served on a platter, while the soup is served in shallow soup bowls, with croutes (toasted rounds of French bread) spread with Rouille. An alternative would be to serve the stew in bowls, with the bread and Rouille served on the side.

Serves 6–8
May be partially prepared in advance

The sea robin feeds mostly on crustaceans and mollusks and its meat is considered mild flavored and good eating. It is a fish that is often discarded by anglers who do not know its worth.

The sea robin is aptly named as its large pectoral (side) fins fan out like a bird's wings. However, it usually uses these "wings" to walk along the ocean floor in search of food.

Although sea robin and sculpin are rarely available from anyone except your friendly amateur angler, their meat makes great eating. After skinning and filleting, they can be sautéed, poached, broiled, or baked according to directions in Chapter 1.

The Individualists:
Monkfish, Ocean Pout, and
Wolffish

It is hard to imagine a more diverse looking group of fishes than the monkfish, ocean pout, and wolffish, and yet they may be related. The degree of relationship is still a matter of debate, but all seem to have evolved from a simple perchlike ancestor. All are examples of complex and specialized species that had plain, generalized ancestors.

The "monkfish" found at the fish market is actually the tail meat of a huge bottom-dweller that is also known as the goosefish. Although this fish bears absolutely no resemblance to either a monk or a goose, there is an old fish tale that someone saw it devouring a goose. A member of the anglerfish family, the monkfish lies in wait for smaller prey to stray near its mouth to be sucked in and swallowed. Occasionally, a diving bird such as a cormorant becomes this fish's lunch. Monkfish is often called "poor man's lobster" because the texture and flavor of the tail remind many diners of lobster.

The wolffish is a long eel-like fish with somewhat flattened sides. It gets its name from its large, powerful jaws filled with long, sharp teeth. The wolffish grows up to five feet in length and weighs over forty pounds. Although they are not yet popular in the United States, hundreds of thousands of pounds of this delicious species are caught every year off Georges Bank, near Cape Cod. The light, white texture and mild flavor are favored on the tables of Europe, which is the final destination of most of the catch.

The ocean pout, or eelpout, resembles the wolffish in form and function but is not closely related. The similarities are a result of convergence—the tendency of animals with similar life-styles to develop similar forms. Ocean pout tastes like wolffish but is somewhat milder.

MONKFISH

OCEAN POUT

WOLFFISH

Monkfish Salad

This salad has great personality. The lime juice, yogurt, and Tabasco sauce give it a tangy zip, and the crisp tortillas are a nice change from ordinary bread or rolls. You can use any firm-fleshed, chunky, white fish, such as wolffish or tilefish in place of the monkfish, and surimi can be used instead of the crabmeat.

1 *recipe Mexican Salad Dressing (see page 255)*
1/4 *cup plain yogurt*
2/3 *cup diced peeled jicama or celery*
2/3 *cup diced sweet red pepper*
2/3 *cup cooked corn*
2 *tablespoons thinly sliced scallions*
2 *cups cooked monkfish (about 1 1/2 pounds), in bite-size pieces*
1/2 *pound crabmeat, picked over, shells and cartilage discarded*
2–3 *teaspoons fresh strained lime juice*
Tabasco sauce to taste
Salt and freshly ground black pepper to taste
6 *flour tortillas, fried in vegetable oil according to package directions*
1 1/2 *cups shredded greens, such as romaine, endive, or radicchio*
1/4 *cup minced cilantro leaves*
2 *tablespoons toasted sesame seeds*
6 *lime wedges*

1. Mix the dressing and yogurt together in a large bowl. Add the jicama, pepper, corn, and scallions.
2. Fold in the monkfish and crabmeat. Add lime juice, Tabasco, salt, and pepper to taste. Refrigerate the mixture, covered, for at least 30 minutes or up to 2 hours.
3. To serve, place a tortilla on each of 6 serving plates and top with equal portions of the shredded greens. Mound the salad on top of the greens and sprinkle with the cilantro and sesame seeds. Garnish with lime wedges.

Variations: To save on calories, grill the tortillas in a nonstick skillet brushed with vegetable oil. The tortillas will be speckled brown, rather than golden.

For an unusual presentation, use basket-shaped tortillas. They can be made at home, but some specialty stores sell them ready-made.

Crunchy jicama is a low-calorie vegetable, native to Latin America. It resembles a large turnip covered with a brown papery skin. The taste is somewhere between that of water chestnuts, potatoes, and celery. It can be found in the produce section of your supermarket.

The edible part of monkfish is the tail. It will have been cleaned by the fishmonger, but you should carefully remove any remaining gray membrane and dark spots. It is a good idea to buy slightly more than you need to allow for waste.

This salad makes an attractive stuffing for home-grown tomatoes. Accompany with tortilla chips.

For an hors d'oeuvre, flake the fish before combining it with the mayonnaise to make a spreadable mixture. Serve with tortilla chips.

Serves 6
Must be partially prepared in advance

Monkfish Kebabs

These are easy to prepare and cook, fun to make, and taste great!

1 *recipe Soy Marinade (see page* 249)
1 *teaspoon minced garlic*
1 *teaspoon minced gingerroot*
1 *tablespoon minced onion*
1 *tablespoon brown sugar*
1 *pound monkfish, trimmed, and cut into 1-inch chunks*
12 *cherry tomatoes*
12 *small white onions, peeled*
12 *large mushrooms*
1 *large green pepper, cored, seeded, and cut into 1-inch squares*
12 *chunks of pineapple or apple*

1. Place the soy marinade in a large bowl. Stir in all the remaining ingredients and toss to coat. Let marinate for 30 minutes, or up to 2 hours.
2. Prepare a charcoal fire, or preheat the broiler.
3. Thread the chunks of fish onto skewers, alternating with the vegetables and the fruit. Reserve the marinade. When the coals are red-hot, but not flaming, place the skewers on a greased rack set 4 to 6 inches above the fire. Turn and baste with the marinade until done, about 15 minutes. Or broil in the broiler, 4 inches from the broiler element.

Serves 4
Must be partially prepared in advance

Monkfish goes by many names; among them are lotte, bellyfish, anglerfish, goosefish, mouthfish, or allmouth.

The firm texture of monkfish make it ideal for kebabs, chowder, and stir-fry dishes, as well as broiling and baking.

Moroccan Monkfish

Couscous is a Moroccan dish, usually served with lamb or chicken, but very good in this recipe. The fish is complemented by the rich blend of spices used in the recipe. Wolffish is a good substitute if you can't find monkfish.

1 *quart fish stock (see page 277) or rich chicken stock*
2 *pounds monkfish, trimmed, and cut into 1-inch pieces*
1 1/4 *pounds large shrimp, shelled and deveined*
4 *tablespoons butter*
2 *tablespoons vegetable oil*
1 1/2 *cups chopped onion (about 4 medium)*
1 *cup chopped celery*
1 *large tart green apple, peeled, cored, and diced (about 1 cup)*
1 *tablespoon minced garlic*
1 *tablespoon minced gingerroot*
1 1/2 *teaspoons ground coriander*
1 1/2 *teaspoons ground cumin*
3/4 *teaspoon turmeric*
1/2 *teaspoon ground cinnamon*
1/4 *teaspoon ground cloves*
1/4 *teaspoon cayenne pepper*
1 *bay leaf*
3 *tablespoons flour*
1 *cup dry vermouth or dry white wine*
2/3 *cup Italian plum tomatoes, peeled, seeded, and chopped*
1 1/2 *cups quick-cooking couscous prepared according to the package directions*
3/4 *cup chopped fresh herbs (a combination of parsley and cilantro)*
1/2 *cup toasted pignolia (pine nuts) or almonds*

1. Bring the stock to a boil in a large saucepan and add the monkfish and shrimp. Reduce heat and simmer 4 to 5 minutes, until the seafood is barely done. With a slotted spoon, remove the monkfish and shrimp from the stock, place in a bowl, cover, and refrigerate. Cover the stock and set aside.
2. In another large saucepan, heat 3 tablespoons of butter and the oil over low heat. Add the onion and celery and cook until softened, stirring frequently, about 15 minutes. Stir in the apple, garlic, and gingerroot and cook 5 minutes, stirring often. Add the

coriander, cumin, turmeric, cinnamon, cloves, cayenne, and bay leaf. Raise heat to medium, and cook the mixture 3 minutes, stirring constantly. If the mixture appears very dry, add another tablespoon of oil.

3. Sprinkle the mixture with 3 tablespoons of flour and cook 2 minutes, stirring. Add the vermouth and stir, scraping up any browned particles. When the mixture begins to bubble, add the reserved stock and the tomatoes and bring to a boil.

4. Lower the heat and simmer 15 minutes. The recipe can be made up to 6 hours in advance to this point. Tightly cover the pan in the refrigerator. Bring to a boil before proceeding with the recipe.

5. Add the monkfish and shrimp to the stock and cook, covered, until the seafood is just heated through, about 3 to 4 minutes.

6. In a large bowl, toss the couscous with the remaining 1 tablespoon butter, herbs, and nuts. Blend well and fluff with a fork.

7. To serve, ladle the monkfish mixture onto a large rimmed platter and spoon the couscous into the center. Serve immediately.

Serves 6
May be partially prepared in advance

Blanquette de Lotte au Saffron et Mirepoix de Legumes

FROM JEAN-LOUIS AT WATERGATE, WASHINGTON, D.C.

Monkfish, sometimes called poor man's lobster, is a firm, mild-flavored white fish. When combined with a lobster-based stock, it masquerades convincingly as the well-known crustacean. Chef Jean-Louis Palladin poaches monkfish medallions and coats them with a light sauce of lobster or fish stock, dotted with colorful bits of crunchy vegetables.

1 ½ pounds monkfish fillet, trimmed
Salt and pepper
6 tablespoons diced carrot
6 tablespoons diced turnip
¼ cup thinly sliced leek, white part only
6 tablespoons diced celery

2 *teaspoons olive oil*
2 *tablespoons minced shallots*
¹/₂ *cup dry vermouth*
1 *cup lobster stock or fish stock (see page 277)*
Pinch of saffron
3 *tablespoons light cream*
1 *quart Wine Court Bouillon (see page 279)*

1. Cut the fillet crosswise into pieces about ¹/₂ inch thick. Salt and pepper both sides lightly. Refrigerate, covered, if not proceeding immediately.
2. In a medium-size saucepan, bring 3 cups of salted water to a boil. Add the carrot, turnip, and leeks and boil 1 minute. Add the celery and boil 1 minute more. Drain and refresh in cold water. The recipe may be completed up to this point 8 hours in advance. Refrigerate the mirepoix of vegetables, tightly covered.
3. In a small nonreactive (such as enamel) saucepan, heat the olive oil over medium heat. Add the shallots and sauté for 2 to 3 minutes. Add the vermouth and reduce over high heat to 6 tablespoons. Pour in the lobster stock and reduce to ¹/₂ cup. Add the saffron and cream and lower heat to a simmer. Stir occasionally while continuing with the recipe.
4. Bring the court bouillon to a boil in a skillet large enough to hold the monkfish in a single layer. Add the fish and reduce heat to a simmer. Cover and poach for 5 to 8 minutes, until the fish is firm to the touch and opaque throughout. Immediately remove from the heat.
5. Add the mirepoix of vegetables to the simmering sauce. Remove the pieces of fish from the court bouillon and arrange them on warm serving plates. Using a paper towel, wipe up any juices that the fish exudes. Place 2 to 3 tablespoons of the lobster sauce at the side of the monkfish pieces and pour a bit of the sauce in a ribbon over the top of the fish.

Serves 4
May be partially prepared in advance

Monkfish Harvest Stew

The name of this recipe is derived from the use of pumpkin or acorn squash. You may substitute other vegetables, but the deep orange pumpkin and the yellow corn make a very attractive autumn supper dish. Members of the cod family or sculpin and sea robin may also be used successfully in place of the monkfish. Serve with a green salad dressed with our Vinaigrette dressing (page 256).

2 slices bacon, diced
2 teaspoons vegetable oil
1/2 cup minced onion (about 1 medium)
1/2 cup diced pumpkin or acorn squash
1/4 cup diced carrot (about 1 medium)
3/4 cup diced fennel or celery (about 2 stalks)
3/4 cup diced sweet red pepper (about 1/2 pepper)
2 tablespoons minced, seeded jalapeño pepper (about 1 pepper)
3/4 cup dry vermouth
1/4 cup dark rum
5 cups fish stock (see page 277) or rich chicken stock
1/2 cup Italian tomatoes, peeled, seeded, and chopped (about 2)
1/2 cup corn, fresh or frozen
1 cup diced zucchini
2 pounds monkfish, trimmed and cut into 1-inch squares
1 pound medium shrimp, shelled and deveined
1 tablespoon fresh strained lemon juice
1/2 teaspoon salt
1 recipe Rouille (see page 251)
12 slices toasted French bread, about 1/2 inch thick
1/4 cup minced cilantro leaves

Monkfish has the dubious distinction of being the ugliest fish in the sea. Its enormous, antenna-topped head, and scaleless, slippery skin belie the fact that its tail contains some of the most delicious meat to be found in the sea.

1. Cook the bacon in a large saucepan over medium heat. When it begins to brown, add the oil, onion, pumpkin, carrot, fennel, red pepper, and jalapeño pepper. Sauté, stirring frequently, for 5 minutes.
2. Add the vermouth and rum. Reduce over high heat by half. Add the stock and bring to a boil. Stir in the tomatoes, corn, zucchini, monkfish, and shrimp. Cover, reduce heat, and simmer for 5 minutes, or until the fish is cooked. Remove from heat. Stir in the lemon juice and salt.
3. To serve: Spread the Rouille on the toast slices. Ladle the stew into 6 warmed shallow soup bowls. Top each serving with 2 slices of toast and sprinkle with the cilantro.

Serves 6

Ocean Pout with Salsa Cruda

This recipe is most appealing in warm summer weather. The cool mild fish is greatly enhanced by the spicy salsa cruda. Use this dish as a luncheon salad, or as a light dinner entree accompanied by a tabouli or rice salad and steamed or grilled fresh garden vegetables.

2 *pounds ocean pout fillets*
Salt and pepper to taste
2–3 *tablespoons vegetable oil*
1 *tablespoon fresh strained lemon juice*
1 *recipe Salsa Cruda (see page 265)*
2 *tablespoons minced fresh cilantro or parsley*

1. Cut the fish into 6 equal portions and score the skin side of the fish at one-inch intervals. Season lightly with salt and pepper to taste.
2. Heat 2 tablespoons of the oil in a nonstick skillet over medium-high heat. When it is hot, add the pieces of fish and sauté them about 2 minutes on each side. Add the remaining tablespoon of oil, if needed. Transfer the fish to a serving platter.
3. Sprinkle the fish with the lemon juice, cover, and refrigerate at least 30 minutes before serving, or up to 2 hours before serving.
4. Just before serving spread the Salsa Cruda over the fish and sprinkle with the cilantro.

Serves 6
Must be prepared in advance

For a fast feast, preheat the oven to 400 degrees. Cut 1 1/2 pounds of ocean pout into 3-inch pieces, and lightly coat with vegetable oil. Place skinned side down on a greased cookie sheet. Sprinkle lightly with the seasoning mix used for Cajun Catfish (see page 122), or a store-bought seasoning for blackened fish. Bake 4 to 6 minutes, depending on thickness. Remove from oven and squeeze copious amounts of fresh lime juice over the top. Serve with tartar sauce. Serves 4.

Ocean pout has an eel-like appearance, but has few bones and sweet white meat. It is caught by fishermen who trawl the bottom, but because there is not much demand for it, ocean pout is an underutilized fish.

Ocean Pout Baked with Yogurt

Ocean pout is a mild fish that profits from the addition of a sauce with some kick! Horseradish and mustard along with crunchy capers provide just the needed touch. Broiling adds an attractive brown glaze. This sauce can be used on any but the most delicate of fish.

1 cup plain yogurt
2 tablespoons prepared horseradish, drained
2 teaspoons grated lemon peel (zest)
4 teaspoons Dijon-style mustard
5 tablespoons freshly grated Parmesan cheese
2 tablespoons capers, rinsed, drained, and minced
Dash cayenne pepper
2 1/2 pounds ocean pout fillets
3 tablespoons snipped fresh dill or minced fresh
  parsley

1. Preheat oven to 400 degrees.
2. Cut the fillets into 6 equal portions and score the skin side of the fish at one-inch intervals.
3. Combine the yogurt, horseradish, lemon peel, mustard, cheese, capers, and cayenne.
4. Place the pieces of fish, skin side down, in one layer in a nonmetallic baking dish. Spread them evenly with the yogurt mixture. Make a tent of aluminum foil over the dish and bake for 12 minutes. Remove from oven.
5. Preheat the broiler, remove the foil, and baste the fish with any juices that may have accumulated in the dish. Run the dish under the broiler until the top just begins to brown. Sprinkle with the dill or parsley and serve immediately.

Serves 6

A very thin, colorless membrane lies between the skin and the flesh of ocean pout. If the membrane is not removed when the fish are filleted, it will cause the fillet to curl up when it is cooked. Scoring the membrane at one-inch intervals will reduce the tendency to curl. The membrane is edible, but you may want to remove it, especially when using cooked ocean pout for a cold fish salad.

Steamed Wolffish in Romaine

This recipe has a striking presentation, is full of flavor, and is easy to prepare. Almost any firm, white-fleshed fish fillet, about 1 inch thick, can be used in this recipe.

2 *pounds wolffish fillet, 1 inch thick, cut into 6*
   equal portions
2 *tablespoons unsalted butter*
2 *tablespoons peanut oil*
1/4 *cup finely chopped onion (about 1 small)*
1/4 *cup finely chopped carrot (about 1 medium)*
1/2 *pound chopped mushrooms*
1/2 *teaspoon minced garlic*
1/2 *teaspoon salt*
1/4 *teaspoon freshly ground black pepper*
10 *large Romaine lettuce leaves*
1 *tablespoon minced shallots*
1/2 *cup dry white wine*
2 *cups fish stock (see page 277) or chicken stock*
1/2 *cup heavy cream*

1. Make a pocket in each fillet by cutting horizontally through the flesh to within 1/2 inch of the edge.
2. Melt the butter and the oil in a nonstick skillet over medium heat. When the butter is foaming, sauté the onion and carrot for 3 minutes. Add the mushrooms and continue to cook over medium heat for 10 minutes, stirring occasionally. Add the garlic and cook 5 more minutes. The mixture should be dry and the vegetables soft. Season with salt and pepper to taste, and cool.
3. Bring a 2-quart saucepan of water to a boil. Add the romaine leaves. Bring the water back to a boil and cook about 2 minutes. (The lettuce should be flexible but still a little crisp.) Drain and refresh in cold water. Dry each leaf with a paper towel. If the central rib is too thick to allow flexibility, trim it down. Arrange the leaves on a flat surface, rib side up.
4. Divide the mushroom mixture into 6 equal portions. Fill the pocket in each fillet with a portion. Season the fish lightly with salt and pepper. Place a stuffed fillet in the center of each of 6 lettuce leaves. Wrap to completely enclose the fillets, using extra leaves if necessary. The recipe may be prepared to this point up to 4 hours in advance. Keep the stuffed fillets in the refrigerator, covered, and let them sit at room temperature for 20 minutes prior to steaming.

Minutemade Wolffish

Preheat oven to 400 degrees. Cut 1 1/2 pounds of wolffish fillets into 6 pieces of equal size. Place skinned side down in a lightly oiled pan. Combine 1/2 cup mayonnaise, 2 teaspoons lemon juice, 1 teaspoon mustard, 1 tablespoon minced scallion, and 3 tablespoons grated Parmesan cheese. Spread over fillets, and add 1 to 2 tablespoons water or dry white wine, just enough to cover the bottom of the pan. Tent with aluminum foil, and bake about 10 minutes, or until fish tests just done. Remove the pan from the oven and throw away the foil. Turn the oven to broil. If desired, sprinkle the fillets with buttered fresh bread crumbs. Broil 5 to 6 inches from heat until brown, about 45 seconds. Serves 6.

5. Transfer to a steamer and steam over simmering water, covered, for about 10 minutes.
6. While the fish is cooking, combine the shallots, wine, and fish stock and boil until the liquid is reduced to $1/2$ cup. Lower the heat, whisk in the cream, and simmer for 5 more minutes.
7. To serve, place a romaine-wrapped fillet on a serving plate and nap with the sauce.

Serves 6

Fish, to taste right, must swim three times—in water, in butter, and in wine.—**Polish proverb**

Wolffish, also called ocean catfish, is a firm, sweet white meat usually sold as "whitefish" or "catch of the day." This fish is sometimes featured in restaurants under its French name, "loup de mer."

Chapter 6

Sweet Roes, Caviars, and Other Delights

Sweet Roes, Caviar, and Other Delights

The roe is a rich and delicious part of the fish that is sometimes overlooked. While many of us are familiar with caviar, which is sturgeon roe, the fresh, tender, roe of shad, herring, mackerel, flounder, carp, salmon, tuna, and cod are delectable treats, as well. The term "roe" applies to the ovaries of the female fish. Consisting of pairs of egg-filled sacs, the ovaries are joined together at one end and covered by a thin, edible membrane. When you cook the roe, you may want to separate the two sacs. Cut them apart carefully, or the eggs will spill out.

Roe appears on the market in both fresh and processed forms. Some, such as shad roe, are available from fish markets. But others have no commercial market and must be obtained from your friend, the amateur angler. As with all fish, the fresher the roe, the better. In the East, fresh shad roe gently sautéed with bacon is a favorite meal, and its appearance heralds the approach of spring.

Caviar, the best known and most expensive of all the roes, comes primarily from three species of sturgeon: beluga, sevruga, and osetra. The roe is priced according to size. The largest and most expensive eggs are from the beluga sturgeon; next in size are from the osetra; and the smallest are from the sevruga sturgeon. Harvesting the sturgeon eggs must take place at a precise stage in their maturity, or the quality of the caviar will suffer. After removing the roe from the sturgeon, the sacs of eggs are placed on a wire-mesh screen to separate them from the membranes that surround them. The eggs are then washed and graded.

Malossol caviar is made from the finest grade of caviar and commands the highest price. Although it is frequently referred to as fresh, malossol is processed (as all caviar is) by immersion in a brine solution. The longer the roe soaks, the less perishable but more salty it becomes. Malossol, meaning little salt, has only 3 to 5 percent salt.

Lesser grades are sold as pasteurized or pressed caviar. Pasteurized caviar is sold in vacuum-packed tins or jars and does not require refrigeration until opened. Pressed caviar, labeled "pausnaya," is made from damaged or broken eggs, which are pressed through cheesecloth until about one third of their liquid has been expelled. It has a consistency of marmalade and is much saltier than other caviar.

CAVIAR

Caviar substitutes are produced from several other fishes, and while they may not satisfy the aficionado, they are more affordable and have a distinctly pleasing flavor of their own. Salmon caviar—called red caviar because of its color—and whitefish caviar—often marketed as golden caviar—have the advantage of being freezable. The lumpfish is native to the Northeast, and its roe is used in making inexpensive caviar. The ripe eggs, which are green, are dyed black to look more like sturgeon caviar. All the cheaper caviars can be combined with other ingredients in recipes, but sturgeon caviar is best served simply, so as not to mask its delicate flavor.

If you have not indulged in roe before, you are in for a treat. If you are already a devotee, the following recipes will merely add to your enjoyment.

Caviar for the Purist

There are many ways of serving caviar, but for the purist there is only one way. Place Beluga Malossol caviar in a small crystal bowl, nestle the bowl in shaved ice in a larger silver bowl on a tray, and provide a small spreader made of mother-of-pearl. Surround the bowl with toast points. True purists dispense with the toast, and carry their own spoon. Serve with the finest champagne or iced Russian vodka. An alternate and perfectly acceptable way of serving caviar is to surround the larger bowl of ice with smaller bowls of finely chopped onion, snipped chives, or thinly sliced scallions, sieved hard-boiled egg yolks, finely chopped egg whites, crème fraîche, and lemon wedges.

Taramosalata

This is an ubiquitous dip, found in Greek restaurants and delicatessens from Boston to the Aegean. We have found it to be addictive.

10 *slices crustless white bread*
1 *cup milk*
4–5 *cloves garlic, smashed*
1 *10-ounce jar of tarama (carp roe, found in Greek markets)*
¼–½ cup fresh strained lemon juice
½–¾ cup olive oil
Cayenne pepper
Pita bread, cucumber rounds, or zucchini sticks for serving
Greek or Italian olives for garnish
Parsley sprig for garnish

1. Soak the bread in the milk for 10 minutes (the milk should just cover the bread). Remove the bread and squeeze it fairly dry.
2. Place 4 cloves of garlic and the bread in a food processor fitted with the steel knife. Process on and off to pulverize. Add the tarama and ¼ cup lemon juice and process until smooth. With the motor running, add ½ cup oil in a steady stream, and process until the mixture is thick, like mayonnaise. Add the remaining ¼ cup of oil by tablespoonfuls, if necessary, to achieve the proper consistency. Taste and add cayenne and the remaining garlic clove and lemon juice, if necessary. Refrigerate, covered, for up to several days, if you wish.
3. Cut the pita into triangles and pile in a small basket. If you wish, serve the cucumbers and zucchini as well. Serve the taramosalta in a bowl, garnished with Greek olives and parsley.

Serves 10
May be prepared in advance

Unopened pasteurized caviar has a shelf life of 6 months if properly stored. Once opened, it should be kept on ice and consumed within several hours.

Sautéed Fish Roe

Roe from freshly caught fish is delicious sautéed in a small amount of butter. From the small delicate roe of flounder and sole, to the more robust haddock roe, to the rich-flavored roe of mackerel, all can be a real treat when fresh. More often than not, the busy fishmonger discards the roe. However, once you have savored this delicacy, you will be asking your fishmonger to save the roe for you.

> 4 *ounces fish roe*
> 1 *tablespoon unsalted butter*
> 3 *lemon wedges*
> *Salt and freshly ground black pepper to taste*

1. Rinse the packets of roe and pat dry.
2. Melt the butter in a small skillet over moderate heat. Place the roe in the hot butter and sauté until golden brown on one side. Turn the roe over and brown the other side.
3. Transfer the roe to a heated plate and keep warm. Squeeze one lemon wedge into the skillet and scrape up the browned bits. Pour the lemon butter over the roe and season to taste with salt and pepper. Serve at once, garnished with the remaining lemon wedges.

Serves 1

The roe of female fish is also called hard roe, while the male fish's sperm is known as soft roe or milt. Both are used in cooking, but hard roe is more valued.

Beggars' Purses

The name of this recipe is certainly ironic, as caviar is one of the most costly foods known. However, the technique can be used equally well with other, less expensive fillings. Impress your dinner guests by serving them these purses as an appetizer, using any caviar of your choice except lumpfish.

> 1 *cup crêpe batter (see page 242)*
> 2 *tablespoons clarified butter (see page 273)*
> 20 *chive or scallion sprigs, at least 10 inches long*
> 6 *tablespoons crème fraîche*
> 4 *ounces caviar*
> 12 *paper-thin slices of lemon for garnish*

1. Heat a crêpe pan or small (5-inch) nonstick skillet over moderate heat. Brush lightly with clarified butter. When the pan is hot, add a full tablespoon of

batter. Rotate the pan to spread the batter out to the edges to make crêpe, 4 to 5 inches in diameter. Cook until it just begins to color on the bottom and appears slightly dry on the top. Turn over and cook for an additional 20 seconds on the other side. Transfer to a plate. Continue to cook crêpes; add more butter as necessary. Place a layer of wax paper between the crêpes and cover them with a tea towel until you are ready to make purses. One cup of batter should yield about 16 crêpes. Select the best ones for the purses.

2. Blanch the chive or scallion sprigs in boiling water for 3 seconds. Drain and refresh in cold water. Dry on paper towel. Because the chives and scallions are fragile, it is a good idea to have a few extras as a back-up.

3. Lay the crêpes on a work surface and place a heaping teaspoon of crème fraîche on each. Top with a scant teaspoon of caviar.

4. Gather the edges of the crêpe together around the filling to form a pouch. Carefully tie a chive sprig around the gathers, about ½ inch from the top. Place the pouches on a lightly oiled baking sheet. The purses may be prepared, covered, and refrigerated for up to 2 hours in advance. If prepared ahead, bring them to room temperature before heating.

5. When ready to cook, preheat oven to 325 degrees.

6. Warm the purses in the oven for 3 to 5 minutes. To serve, place 3 purses on each of 4 heated plates. Garnish with paper-thin slices of lemon.

Serves 4
May be prepared in advance

For ease in handling and cooking, the pair of roe-filled sacs may be separated by carefully cutting through the portion of the membrane joining the sacs.

Fresh caviar must be kept refrigerated. A temperature of 28 to 32 degrees is optimal. Because of its salt content, the caviar will not freeze.

Herring Roe with Anchovy Butter

In England this dish is often served as a "Savoury," a course that follows the entree. It is equally good as an appetizer served with toast squares.

$1/2$ *pound herring roe*
1 *anchovy fillet or 1 tablespoon anchovy paste*
6 *tablespoons unsalted butter, softened*
2 *tablespoons flour*
3 *tablespoons clarified butter (see page 273)*
4 *slices white bread, crusts removed*
1 *teaspoon fresh strained lemon juice*
Dash cayenne pepper
Paprika

1. Rinse the herring roe under running water and place in a colander. Pour 2 to 3 cups of boiling water over the roe and drain well. Allow to cool for 10 minutes.
2. In a very small bowl, mash the anchovy with 4 tablespoons of the softened butter to make anchovy butter. Set aside.
3. Coat the roe with the flour. Heat the clarified butter in a small skillet and gently fry the roe until crisp and golden brown.
4. Toast the bread and spread with the anchovy butter. Cut the toast in half and place on a warm serving dish. Arrange the roe on top of the toast and keep warm.
5. Heat the remaining 2 tablespoons of unsalted butter and cook until nut brown. Add the lemon juice and cayenne pepper. While the butter is foaming, pour it over the roe. Sprinkle with paprika and serve immediately.

Serves 4

Caviar is high in protein, fat, cholesterol, and sodium. It is also a source of B vitamins, calcium, potassium, iron, phosphorous, and the healthful Omega-3 fatty acids.

Sautéed Shad Roe

Cooking the roe in wax paper packets keeps the roe intact, and the bacon fat gives it a mild smoky flavor.

4 strips bacon, preferably a smoky brand
1 pair fresh shad roe
Freshly ground black pepper to taste
Parsley sprigs for garnish

1. Sauté the bacon in a heavy skillet until crisp. Remove the bacon, crumble the pieces, and set aside. Retain the bacon fat in the skillet.
2. Carefully cut the membrane between the pair of roe, rinse under cold water, and pat dry. Cut two 10-inch squares of wax paper. Wrap each sac of roe in a square of wax paper and twist the ends of the paper to seal.
3. Place the roe packets in the hot bacon fat and sauté over moderate heat for 3 to 4 minutes on each side. Remove the packets from the skillet and unwrap the roe.
4. Grind black pepper to taste over the roe. Serve the roe garnished with the crumbled bacon and parsley sprigs.

Serves 2

Because caviar tarnishes silver very quickly, it is traditionally served in crystal bowls set in ice, with mother-of-pearl utensils. Perfectionists feel that gold is the only suitable metal with which to serve caviar.

Good caviar, like good wine, stands best by itself.

Salmon Caviar Roulades

This festive party hors d'oeuvre combines a delicious mousse with delicate crêpes to make roulades, which are then topped with glistening grains of salmon caviar. This recipe is prepared ahead of serving time. The crêpes may even be frozen, separated by pieces of wax paper and sealed in a heavy-duty plastic bag.

Crêpes

2 *eggs*
½ cup milk
¾ cup water
¾ cup flour
¼ teaspoon salt

1. In the work bowl of a food processor, combine the eggs, milk, and water. Pulse on and off to mix well. Add the flour and salt and process until thoroughly combined. Pour into a bowl, cover, and refrigerate for at least 1 hour or up to 4 hours.

According to an FDA ruling, only sturgeon roe may be labeled caviar. Any substitutes must indicate the species from which the roe was obtained. Thus red caviar must be labeled "salmon caviar."

Roulades

3 *hard-boiled eggs, sieved*
¾ cup mayonnaise
1 *tablespoon minced scallions*
1 *teaspoon Worcestershire sauce*
4 *teaspoons fresh strained lemon juice*
6 *drops Tabasco sauce*
Salt and freshly ground white pepper to taste
¼ cup minced fresh dill
1 *recipe crêpes (see recipe above)*
2 *tablespoons clarified butter (see page 273)*
¼ cup cold water
1 *tablespoon unflavored gelatin*
6–8 ounces salmon caviar
Dill sprigs for garnish (optional)

1. In a small bowl, combine the sieved eggs, mayonnaise, scallions, Worcestershire, lemon juice, Tabasco, salt, and pepper. Mix well. Cover this mousse mixture and refrigerate for at least 1 hour or up to 24 hours.
2. Stir the dill into the crêpe batter.
3. Heat a 9-inch nonstick skillet over moderate heat. Brush lightly with clarified butter. When the pan is hot, pour in a scant ¼ cup of the crêpe batter and rotate the skillet to evenly distribute. Cook until tiny

bubbles appear at the surface and the bottom is just beginning to color. Flip over and cook for an additional 20 seconds. When cooked, transfer to a plate. Continue to cook the crêpes, using the remaining batter. Add more clarified butter to the pan as necessary. Place a layer of wax paper between the crêpes and cover with a tea towel until ready to use.

4. Shortly before assembling the roulades, pour the ¼ cup cold water into a small flameproof bowl. Sprinkle the gelatin over the water and allow it to soften for 10 minutes. Meanwhile, lay each crêpe on a piece of dry wax paper on a work surface and cover with a tea towel to prevent drying during the final preparation of the mousse.

5. When the gelatin has softened, place the bowl in a pan of simmering water to dissolve the gelatin. When all the granules have dissolved, remove from heat and allow to cool for 5 minutes. Fold the gelatin into the mousse mixture and immediately proceed with making the roulades as the mousse will firm up rapidly now that the gelatin has been added.

6. Spread each crêpe with a layer of the mousse. Roll the crêpes to form roulades and place on a baking sheet, seam side down. Cover and refrigerate for at least 1 hour or up to 4 hours.

7. To serve, trim of the ends of the roulades, then slice the roulades into ½-inch rounds. Lay the rounds on their sides on a serving tray. Top each slice with several grains (about ¼ teaspoon) of salmon caviar. Decorate with a dill sprig if desired.

Yield: 6–7 dozen roulades
Must be prepared in advance

The huge beluga sturgeon may weigh as much as 2,500 pounds, but 900 pounds is the average. Osetra sturgeon weigh in at 200 pounds and are 6 to 7 feet long. Sevruga sturgeon average about 50 pounds.

Corncakes with Salmon Caviar

This recipe is similar to but simpler than blinis. Using cornmeal makes it a more American dish. We recommend you use salmon caviar in this recipe because it is an American product that goes well with the American corncakes. Also, the coarse-grained texture of the corncakes is not appropriate for more costly caviar.

1 ½ cups buttermilk
3 eggs, separated
¼ cup butter, melted
1 ¼ cups yellow cornmeal
½ cup all-purpose flour
1 teaspoon salt, plus a pinch more
2 teaspoons sugar
3 tablespoons vegetable oil
1 ¼ cups crème fraîche
4 ounces salmon caviar

Lumpfish eggs benefit from a rinse in cold water.

1. Combine the milk and egg yolks in a small bowl. Stir in the butter.
2. Sift together the cornmeal, flour, sugar, and salt in a large bowl. Make a well in the center of the dry ingredients and add the liquid mixture. Stir to combine well.
3. Whisk the egg whites until frothy, add a pinch of salt, and continue to beat until they hold stiff peaks. Stir one-third of the egg whites into the batter, then fold in the remaining whites.
4. Heat a nonstick skillet or a griddle over moderate heat. Brush lightly with vegetable oil. Drop the batter onto the heated griddle by scant tablespoons and quickly spread to a 3-inch-diameter circle. Cook until the undersides are lightly browned and the tops have developed tiny bubbles. Flip the corncakes over and continue to cook until lightly browned. Remove to a heated plate and keep warm, continue to cook corncakes, adding more oil as necessary, until all the batter has been used.
5. To serve, center a spoonful of crème fraîche on each corncake and top with salmon caviar.

Yield: 5 dozen

Pasta with Caviar

FROM THE OFFICE OF THE ROMIAGNOLI'S TABLE, BOSTON

Serve this elegant pasta and caviar creation as a pre- or post-theater entree. The recipe is quick and simple to prepare, and the dinner needs only a salad of impeccably fresh greens and a flute of cold dry champagne. Serve a fresh fruit salad for dessert.

> $2/3$ *cup sour cream*
> $1/4$ *cup light cream*
> 2 *ounces caviar (lumpfish, whitefish, salmon, or American malossol)*
> 1 *tablespoon minced Italian parsley*
> 7 *ounces fresh pasta, fettuccine or linguine*

1. Place the sour cream in a small bowl and gently mix in the light cream until well blended. Stir in half the caviar and the parsley.
2. Cook the pasta until "al dente," drain, and dress with the cream and caviar mixture. Place the rest of the caviar in the center of the dish. Serve immediately.

Serves 2

Fresh malossol caviar—whether it is beluga, osetra or sevruga—has a nutty, barely salty taste. The eggs, or berries, are soft yet firm, neither mushy nor hard and crunchy. One taste will tell you why true caviar is the queen of all roe.

Chapter 7

Spicing the Catch

Marinades

Depending upon the ingredients, a marinade will add flavor, ensure moistness, and tenderize. The ingredients will add the flavor; the liquid is responsible for moistness; and acids such as lemon or lime juice, vinegar, and wine have a tenderizing effect. Because fish seldom needs tenderizing, we suggest a short marinating time for acidic marinades, since more than 30 minutes will produce too soft a texture. In some instances, a marinade actually "cooks" the fish, as in seviche, the lime-marinated dish of Latin America. Vinaigrette salad dressings make good marinades. Try your own favorite, or refer to the vinaigrette section in this chapter. Marinades are often equally good used as a basting sauce.

SAUCES

Soy Marinade

The soy imparts an attractive brown glaze as well as a distinct Oriental flavor. Since the flavors are assertive, marinate for no longer than 15 to 30 minutes. It is particularly well suited to bluefish, swordfish, tuna, mackerel, and salmon.

> 2 tablespoons soy sauce
> 2 tablespoons fresh strained lemon juice
> 2 teaspoons minced gingerroot
> 1 clove garlic, smashed
> ¼ teaspoon freshly ground black pepper
> ⅓ cup olive or vegetable oil

1. Combine all the ingredients. Place the fish in a shallow dish and pour the marinade over it. Remove the garlic just before cooking. Use the marinade to baste the fish while it cooks.

Variation: Try adding several tablespoons of sesame seeds, a teaspoon of mustard, crushed coriander seeds, or grated lemon, lime, or orange zest—the possibilities are almost limitless. Substitute lime or orange juice for the lemon juice or add a few drops of sesame oil.

Yield: ½ cup

Cutting slits in the surface of fish or meat—"scoring"—increases its tenderness and, if a marinade is being used, increases the rapidity of its absorption.

Fresh gingerroot may be placed in a plastic bag and frozen for long-term storage. Slice or shred while it is still frozen. Or peel the gingerroot and place it in a jar, adding dry sherry to cover. Keep it tightly covered in the refrigerator.

Quick Soy-Lime Basting Sauce

This sauce is a terrific way to add last minute pizzazz to grilled fish steaks and fillets. It is especially good with salmon, swordfish, tuna, mullet, and bluefish. Do not marinate fish in this sauce. It should be brushed over the fish just before grilling, and used to baste the fish while it cooks.

2 *tablespoons fresh strained lime or lemon juice*
2 *tablespoons soy sauce*

1. Combine the lime juice and soy sauce and mix well. Spoon over each side of the fish as it grills over coals.

Yield: ¼ **cup**

Herbal Wine Marinade

Fresh herbs provide a subtle flavor that can be used with any fish, but they are particularly complementary with halibut, striped bass, and other mildly flavored fish. For more intensely flavored fish, such as swordfish, tuna, mackerel, or bluefish, use more pungent herbs.

2 *tablespoons dry white wine or sherry*
1 *tablespoon fresh strained lemon juice*
1 *tablespoon minced shallot or scallion*
2 *tablespoons chopped fresh herbs, such as thyme, basil, and dill*
Pinch freshly ground black pepper
6 *tablespoons olive oil*

1. Combine all the ingredients. Mix well. Pour over the fish in a shallow dish and let marinate for up to 30 minutes.

Variation: Add a clove of smashed garlic or a teaspoon of mustard.

Yield: ⅔ **cup**

It is always a good idea to rinse any fresh fish product in cold water, and then pat dry with paper toweling before proceeding with a recipe.

Salad Dressings

Old standbys like mayonnaise and vinaigrette are familiar to almost everyone. The recipes in this section include not only basic recipes, but also variations infused with some surprise ingredients that complement the taste of fish. We hope our recipes will inspire you to go beyond the usual application of a vinaigrette to salad greens and mayonnaise to tuna fish.

Rouille

This is a classic French sauce served with bouillabaisse or fish stew. It is also quite good on baked fish steaks or fillets. We are including it here because the method of preparation is the same as for mayonnaise.

1 cup diced French bread
¹/₃ cup fish stock (use liquid from bouillabaisse or stew)
4 garlic cloves, mashed
1 3-ounce jar pimientos, drained
1 egg yolk
¹/₂ cup olive oil
¹/₄ teaspoon cayenne pepper

1. In a small bowl, soak the bread in the fish stock, until it can be mashed to a paste. Blend the mashed garlic cloves into the bread paste.
2. In a food processor fitted with the steel knife, process the pimientos until pureed. With the motor still running, drop the bread and garlic paste through the feed tube and process until combined. Add the egg yolk and blend. Pour in the oil in a slow, steady stream and process until thick. Add the cayenne. Taste and correct the seasoning if necessary. If the sauce is too thick, blend in 2 or 3 additional tablespoons of hot fish stock. Serve.

Yield: 1 cup

"Of all the items on the menu, soup is that which exacts the most delicate perfection and the strictest attention."—Escoffier

Mayonnaise

We prefer using homemade mayonnaise in all our recipes, although we know it is not always possible. This is a simple mayonnaise recipe that will keep at least a week, covered, in the refrigerator. One secret of making mayonnaise is to have all the ingredients at room temperature.

2 *egg yolks*
¹/₂ teaspoon salt
¹/₂ teaspoon dry mustard
1 *cup olive or vegetable oil*
1 *tablespoon fresh strained lemon juice*

The addition of an herb, such as thyme or rosemary, gives the lemon mayonnaise a different but delicate flavor.

1. In a blender or food processor, whir the egg yolks, salt and mustard until slightly thickened. With the motor running, add about ¹/₂ cup oil in a slow, steady stream. Add the lemon juice, then continue adding the oil until it is thoroughly incorporated. Taste for seasoning. If it seems to need salt, add more lemon juice before adding more salt. Cover and refrigerate until ready to use.

Variations: Aioli: Place 5 garlic cloves, mashed to a paste, in the food processor, then add the egg yolks and continue with the above recipe.

Red Pepper Mayonnaise is fun to use because of its lovely color. Create a startlingly beautiful, delicious salad using red pepper mayonnaise as a binder (for cooked and cooled pieces of fish, such as grouper or snapper). Serve on magenta colored radicchio, or a chiffonade of spinach, and top it off with a teaspoon of red salmon or golden whitefish caviar.

Lemon: Add 3 tablespoons fresh strained lemon juice and 1 tablespoon lemon zest to 1 cup mayonnaise. It is particularly good with smoked trout and smoked bluefish.

Red Pepper: Broil an 8-ounce sweet red pepper, turning it until the skin is charred on all sides. Remove from heat and place in a paper bag. Fold over the top of the bag and allow the pepper to cool for 10 minutes. Slip off the skin, remove the seeds, and puree. Stir into 1 cup mayonnaise. Add salt and pepper to taste.

Yield: 1 ¹/₂ cups
May be prepared in advance

Sauce Verte

This traditional green mayonnaise is excellent with a wide variety of seafood. Easy to make, this sauce is a taste treat for all diners.

> 1 *ounce spinach leaves, stemmed, washed, and patted dry*
> 1 *ounce watercress, stemmed, washed, and patted dry*
> ½ *ounce parsley, stemmed, washed, and patted dry*
> ½ *ounce tarragon leaves, washed, and patted dry*
> 1 *tablespoon minced fresh chives*
> 2 *teaspoons minced fresh dill*
> 1½ *cups mayonnaise, preferably homemade*
> *Salt and freshly ground black pepper to taste*

1. Bring several cups of water to a boil in a small saucepan. Blanch the spinach, watercress, parsley, and tarragon in the boiling water for 1 minute.
2. Place the blanched spinach, watercress, parsley, and tarragon, and the dill and chives in the blender and puree.
3. Stir the puree into the mayonnaise and blend well. Season with salt and pepper to taste. Cover and refrigerate for at least 30 minutes or no more than 4 hours before serving.

Yield: 2 cups
Must be prepared in advance

Chives are the most delicately flavored member of the onion family. They are easily grown in a sunny kitchen window and can be snipped for any number of dishes. The small flowers are also edible and make lovely garnishes.

A fish salad bound with Sauce Verte looks tantalizing served in yellow or red pepper halves. Cut the peppers in half lengthwise and remove the cores and seeds. Broil or steam briefly, until barely tender. Cool and fill with salad.

Tarragon Mayonnaise

Tarragon enhances the flavor of all fish. This recipe can either create a salad from cooked leftover pieces of fish, or be served alongside (cool) poached salmon, grouper, snapper, or striped bass. The flavor of the tarragon will be more noticeable if added just before serving.

1 *cup mayonnaise, preferably homemade*
2 *tablespoons light cream*
1 *tablespoon tarragon vinegar*
1 *tablespoon lemon juice*
3 *tablespoons minced fresh tarragon*
Freshly ground white pepper to taste

1. Combine the mayonnaise and cream in a small bowl. Stir in the vinegar and lemon juice. Add the tarragon and pepper to taste.
2. Cover and refrigerate for at least 30 minutes before serving. If necessary, the mayonnaise may be refrigerated up to 8 hours before serving.

Yield: 1 ¼ cups
Must be prepared in advance

Scallions are easily chopped by holding a clean bunch in one hand and snipping them with scissors.

Try folding in a handful of lightly toasted pecans when you make your next salad with Mustard Salad Dressing.

Bind cooked shellfish with any salad dressing variation. Add a dice of your favorite vegetables, including one that is brightly colored such as red or yellow bell pepper, red radish, or carrot.

New England Aquarium Salad Dressing

This dressing was created by Aquarium testers to enhance basic fish salads. The recipe will bind approximately 2 pounds or 4 cups of cooked and cooled seafood.

½ *cup mayonnaise, preferably homemade*
2 *tablespoons light cream*
1 *tablespoon Dijon-style mustard*
2 *teaspoons fresh strained lemon juice*
2 *teaspoons thinly sliced scallions*

1. Combine all the ingredients in a small bowl. Mix to blend thoroughly. This will keep, tightly covered, in the refrigerator for at least 48 hours.

Variations Marie Rose: Stir in 2 tablespoons ketchup and 1 teaspoon paprika. This is good with canned tiny shrimp and served in half an avocado, or with any of the crustaceans.

Mustard: Stir 1 tablespoon whole-grain mustard, such as Moutarde de Meaux. Strongly flavored fish, such as bluefish, mackerel, and swordfish, seem to respond well to a heavy dose of mustard.

Pesto: Stir in ¼ cup Pesto Sauce (see page 262)

Chinese: Omit the cream and add 1 teaspoon sesame oil, 2 teaspoons soy sauce, 1 teaspoon grated gingerroot, and 2 teaspoons minced cilantro. This variation perks up a surimi (imitation crabmeat) salad, and is also excellent with salmon or tuna, especially with a tablespoon of toasted sesame seeds sprinkled on top.

Mexican: Substitute lime juice for the lemon and add 4 drops of Tabasco, 2 teaspoons minced jalapeño pepper, 1 small peeled, seeded, and chopped plum tomato, and 2 teaspoons minced cilantro. Try it with rich-flavored fishes, such a tuna and swordfish, or monkfish or halibut.

Tropical: Substitute 2 tablespoons fresh strained orange juice for the lemon juice and omit the mustard. Stir in 1 teaspoon grated orange rind, 1 teaspoon grated gingerroot, ¼ cup sour cream, and 2 teaspoons minced fresh parsley. This is very good with simply poached fish, such as halibut, monkfish, or hake, and even steamed lobster. We enjoyed a touch of toasted almonds and red grapes with this variation.

Yield: ¾ to 1 cup
Must be prepared in advance

Toss a salad with Mexican Salad Dressing, and serve it on a fried tortilla.

Scatter crispy fried wonton strips over a salad using Chinese Salad Dressing.

Rings of cooked, cooled squid or octopus make a tasty and unusual hors d'oeuvre when served with Chinese Salad Dressing as a dipping sauce.

Serve monkfish cubes on a slice of melon, garnished with small clusters of seedless grapes and a dollop of Tropical Salad Dressing.

Vinaigrette

A basic vinaigrette dressing may be made up to 5 days in advance. If fresh herbs are used, add them just before serving. As with any vinaigrette, the quality of the vinegar and oil will directly affect the taste.

> ^{1}/3 *cup red or white wine or tarragon vinegar*
> 1 *teaspoon salt*
> 1 *teaspoon freshly ground black pepper*
> 1 *teaspoon dry mustard or 2 teaspoons Dijon-style mustard*
> 1 *cup olive oil*

1. In a small bowl, whisk the vinegar with the salt, pepper, and dry mustard. Add the oil slowly, while continuing to whisk. When the dressing has thickened, taste and correct seasoning. Cover and refrigerate until ready to serve.

Variations Herb: Stir in 3 tablespoons chopped fresh herbs such as thyme, basil, parsley, or tarragon after the vinaigrette has thickened.

Sesame: Substitute ^{1}/3 cup sesame oil for ^{1}/3 cup of the olive oil. Try this as a dipping sauce with octopus as an hors d'oeuvre.

Tomato: Add 1 tablespoon tomato paste and 3 tablespoons minced fresh basil.

Walnut Oil: Substitute ^{1}/2 cup walnut (or other nut) oil for the ^{1}/2 cup olive oil.

Yield: 1 ^{1}/3 cups
May be prepared in advance

Don't limit your use of vinaigrettes to salad greens. Pasta cooked *al dente* is great when dressed with one of our vinaigrettes, arranged on a plate, and topped off with chunks of cooked fish briefly marinated in the same dressing. Try monkfish, wolffish, or scallops with the herbal variation. Tomato Vinaigrette is delicious with bluefish, swordfish, and mahi mahi. Rings of squid and octopus work nicely with the Sesame Vinaigrette, served on black squid ink pasta.

Pour ^{1}/4 cup vinaigrette, or one of the variations, over 2 cups of cooked and cooled fish cut into bite-size pieces. Cover and marinate in the refrigerator for 1 to 3 hours, stirring once or twice. Remove from the refrigerator and add 5 or 6 tablespoons of mayonnaise, or one of the mayonnaise variations, 3 tablespoons each minced scallions and chopped fresh herbs, and 3 tablespoons rinsed and drained capers. Season to taste with salt and pepper. Garnish with wedges of hard-boiled eggs and tomato wedges, if desired. This is great in lunch boxes or for a light lunch anywhere, anytime.

Lemon-Thyme Vinaigrette

Thyme combines nicely with almost any fish, but seems to have a special affinity for the stronger flavored fishes. Toss cooked rice or couscous with thyme vinaigrette to moisten, add your choice of diced vegetable, and fold in bite-size pieces of cooked and cooled swordfish, bluefish, or tuna. Squid or octopus rings and members of the codfish family also work well.

3 *tablespoons white wine vinegar*
2 *tablespoons fresh strained lemon juice*
1 *teaspoon salt*
1 *teaspoon freshly ground black pepper*
1 *cup olive oil*
2 *tablespoons chopped fresh thyme*

1. In a small bowl, whisk the vinegar with the lemon juice, salt, and pepper. Add the oil slowly, while continuing to whisk. When the dressing has thickened, stir in the thyme and serve.

Yield: 1 ⅓ cups

Gently warm one of our vinaigrettes and spoon a tablespoon over a poached or steamed fish fillet or steak.

Cooked pieces of squid and octopus will brighten the next cocktail party when marinated in Sesame Vinaigrette. Serve with toothpicks and lots of napkins.

Make a potato salad with Lemon-Thyme Vinaigrette and your favorite firm-fleshed fish, cooked and cooled. Dress about 2 cups of warm, quartered, cooked new potatoes with ½ cup of gently heated Lemon-Thyme Vinaigrette. Toss to coat and add chopped black olives and celery to taste. Let marinate at room temperature for at least 15 minutes, or up to an hour. Then add 1 ½ cups cooked fish, cut into bite-sized pieces. Add more vinaigrette, if needed, to moisten fish, and stir to combine. Add salt and freshly ground black pepper to taste. Leftover chunks of broiled or grilled fish seem to work particularly well when used this way.

Sauces and Toppings

The diversity of recipes in this section is testimony to the wide range of tastes and textures that we find in fishes, and to the variety of cooking methods that can be used in preparing them. Sauces and toppings are vehicles for enhancing rather than masking the characteristic taste of fishes.

Although there are no definitive rules for using sauces and toppings, a few guidelines emerged during our testings that we would like to share with you. First, the less involved the preparation of the fish, the more likely it will take to a sauce or topping. Second, we found that grilled and broiled fish, especially those we call rich fishes such as tuna, swordfish, bluefish, marlin, and mahi mahi, have a special affinity for acidic-based tomato sauces. These rich, oily fishes also combine well with the assertive qualities of such foods as mustard, peppercorns, and anchovies, while the mild fishes marry well with herbal and citrus flavors. Finally, the imagination and creativity of the cook, plus the use of top-quality ingredients, are very important when adding these finishing touches.

Cocktail Sauce

No fish cookbook is complete without a chili sauce-based cocktail dipping sauce. Served with boiled shrimp, it guarantees the crustaceans will quickly disappear. Feel free to vary the amounts of the ingredients to suit your own palate.

> $^1/_2$ *cup ketchup*
> $^1/_2$ *cup chili sauce*
> 2–3 *tablespoons prepared horseradish*
> 3 *tablespoons fresh strained lemon juice*
> 1 *tablespoon Worcestershire sauce*
> 6 *drops Tabasco sauce*

1. Combine the ingredients in a small bowl. Mix well until thoroughly blended. Cover and refrigerate. Serve within 24 hours.

Yield: 1 $^1/_2$ cups
May be prepared in advance

Cucumber and Tomato Sauce

Serve this sauce with either hot or cold entrees. The tart flavor of the yogurt, tempered with mayonnaise, is a perfect foil for the tomatoes and cucumbers. The sauce is delicious on its own, but will do a favor for any rich-flavored fish with which it is served. It is especially good with salmon.

$^1/_2$ cup yogurt or sour cream
$^1/_2$ cup mayonnaise
1 tablespoon fresh strained lemon juice
1 tablespoon Dijon-style mustard
2 tablespoons minced fresh dill
1 tablespoon thinly sliced scallion
1 tablespoon minced fresh parsley
2 medium tomatoes, peeled, seeded and finely chopped (about $^2/_3$ cup)
1 medium cucumber, peeled, seeded, and diced (about $^1/_4$ cup)
Freshly ground white pepper to taste

1. In a small bowl combine yogurt or sour cream, mayonnaise, lemon juice, mustard, dill, scallion, and parsley. Mix to blend. Refrigerate, if desired, up to 4 hours.
2. At serving time, drain any liquid from the tomatoes and cucumbers and discard. Fold the tomatoes and cucumbers into the sauce. Taste, adjust seasoning, adding pepper if necessary.

Yield: 1 $^1/_2$ cups
May be partially prepared in advance

The Greeks believed dill to be so nourishing that athletes were required to eat it in all their food.

Dill is a natural with fish. Try it as an accompaniment on simply grilled or broiled fillets or steaks. With the addition of some diced cucumber and scallions, it will serve as a base for a fish salad.

Gremolata

This refreshing, low-calorie, Italian herbal garnish is particularly good with broiled or grilled fish, such as bluefish, salmon, or swordfish.

$1/2$ cup minced fresh parsley
2 tablespoons grated lemon rind (zest)
$1 1/2$ teaspoons minced garlic
$1/4$ teaspoon salt
1 teaspoon freshly ground black pepper

1. In a small bowl, combine the parsley, lemon zest, garlic, salt, and pepper. Serve within 1 or 2 hours.

Yield: $2/3$ cup
May be prepared in advance

From a nutritional viewpoint, steaming fish in aluminum foil is an excellent method of cooking. Fats and calories are kept to a minimum, and the end product is a moist and tasty portion of fish. Preparation and cleanup time are minimal, and the recipe can be made in advance. Everyone wins with foil-steamed fish.

Guacamole Sauce

Our guacamole is not prepared in a blender or food processor, as we like a roughly textured sauce rather than a smooth one. You can do everything in advance, except mashing the avocados.

2 ripe avocados, pitted and peeled
2 teaspoons fresh strained lemon juice
12 drops Tabasco sauce
$1/2$ cup chopped onion
1–2 teaspoons minced garlic
2 medium tomatoes, peeled, seeded, and chopped
    (about $2/3$ cup)
Salt and freshly ground black pepper to taste.

1. Mash the avocados in a shallow bowl. Blend in the lemon juice and Tabasco. Add onion and garlic and mix well. Fold in the tomatoes. Add salt and pepper to taste.
2. If you want to prepare this in advance, mix together all the ingredients except the avocados. Do not add the avocados until the last minute. If necessary, you may add the avocados up to one hour in advance and cover the bowl with plastic wrap, letting the wrap touch the sauce to prevent discoloration.

Yield: 2 cups
May be prepared in advance

260

Horseradish Sauce

Horseradish and trout embellish one another. Although we like the zing of fresh horseradish, you may substitute drained bottled horseradish, if the jar is very fresh. This is also delicious with smoked bluefish.

1 *cup whipped cream*
¹/₃ *cup freshly grated horseradish*
1 *teaspoon sugar*
Pinch *freshly ground white pepper*

1. In a small bowl, combine the cream, horseradish, sugar, and pepper. Cover and refrigerate for 1 hour before serving.

Yield: 1¹/₄ cups
Must be prepared in advance

Mustard Sauce

This sauce is traditionally Scandinavian and is excellent as a dip with shrimp or raw vegetables. It is also good on meat.

4 *tablespoons whole-grain Dijon-style mustard*
1 *teaspoon dry mustard*
3 *tablespoons sugar*
2 *tablespoons white vinegar*
¹/₃ *cup vegetable oil*
4 *tablespoons minced fresh dill*

1. Combine the Dijon-style mustard and dry mustard in a small bowl. Stir in the sugar and vinegar. Add the oil very slowly, whisking until the sauce thickens. Stir in the dill and refrigerate until serving. It will keep up to 2 weeks.

Yield: 1 cup
May be prepared in advance

A piece of horseradish root will keep for several weeks in the refrigerator. Sauces calling for grated horseradish are enhanced by the use of a fresh root rather than the bottled product. If using prepared horseradish, be sure to use a freshly opened bottle for the best results. The bottled horseradish quickly loses its punch once opened.

Mustard Topping

This is a pungent spread, and should be used with a strongly flavored fish, such as bluefish or shark.

> ¹/₄ *cup coarse-grain mustard, such as Moutarde de Meaux*
> 1 *teaspoon minced garlic*
> 2 *teaspoons fresh strained lime juice*
> 1 *tablespoon honey*

1. Combine the ingredients in a small bowl. Spread on fish fillets or steaks. Adjust oven rack so that the fish will be about 5 inches from the broiler element. Broil, watching carefully so that it doesn't burn. (If necessary, tent fish with aluminum foil.)

Yield: 6 tablespoons

If using a garlic press, leave the skin on the garlic. This will assure easier cleaning of the press.

Try a generous dollop of Pesto Sauce on top of a baked potato for a real taste treat.

Pesto Sauce

This is a kitchen basic and easy to make with a food processor. Although traditionally used on pasta, it is very good on grilled or broiled fish. Simply place a spoonful on top of the fish just before removing it from the heat. It may be served hot or cold.

> 2¹/₂ *cups lightly packed fresh basil leaves*
> 3 *cloves garlic, quartered*
> ¹/₂ *cup pignolia (pine nuts)*
> ³/₄ *cup olive oil*
> 6 *tablespoons freshly grated Parmesan cheese*
> *Salt and freshly ground black pepper*

1. In a food processor fitted with the steel knife, chop the basil, garlic, and pine nuts until reduced to medium-fine. Add the olive oil in a stream through the food tube. Add the Parmesan and process to combine. Add salt and pepper to taste.
2. For the best color and strongest basil taste, serve immediately. If necessary, store in the refrigerator, covered with a thin film of olive oil and plastic wrap. It will keep for a week. If you wish a more liquid puree, add up to ¹/₄ cup additional olive oil.

Variation: Almonds or walnuts may be substituted for the pignolia.

Yield: 1 1/4 cups
May be prepared ahead

Red Tomato Salsa

Fresh tomatoes are essential for this salsa; the better the tomato, the better the salsa. It goes well with any broiled or grilled fish, and is wonderful with a fish terrine.

2 *tomatoes, peeled, seeded and coarsely chopped*
(about 1/2 cup)
2 *tablespoons minced fresh cilantro*
2 *tablespoons minced red onion*
2 *teaspoons fresh strained lime juice*
Salt and freshly ground black pepper to taste
Tabasco sauce to taste

1. In a nonmetal bowl, combine the tomatoes, cilantro, onion, and lime juice. Add salt, pepper, and Tabasco to taste.
2. Cover and refrigerate for at least 1 hour to let the flavors blend. The salsa is best if made less than six hours in advance.

Yield: 3/4 cup
Must be prepared in advance

In England, in early times, anxious parents inserted cloves of garlic into the stockings of a child with whooping cough. Garlic was thought of as an effective charm against witches, and anyone who purchased garlic on St. John's Day believed that he would be safe from poverty for the coming year.

Roasted Red Pepper Sauce

This sauce enhances broiled or baked fish. It also provides a colorful touch on a fish terrine.

4 *medium-size sweet red peppers*
2 *tablespoons olive oil*
3 *tablespoons minced shallots*
2 *teaspoons minced garlic*
1/4 *cup chicken stock*
1/8 *teaspoon cayenne pepper*
1 *teaspoon fresh strained lemon juice*
Salt and freshly ground black pepper to taste

1. Broil peppers, turning, until charred on all sides. Immediately place them in a paper bag and fold the top over. Let cool 10 minutes, then slip the skins off. Remove and discard seeds; chop the peppers coarsely.
2. Heat the oil in a heavy 2-quart saucepan over medium heat. Add the peppers, shallots, and garlic. Lower heat and cook until the shallots and garlic are softened. Add the chicken stock and cayenne and cook for 2 to 3 minutes.
3. Puree the pepper mixture in a food processor fitted with a steel knife, or in a blender. Add the lemon juice and season to taste with salt and pepper. If the sauce is too thick, add a bit more chicken stock. The sauce keeps well in the refrigerator for up to 2 days. It can be frozen up to 3 months.

Yield: 1 cup
May be prepared in advance

Salsa Cruda

This is a refreshing, low-calorie garnish for grilled and broiled fish such as mullet, shark, swordfish, or tuna steak. The toasted cumin seeds really make it special.

1 1/2 teaspoons cumin seeds, or 1 1/4 teaspoons
    ground cumin
1 3/4 cups peeled, seeded, and chopped tomatoes, or
    1 pint cherry tomatoes, halved
2 teaspoons minced jalapeño peppers
1/4 cup diced red onion
1 teaspoon minced garlic
3 tablespoons minced fresh cilantro
1–2 tablespoons fresh strained lemon juice
1/2 teaspoon salt
Freshly ground black pepper to taste

1. In a heavy skillet over medium-high heat, toast the cumin seeds, for 2 or 3 minutes until they give off a pungent smell. Cool and pulverize in a mortar and pestle, or grind in a spice grinder.
2. Combine all the ingredients in a glass or china bowl. Mix well. It may be made up to 2 hours in advance and kept covered.

Variation: Add 1 avocado, peeled, pitted, and cut into 1/2-inch cubes. This version is good with mahi mahi, shark, and swordfish.

Yield: 2 cups
May be prepared in advance

Salsa Verde

Serve Salsa Verde rather than guacamole with shrimp for an interesting hors d'oeuvre. Or use it as a garnish for grilled shrimp, grouper, bluefish, marlin, or swordfish.

1 *pound tomatillos, or 1 13-ounce can tomatillos*
1/4 *cup diced red onion*
1 *teaspoon minced garlic*
2 *teaspoons minced jalapeño peppers*
1 *teaspoon ground cumin*
1/4 *cup chopped fresh cilantro*
1 *tablespoon fresh strained lime juice*
Salt and freshly ground black pepper to taste

1. If using fresh tomatillos, remove and discard their husks. Rinse. Bring a pan of water to a boil and simmer the tomatillos for 5 minutes. Drain. If using canned tomatillos, rinse and drain.
2. In a food processor fitted with the steel knife, combine the onion, garlic, and jalapeño peppers. Process on and off until finely minced. Add the tomatillos and cumin and process, on and off, until coarsely pureed. Do not overprocess.
3. Transfer to a glass or china bowl and add the cilantro and lime juice. Season to taste with the salt and pepper. Add additional lime juice if desired. Serve within 4 hours.

Yield: 1 1/4 cups

Salsa verde can be warmed gently and served under a fish steak or fillet. Simply ladle a pool of the sauce on a serving plate, and center the fish on top. This is an especially nice treatment for grilled or broiled fish.

Tomato Concassée

This simple uncooked sauce needs to be made from top-quality tomatoes. The refreshing acid quality of tomatoes make the concassée good with rich dishes, such as a fish terrine, or with rich fishes.

> 3 *medium tomatoes, peeled, seeded, and diced (about 1 cup)*
> 1–2 *teaspoons olive oil*
> *Salt and freshly ground black pepper to taste*

1. In a small bowl, combine the tomatoes with the oil. Season to taste with salt and pepper. Serve, or cover tightly and keep at room temperature for no more than 3 hours before serving.

Yield: 1 cup
May be prepared in advance

This sauce is a quick enhancement to most of the rich, strong-flavored fish, such as swordfish, tuna, mullet, mahi mahi, mackerel, or salmon.

Oregano is a perennial in the mint family. It is one of the more pungent herbs and mixes well with all tomato dishes.

Tapenade

Tapenade is salty and should be used with discretion. It is a good complement for plain grilled tuna, swordfish, marlin, and shark. Its velvety black color provides the artistic chef with some interesting opportunities for hors d'oeuvres. Surrounded with pale green fennel spears, red radishes, and carrots, the effect is quite dramatic.

> 3 *garlic cloves*
> 1 *cup pitted Italian or Greek black olives*
> 2 *2-ounce cans anchovy fillets, rinsed and drained*
> 3 *tablespoons capers, rinsed and drained*
> 1/2–3/4 *cup olive oil*
> 1/2 *teaspoon freshly ground black pepper*

1. In a food processor fitted with the steel knife, finely mince the garlic. Add the olives, anchovies, and capers, and process until smooth. Add the oil in a thin stream, processing until thick. Add the pepper. Serve, or tightly cover and refrigerate for up to 2 days.

Yield: 1 1/2 cups
May be prepared in advance

Capers are the unopened flower buds of a shrub (*Capparidaceae* family) native to the Mediterranean region. The buds are picked in the early morning before they open, then pickled in vinegar and brine.

Stuff hollowed-out cherry tomatoes with Tapenade for an easy hors d'oeuvre.

Yellow Pepper Puree

Sautéing and stewing the peppers, rather than roasting, ensures a puree with a bright yellow color. Serve several tablespoons of this mild, sweet-tasting sauce alongside a mild fish such as halibut or grouper.

> 2 tablespoons olive oil
> 3 sweet yellow peppers, 6 to 8 ounces each, cored, seeded, and cut into thin slivers
> 2 tablespoons minced shallots
> 3/4 cup chicken stock
> Dash cayenne pepper
> Dash dried thyme
> Dash salt

1. Heat the olive oil in a large nonstick skillet over medium heat. Add the peppers and shallots and toss to coat with oil. Sauté 4 to 5 minutes, stirring frequently.
2. Add the chicken stock and bring to a boil over high heat. Reduce heat, cover, and simmer 30 minutes.
3. Uncover and increase the heat to medium. Cook until most of the liquid has evaporated. Remove from heat and stir in the cayenne and thyme. Taste and add salt if necessary.
4. Puree the mixture in a food processor fitted with the steel knife, or in a blender. Strain through a sieve into a small bowl, pressing hard on the solids to extract as much puree as possible. Discard the remaining solids.
5. The puree will keep, tightly covered, in the refrigerator for 4 days. It may also be frozen for up to 3 months. To serve, heat the puree over low heat.

Yield: 3/4 cup
May be prepared in advance

Dried herbs should be stored in a cool, preferably dark area and used within a short time. Once opened, a jar of dried herbs starts to lose its pungency and becomes stale in a matter of months. Buying herbs in small quantities will make your recipes taste better. Paprika is best when stored in the refrigerator, because it has a very short shelf life once it has been opened.

Tartar Sauce

If you've never had homemade tartar sauce, you'll marvel at the taste of a freshly prepared variety. Although tartar sauce is traditionally served with deep-fried and pan-fried fish, we think it makes an interesting binder for a tuna salad sandwich.

1 *cup mayonnaise, preferably homemade*
1 *tablespoon capers, rinsed and drained*
1 *tablespoon thinly sliced scallion*
1 *tablespoon fresh strained lemon juice*
1 *tablespoon finely chopped dill pickle*

1. Combine all the ingredients in a small bowl. Mix thoroughly. Refrigerate for at least 1 hour or up to 24 hours before serving.

Yield: 1 ¼ cups
Must be prepared in advance

Quick Tartar Sauce

This tartar sauce has a sweet taste, which many people enjoy.

¼ *cup mayonnaise*
2 *tablespoons dill pickle relish*
1 *tablespoon chili sauce*
1 *teaspoon prepared horseradish*

1. Combine all the ingredients in a small bowl. Mix well. Refrigerate at least 1 hour or up to 24 hours before serving.

Yield: ½ cup
Must be prepared in advance

Substitute yogurt for part of the mayonnaise in a recipe; this cuts the calories and adds a pleasant piquant flavor.

Sauce Remoulade

Though French in origin, Sauce Remoulade has become an international, and for some, an indispensable, accompaniment to boiled shrimp and crab claws. It is also appropriate as a binder for any cooked and cooled fish. If you like a grainy texture, use a whole-grain mustard. The sauce will keep 3 days in the refrigerator, but is best if used within 24 hours.

> 1 *cup mayonnaise, preferably homemade*
> 2 *teaspoons capers, rinsed and drained*
> 2 *teaspoons chopped dill pickle*
> 1 *tablespoon Dijon-style mustard*
> 1 *tablespoon chopped scallion*
> 2 *teaspoons minced fresh parsley*
> 1 *teaspoon minced fresh tarragon*
> *Salt and pepper to taste*

1. Combine all the ingredients in a small bowl. Mix well, cover, and refrigerate for 1 hour or up to 24 hours before using.

Yield: 1 ¼ cups
Must be prepared in advance

Butter sauces add flair to many types of simply prepared fishes. Sole, turbot, scrod, cusk, and hake are delicate fishes that are wonderful with mild-flavored sauces, such as herb, toasted nut, or maitre d'hôtel butters. Stronger flavored fishes, such as bluefish, tuna, swordfish, and mahi mahi, can stand up to more robust sauces, including anchovy, mustard-shallot, and green peppercorn butters.

Simple Butter Sauces

Simple butter sauces are formed by adding flavorings to ¼ cup hot, melted unsalted butter and blending thoroughly. They are made right before serving. Suggested flavorings follow:

Anchovy: Add 1 teaspoon anchovy paste and 1 ½ teaspoons fresh strained lemon juice.

Caper: Add 1 tablespoon capers, rinsed and drained.

Ginger: Add 2 teaspoons minced gingerroot and 1 teaspoon thinly sliced scallion.

Green Peppercorn: Add 1 tablespoon green peppercorns, rinsed, drained, and smashed.

Herb: Add 3 tablespoons minced fresh herbs and 1 teaspoon fresh strained lemon juice.

Lemon or Lime: Add 1 tablespoon fresh strained lemon or lime juice and 1 teaspoon grated lemon or lime peel.

Maitre d'Hôtel: Add 2 teaspoons minced fresh parsley, 1 teaspoon fresh strained lemon juice, and freshly ground black pepper to taste.

Mustard-Shallot: Add 1 tablespoon whole-grain mustard, 1 tablespoon minced shallots, 1/4 teaspoon salt, and 1/4 teaspoon freshly ground white pepper.

Nut: Add 2 teaspoons coarsely chopped toasted nuts (almonds, pecans, walnuts, etc.).

Oriental: Add 1 tablespoon soy sauce, 1 teaspoon minced garlic, and 1 teaspoon minced gingerroot.

Tarragon: Add 3 tablespoons blanched and minced fresh tarragon or 1 tablespoon dried tarragon.

Yield: Approximately 1/3 cup

Compound Butters

These butters are as easy and as versatile as the Simple Butter Sauces, but they have the advantage of advance preparation.

1/2 cup unsalted butter (1 stick), softened
Flavoring of your choice (from list of Simple Butters)

1. In a small bowl, mix the softened butter with your chosen flavoring until thoroughly blended. Roll the butter into a log and cover with plastic wrap. Store in the freezer until hard, then in the refrigerator.
2. To use, slice off rounds of the butter, and serve on top of hot fish.

Yield: 1/2 cup
Must be prepared in advance

Give an added dimension to poached pike by serving an herbal or ginger simple butter sauce alongside. Broiled mullet would benefit from a spoonful of Anchovy or Mustard-Shallot Butter Sauce, while broiled sculpin and sea robin would taste ambrosial with a soupçon of Oriental or Maitre d'Hôtel Simple Butter Sauce.

A round of Caper or Nut Compound Butter on a simply baked or grilled fillet of tilapia adds a note of distinction to this mild tasting fish.

New England Aquarium Beurre Blanc

Many cooks are familiar with beurre blancs. We feel that this beurre blanc, with its use of a rich fish stock, is an excellent complement for our seafood dishes.

> 3 *tablespoons minced shallots*
> 2 *tablespoons white wine*
> 1/4 *cup rich fish stock (see page 277)*
> 2 *tablespoons white wine vinegar*
> 1 *cup unsalted butter, at room temperature (2 sticks), cut in small pieces*

These silky smooth sauces, known as Beurre Blancs, are based on a reduction of wine, vinegar, lemon juice or stock, to which butter is added. The flavoring combinations are almost limitless. They can be prepared about an hour in advance and kept warm over water (which should not exceed 140 degrees). To serve, spread several spoonfuls of sauce on a serving plate and position the seafood on top of the sauce. A ribbon of sauce may be drawn across the seafood to complete the presentation.

1. Place the shallots, wine, stock, and vinegar in a 2-quart heavy enamel or stainless steel saucepan. Bring to a boil. Reduce over high heat until 3 tablespoons remain. Take care not to let the reduction burn.
2. Over very low heat, beat in the butter, one piece at a time, until the butter is fully incorporated. For a smoother sauce, strain through a fine sieve. Keep warm until serving. Be aware that this sauce is very difficult to reheat, and separates easily.

Variations: To the basic recipe above, stir in any of the following flavorings after the butter:

Herb: 2 to 4 tablespoons minced fresh herbs, such as basil, cilantro, dill, parsley, tarragon, etc.

Ginger: 1 tablespoon minced gingerroot and 2 teaspoons grated lemon peel.

Tomato: 2 teaspoons tomato paste.

Champagne-Caviar: Substitute champagne for the white wine and lemon juice for the vinegar and stir in a 2-ounce jar of rinsed and drained caviar.

Beurre Rouge: Substitute red wine for the white wine and red wine vinegar for the white wine vinegar. This is particularly good with charcoal-grilled seafood.

Tomato-Basil: Add 1 tablespoon tomato paste and 2 tablespoons minced fresh basil to the Beurre Rouge.

Yield: approximately 1 cup
May be prepared in advance

Champagne Sauce for Lobster

FROM LE BOCAGE, WATERTOWN, MASSACHUSETTS

This recipe, developed by the late Chef Enzo Danesi, former owner of Le Bocage Restaurant in Watertown, Massachusetts, was contributed by his daughter, Gioia. It is superb with lobster as well as with lean fish such as red snapper or halibut.

1 *cup unsalted butter (2 sticks)*
2 *cups champagne*
1 *teaspoon fresh strained lemon juice*
1 *egg yolk, lightly beaten*

1. Cut the butter into small pieces and set aside to let soften at room temperature.
2. Bring the champagne and lemon juice to a boil in a 2-quart heavy enamel or stainless steel saucepan. Reduce over high heat until 2 tablespoons remain. Take care not to let the reduction burn.
3. Whisk in the butter, one piece at a time, until it has been fully incorporated. Gradually drizzle the butter sauce into the beaten egg yolk, whisking constantly, until thoroughly blended. Keep warm; use as soon as possible.

Yield: 1 1/4 cups

Clarified Butter

Once butter is clarified, it can be heated to a higher temperature without burning. Use clarified butter instead of oil, if you wish, for sautéing foods.

1/2 cup unsalted butter (1 stick)

1. In a small saucepan, over low to medium heat, allow the butter to melt, being careful that it does not brown. Continue to heat slowly until the butter begins to separate. The milky whey will settle on the bottom of the pan, while the fat, now clear, will rise to the top. Pour off the clear fat and set aside. Discard the whey. Cover and refrigerate; it will keep indefinitely.

Yield: 1/2 cup
May be prepared in advance

Green Peppercorn Sauce

FROM LOUIE'S BACKYARD RESTAURANT, KEY WEST, FLORIDA

This sauce is served with charcoal-grilled tuna steaks at Louie's Restaurant. It would work equally well with shark or swordfish. Serve small portions of this very rich sauce.

1 *cup unsalted butter (2 sticks)*
3 *tablespoons minced shallots*
2 *tablespoons green peppercorns*
1/3 *cup heavy cream*

1. Cut the butter into small pieces and set aside to soften at room temperature.
2. Melt 1 tablespoon of the butter in a heavy 2-quart saucepan. Sauté the shallots and green peppercorns until soft. Add the heavy cream and reduce over high heat to 2 tablespoons.
3. Lower heat and add the butter, one piece at a time, whisking constantly, until it is fully incorporated. Keep warm; use as soon as possible.

Yield: 1 cup

Saffron is available in two forms: deep orange threads and powder. Buy the threads, which are the dried stigma of the saffron crocus, as they have much more flavor. Close to 70,000 flowers and a very labor-intensive harvesting process are required to produce one pound of the spice. Thus, saffron is expensive, but worth every penny in taste.

Orange-Saffron Beurre Blanc

The light orange hue of this sauce with its dark orange specks of saffron creates an unusually attractive sauce with a hint of citrus sweetness. Monkfish steaks, poached, baked, or broiled, are particularly good with this beurre blanc.

1/2 *cup unsalted butter (1 stick)*
3 *tablespoons fresh strained orange juice*
3 *tablespoons dry white wine*
1 *tablespoon minced shallots*
1/4 *teaspoon crushed saffron*
1 *teaspoon grated orange rind (zest)*
Salt and freshly ground white pepper to taste

1. Cut the butter into small pieces and set aside to soften at room temperature.
2. Combine the orange juice, wine, and shallots in a one-quart heavy enamel or stainless steel pan. Bring to a boil and reduce the liquid over high heat to 1 tablespoon. Take care not to let the reduction burn.

3. Remove the pan from the heat and lower the heat to its lowest setting. Whisk in the saffron and one piece of butter. Return to the heat and continue to whisk in the butter, one piece at a time, until it has been fully incorporated. Remove from the heat and add the orange zest. Taste and add salt and pepper if desired. Keep warm; serve as soon as possible.

Yield: approximately ¹/₂ cup

Hollandaise in a Flash

This is an easy technique for making small amounts of Hollandaise sauce. Because eggs cook very rapidly in a microwave oven, constant attention is essential in producing a smooth sauce.

1 *egg*
1 *egg yolk*
1 *tablespoon fresh strained lemon juice*
6 *tablespoons unsalted butter, cut in small pieces*
Freshly ground white pepper

Microwave a lemon for 10 seconds on high to produce more juice.

1. In a microwave-proof bowl, combine the egg, egg yolk, and lemon juice. Beat until well mixed. Stir in the pieces of butter.
2. Place the bowl in the center of a microwave oven and cook for 2 to 3 seconds. Remove and whisk. Return to the microwave and cook for a few more seconds. Remove and whisk again. Repeat these two procedures until the sauce is slightly thickened. The sauce will continue to thicken for a few seconds after it is removed from the oven, so it is vital to keep whisking.
3. Serve at once or keep warm over water

Yield: ³/₄ cup
May be prepared in advance

Fish Stock and Court Bouillons

Fish stock and court bouillons are building blocks of serious fish cookery. A good fish stock gives depth of flavor and real personality to a recipe, whether it is an emulsified butter sauce, a stew, or a chowder.

Court bouillon, the classic poaching medium for seafood, is made from water flavored with wine, vinegar, or lemon juice, and herbs and spices. It is usually very simple and requires a short preparation time. (The word court means short.) Shellfish are usually poached in an "all-purpose" court bouillon made with water, wine, and herbs. Vegetables may be added for additional taste, particularly if the liquid is to be saved for further use.

Vinegar is often substituted for part of the wine when poaching a strong-flavored fish with a high oil content. Salmon is particularly well suited for a vinegar court bouillon, but the bouillon is generally not saved for further use. A combination of water, milk, and lemon juice makes a very fine court bouillon for poaching a delicate fish.

As in any basic stock, the ingredients should depend on availability. Do not hesitate to experiment—a new and exciting recipe may be in the making. Court bouillons may be strained after use and frozen for the future, as they will make a very fine base for a fish stock or stew.

Fish Stock

Fish stock has many variations, but one rule is hard and fast: Never add salt, because as the stock is reduced, the salt will become too concentrated.

1 *tablespoon unsalted butter*
1 *onion, thinly sliced*
3 *stalks celery, sliced*
2 *carrots, peeled and thinly sliced*
6 *parsley stems, leaves removed*
1 *bay leaf*
3 *pounds fish bones, including heads if available*
8 *whole black peppercorns*
2 *quarts (approximately) cold water*

1. In a large stainless or enamel kettle, melt the butter over medium heat. Add the onion and celery and sauté about 5 minutes, until soft. Do not brown. Add the carrots, parsley stems, bay leaf, fish bones, and peppercorns.
2. Add as much of the cold water as needed to cover. Bring to a boil. Reduce the heat to a gentle simmer. Skim off the foam that rises to the top. Simmer, uncovered, about 40 minutes. Strain the stock through a fine sieve lined with cheesecloth.
3. To store, freeze in individual 1-cup containers. For a stronger stock, reduce the strained liquid by half, and then freeze in ½-cup containers. The reduction can be reconstituted by adding ½ cup water.

Variations: Use shrimp heads and shells or lobster heads and shells in place of the fish bones.

Use 1 pound of cod, haddock, or any firm-fleshed, non-oily fish in place of the 3 pounds of fish bones.

Use 1 cup of dry white or red wine for part of the water.

Fish stock cubes are a reasonable substitution for homemade stock if the recipe does not call for reducing the stock or when a gelling quality is not necessary. They are best suited for use as a poaching medium or in soups and stews. Be aware that these cubes have a salty taste.

Aspic

Aspic is usually used as a decorative glaze for poached whole fish, such as carp, salmon, and striped bass. The aspic gives the fish a glistening sheen and provides a base into which colorful slices of vegetables are embedded to produce a design. Aspic-coated fish are always served cool or at room temperature.

> 2 *cups* Wine Court Bouillon (*see page* 279)
> 1 *envelope unflavored gelatin*
> ¹/₄ *cup dry vermouth*

1. Bring the court bouillon to a boil in a one-quart saucepan. Meanwhile, soften the gelatin in the dry vermouth in a glass measuring cup for 5 minutes.
2. Remove the court bouillon from the burner. Add ¹/₄ cup of the hot bouillon to the gelatin and stir to dissolve the gelatin. Stir this mixture into the rest of the court bouillon. Let cool at room temperature. The mixture is ready to use when it just begins to gel and has the consistency of an unbeaten egg white.
3. To glaze, place a cold poached skinned fish on a rack, and place the rack on a sheet pan. Ladle spoonfuls of the gelatin mixture over the top flesh of the fish until it is covered with a thin layer. Refrigerate until the aspic is just firm, about 3 to 5 minutes; it will still be a bit sticky when touched. Remove from refrigerator and decorate with thinly sliced (about ¹/₁₀-inch thick) pieces of vegetable, as follows. Dip each piece of vegetable in the gelatin mixture to coat, and place on fish, using the slightest of pressure. Return to refrigerator again, to firm up. Remove, and cover with a final layer of aspic, as in preceding step. Refrigerate until aspic is completely firm. Approximately 30 to 60 minutes before serving, transfer the fish to a serving platter.
4. The remaining gelatin mixture may be softened by placing it in hot water, and then poured into a pan to form a layer about ¹/₈ inch to ¹/₄ inch thick. When firm, cut into cubes or small rectangles and arrange around the fish.

A whole aspic-glazed fish is a stunning addition to a buffet table. Although it appears involved, and labor intensive, it is really quite simple.

Poaching is one of the healthiest and easiest methods of cooking fish.

Wine Court Bouillon

This is an all-purpose court bouillon, the classic medium for poaching seafood.

8 *cups water*
2 *cups dry white wine*
1 *medium onion, quartered*
2 *carrots, peeled and cut into large chunks*
1 *celery stalk, with leaves*
1 *bay leaf*
6 *parsley sprigs*
1 *teaspoon black peppercorns*
1/4 *teaspoon salt*

1. Combine all the ingredients (except salt) in a large kettle. Bring to a boil over high heat, then reduce heat and simmer 20 minutes.
2. Strain the court bouillon. Use it immediately or refrigerate or freeze. Add 1/4 teaspoon salt just prior to use.

Variation: Vinegar Court Bouillon: Substitute 1 cup of white wine vinegar for 1 cup of the white wine.

Yield: 2 1/2 quarts
May be prepared in advance

Milk and Lemon Court Bouillon

Poach delicate white fish such as halibut or sole in this court bouillon.

5 *cups water*
1 *cup low-fat milk*
1 *lemon, thinly sliced*
4 *white peppercorns*
Salt to taste

1. In a large saucepan, combine the water, milk, lemon slices, and peppercorns. Taste and add salt if desired. This does not need to be cooked before using.
2. Add the fish and bring to a simmer over moderate heat. Discard when you have finished cooking.

Yield: 6 cups

Bottled clam juice, diluted with an equal amount of water, may be substituted for part of the fish stock called for in a recipe, but do not use any salt until you have tasted it. Clam juice contains high levels of sodium, and the salty taste is intense.

Appendix I
Harvesting Good Health from the Sea,
by Joyce A. Nettleton, D.Sc., R.D.

Nutritional Benefits of Seafood

Most people know that fish is good for you and may recall the old wives' tale about fish being brain food. We can't guarantee that eating seafood will make you smarter, but we do know that it is smart to eat seafood. Studies show that people who eat fish and shellfish on a regular basis have less heart disease, America's leading cause of death. They also have lower blood pressure, fewer of certain cancers, less diabetes, asthma, arthritis, and strokes. How can eating fish be so beneficial?

What makes seafood so extraordinarily good for you is its unique fat profile. It is low in total fat (most of us eat too many fats); it is low in saturated fat (that's the kind that raises blood cholesterol levels, increasing the risk of heart disease); and its oil actually discourages heart disease. Seafood contains certain fatty acids called omega-3's, which are highly polyunsaturated. Unlike their vegetable oil counterparts, these fatty acids work to reduce blood clotting, making heart attack and stroke less likely. They also influence our immune and inflammatory responses, suggesting benefits in such conditions as asthma and arthritis.

Cholesterol is strongly linked with the development of heart disease. Excess cholesterol in the blood builds up in blood vessel walls. These deposits narrow the passageways and increase the work of the heart. By reducing the amount of cholesterol we carry in our bloodstream, we can reduce the likelihood of heart disease. We can reduce our blood cholesterol levels by maintaining appropriate body weight, exercising more, trimming our intake of fat and saturated fat, and reducing the amount of cholesterol we eat. Because seafood has little fat, very little saturated fat, and not much cholesterol, eating seafood can help lower blood cholesterol levels. Even the richest fish have less fat than most meats. Only by frying or adding butter and cream do we undermine the heart-healthy advantages of seafood.

You may be surprised to know that even shellfish are low in cholesterol. We used to think that most shellfish (mollusks and crustaceans) were relatively high in cholesterol. While a few are, most are not. In fact, mollusks like oysters, clams, and mussels are very low in cholesterol. With improvements in labora-

281

tory measurements, we discovered that what used to be counted as cholesterol in these mollusks is actually harmless plant material resembling cholesterol. Lobsters and crabs, too, are comparatively low in cholesterol, though not as low as the mollusks. You can still enjoy these delicacies and stay within the recommended cholesterol level for the day—just leave the omelettes for a future date. All have the important advantage of being very low in fat and saturated fat.

There are a few seafoods, however, that are fairly high in cholesterol. These are squid (200 to 300 milligrams per $3^1/2$ ounces), shrimp (125 to 180 milligrams per $3^1/2$ ounces), abalone and octopus (about 120 milligrams per $3^1/2$ ounces), and all fish roe (more than 250 milligrams per $3^1/2$ ounces). Most of us do not eat enough of any of these high cholesterol seafoods to make much difference to our average intake. Of course people with certain hyperlipidemias should use these foods with discretion.

Eating seafood has other nutritional bonuses. Fish and shellfish are good sources of several B vitamins and many minerals. In fact, mollusks and dark-fleshed fish, like sardines and Atlantic bluefish, are widely overlooked sources of iron. Also, mussels, clams, and oysters are rich in zinc, selenium, and other trace minerals.

In addition, fish is nutritious because it furnishes the complete protein you need without containing large amounts of substances that undermine your health. When you eat seafood instead of fatty meats and dairy products, you are cutting down on saturated fats, cholesterol, and sodium. Of course, if you fry the fish or add a sauce with lots of cream and butter, you sacrifice much of the health advantage. Wine or evaporated skimmed milk are good substitutes that save calories and fat.

Seafood Preservation

Processed Seafood

Canned seafoods are some of the most convenient, reliable, nutritious foods on the market. They are low in acid and are handled under exacting conditions to prevent the development of botulinus toxin. Protein and most vitamins and minerals are retained well, and enamel linings have reduced the transfer of minerals from the can to the contents.

An important advantage of canned fish over its fresh or frozen counterpart is that any bones present become soft and digestible in this process. This makes canned seafood such as salmon and sardines especially rich sources of calcium.

Fish is usually canned with the addition of water, broth, or oil. The use of broth or water increases the sodium content except in specially marked "diet pack" fish. You can remove much of the sodium by discarding the canned fluid and by rinsing the solid contents under cold water. Only a small amount of fish oils will be lost when you do this; most will be retained in the flesh.

Don't be misled by fish canned in oil. It is nearly always vegetable oil, not fish oil, and adds many unnecessary calories. Remove the oil (and calories) by rinsing the drained fish solids under cold water.

Smoked Seafood

Seafood is smoked by first removing much of its moisture by adding brine or dry salt. The fish is then smoked over aromatic embers that impart flavor and color. This process leaves the seafood relatively high in sodium. Smoked fish may have nitrites and color added, as well. Not all seafood smoking methods achieve a high enough temperature to cook the fish. For this reason, you should treat smoked fish as though it were fresh, and use it quickly.

Experts are advising us to limit our consumption of smoked foods in general, because of the formation of potentially harmful hydrocarbons during the smoking process. However, modern kilns that allow the control of temperature, humidity, and air flow enable the production of high-quality smoked seafood that is both safe and tasty.

Smoked and fresh seafood are often packaged in vacuum-packed containers that extend shelf life and preserve quality. These packages also create an environment where certain types of spoilage bacteria can thrive, so be sure to rewrap them carefully and refrigerate.

Frozen Seafood

Fish frozen shortly after it is caught is virtually fresher than fresh. It is important that seafood remain thoroughly frozen during its distribution and storage. Fish that has been partially thawed and then refrozen quickly loses quality. Choose frozen fish with confidence when the package is frozen hard and is wrapped to exclude as much air as possible. Packages with accumulated frost have likely suffered temperature abuse.

Environmental Concerns about Seafood

The use of our waterways as sewers has taken a heavy toll on seafood. The good news is that we have recognized many abuses and have taken steps to reverse the process. Federal funds have helped the cleanup, and in some cases, fish species are returning to their former habitats.

Awareness of the potential health problems from environmental contamination has led to monitoring programs for seafood. States are required to check fish sold in interstate commerce to ensure that they do not contain unsafe levels of organic residues and heavy metals. Any shipments found to have high levels of dangerous substances are impounded and destroyed. If necessary, fishing grounds may be closed. Fish caught by the recreational fisherman, however, are not subject to monitoring programs. To be safe, buy your seafood only from reputable dealers, not from itinerant merchants selling bargains from the back of a truck.

Actually, the possibility of someone's health being adversely affected from environmental contaminants in fish is miniscule. Most of the nasty substances in the environment that find their way into a fish's diet are retained in the liver and viscera, parts of the fish we don't usually eat. Very little is found in the flesh. Some substances may collect in the fatty parts of the fish. By discarding these portions—mainly the skin, belly flaps, sections close to the head, and the dark red muscle parts—we can further reduce the chance of consuming substances we should avoid. It is a good idea, also, to eat a variety of species.

There are other dangers associated with seafood that we can avoid. One of these is red tide, the seasonal bloom of certain phytoplankton that is toxic to humans. Shellfish harvesting is prohibited in areas affected by red tide bloom. Finally, eating raw seafood presents certain risks, because seafood, like other fresh foods, is highly perishable and can support the growth of disease-causing organisms. Raw fish not previously frozen may contain parasites. Most restaurants serving raw seafood are very careful about the quality and handling of their seafood. If you are doubtful, the risk may not be worth it.

Tips for Healthy Cooking/Eating

The wonderfully nutritious and beneficial qualities of fish are sometimes obscured in recipes that call for large amounts of cream, butter, oil, and/or eggs. Eliminating or cutting down on these ingredients will produce a slightly different appearance and taste, but the results will not disappoint the palate. There's nothing dull about food cooked with small amounts of fat. The alternatives taste superb and are good for you.

Here are some tips to help you minimize the amount of fat when preparing seafood:

Choose recipes and cooking methods that require minimal amounts of fat, such as poaching, steaming, grilling, and broiling.

Eliminate or decrease the amount of cream, butter, or oil whenever possible. For instance, if a soup calls for a final enrichment of cream or butter, taste before adding the indicated amount of fat. You may find that it tastes wonderful without any cream or with just a tablespoon or two.

Substitute a low-fat liquid for a high-fat liquid. Yogurt and buttermilk give a lively piquant taste, while evaporated skim milk gives a creamy subtle effect. Chicken or fish stock can also be used as a substitute for some fats in certain recipes.

Minced fresh herbs add vitality and eye appeal to recipes from which the cream and butter have been subtracted.

Concentrate the flavors of a poaching or steaming liquid by reducing it to a few tablespoons of syrupy liquid. A few teaspoons of the rich glaze add a touch of elegance to a simply prepared fish fillet or steak.

Use cooking utensils, such as nonstick frying pans, to sauté ingredients. (That way you will need only a teaspoon or two of fat to sauté a large amount of vegetables.

Species	Calories (K Cal)	Protein (Gm)	Average Fat (Gm)
Anchovy	127	19.6	4.8
Bass, black sea	96	18.4	1.9
Bass, freshwater	NA	NA	NA
Bass, striped	94	17.3	2.2
Bluefish	112	20.1	2.9
Carp	147	16.4	8.5
Catfish, freshwater	115	17.6	4.4
Clam, soft-shell, whole (lpswich, belly, steamer)	65	10.7	1.2
Clam, hard-shell, whole (Quahog, cherrystone)	60	9.2	1.0
Clam, razor	75	11.2	1.5
Cod, Atlantic	75	16.4	0.6
Conch*	275	47.7	0.8
Crab, blue or soft-shell	81	16.2	1.0
Crab, dungeness	87	17.3	1.2
Crab, Jonah	95	16.2	1.9
Crab, king	74	15.2	0.8
Crab, snow	90	18.4	1.3
Crayfish	76	16.0	.05

*data for cooked whelk, a similar annual

Species	Calories (K Cal)	Protein (Gm)	Average Fat (Gm)
Cusk	84	18.5	0.6
Eel, American	223	18.8	15.8
Flounder (unspecified)	89	25.9	1.4
Grouper, black	93	20.4	0.7
Grunt	NA	NA	NA
Haddock	83	18.2	0.6
Hake	70	15.2	0.6
Halibut, Atlantic	115	19.3	3.6
Halibut, Pacific	105	20.0	2.2
Herring	101	17.7	2.8

Species	Calories (K Cal)	Protein (Gm)	Average Fat (Gm)
Herring, Atlantic	149	18.0	8.0
Herring, Pacific	162	17.3	9.8
Lobster	113	18.2	1.5
Lobster, spiny or rock	100	19.2	1.2
Mackerel, Atlantic	176	18.5	10.7
Mackerel, Pacific (chub)	129	20.8	4.8
Mackerel, king	140	23.0	4.6
Mackerel, Spanish	138	19.8	5.9
Mackerel, jack	98	19.1	1.8
Mahi mahi, dolphin fish	89	18.9	0.9
Marlin, blue	121	23.1	3.2
Marlin, striped	109	21.1	2.7
Monkfish, goosefish, anglerfish	80	15.5	1.5
Mullet	115	19.2	3.7
Mullet, red	NA	NA	NA
Mussel, Atlantic	89	12.0	2.2
Octopus	77	14.8	.8
Oyster, Eastern, American	74	8.2	2.2
Oyster, Western, Olympia	85	9.6	2.5
Oyster, European, French	79	10.3	1.7
Perch, freshwater, yellow	86	18.1	1.0
Perch, ocean, redfish	105	18.7	2.8
Pike, Northern	87	18.5	0.9
Pike, walleye	90	19.2	1.4
Pollock, Atlantic	90	19.2	0.9
Pollock, Pacific	78	16.7	0.8
Porgy, scup, seabroom	109	18.8	3.2
Pout, ocean	79	16.6	0.9
Salmon, Atlantic	129	18.4	5.6
Salmon, Pacific (Chinook, king)	184	19.0	11.4
Salmon, Pacific (Coho, silver)	150	21.1	6.6
Sardine	142	18.9	6.8
Scallop, sea	87	16.2	.81
Scallop, Bay, Cape, Long Island	80	14.8	0.6
Scallop, Calico	84	16.1	0.6
Sculpin	NA	NA	NA
Sea robin	NA	NA	NA
Sea trout, weakfish	106	17.5	3.5
Shad, American	187	17.4	12.5
Shark, spiny dogfish	167	15.1	11.4
Shark, blue	82	18.9	0.1
Shark, Mako	NA	NA	NA
Shrimp (mixed species)	91	18.7	1.2
Skate	93	20.3	1.3

Species	Calories (K Cal)	Protein (Gm)	Average Fat (Gm)
Smelt	98	18.6	2.1
Snapper, red	110	20.2	2.6
Sole, Dover	91	16.1	2.5
Squid, short-finned	99	17.3	1.8
Squid, California	90	16.6	1.4
Sturgeon, Atlantic	98	16.3	3.2
Sturgeon, lake	169	16.8	10.8
Swordfish	122	19.4	4.4
Tautog	75	18.3	2.0
Tilapia	87	18.6	1.4
Tilefish	90	18.6	1.2
Trout, rainbow	131	18.4	5.8
Trout, brook	108	20.0	2.5
Trout, lake	162	18.1	9.4
Tuna, albacore, longfin	172	25.2	7.2
Tuna, bigeye	112	22.8	1.6
Tuna, bluefin	158	24.0	6.1
Tuna, skipjack	130	24.9	2.7
Tuna, yellowfin	124	23.8	2.5
Turbot, greenland	147	13.2	10.0*
Whitefish	162	18.8	9.0
Whiting, Atlantic	87	15.8	2.2
Whiting, Pacific	85	16.6	1.6
Wolffish	101	17.6	2.9

*Fat content unusually high and
may be questioned

Kcal   (Kilocalories)
Gm   (grams)
NA   (not available)

Appendix II
Aquaculture: The Wave of the Future?

Those fabulous steamed mussels you enjoyed the other night (see page 31) were probably raised commercially. Very likely, they were cultured—that is, they were grown and harvested as a crop. Also known as fish farming, aquaculture is to the world's waters what agriculture is to the land. In fact, many scientists think that nutrient-rich fish crops can help provide protein to feed the world's hungry people. Tilapia, a freshwater fish that is easy to cultivate, is fifty times cheaper to produce per pound than beef.*

Practiced for centuries in China and Japan, fish farming was also known to the ancient Greeks and Romans. Aquaculture is still a major source of fishes in Asia and Europe, but it is only in its infancy in the United States.

Why is aquaculture important to cooks? There are at least three good reasons: quality, availability, and price. Cultured fish are often higher quality than their wild relatives. Our steamed mussels, for example, are mercifully free of the sand and grit that so frequently accompany noncultured varieties. The fish for that special recipe you wanted to make is not "in season"? Many species of farmed fish are available all year long. And threatened species that may have disappeared from your fishmonger's display case will have a greater

chance of reappearing if actively cultured.

Finally, as consumers, we are concerned with price. If we can augment the supply of an over-fished species like the American lobster, the resulting abundance should drive down the cost. Researchers in Martha's Vineyard and California are among the scientists working toward this goal.

There are two broad classifications of aquaculture, distinguished by the degree of control over production factors. "Extensive" farming depends on nature to provide some of the basic requirements for nutrition and maturation of the fish, while relying on a minimum of planned control by man. "Intensive" aquaculture is more involved, with close control at all stages of development. In both methods, the process begins with young fish or seed stock obtained either from the environment or from hatcheries. What happens after that can vary considerably.

Some species are placed in ponds or in pens floating in a body of water. The fish are either fed or, in some cases, fertilizer is added to enhance growth of natural organisms in the habitat. Another method is called sea ranching. In this process, often used for salmon, hatchery-grown young are released into privately controlled sections of rivers or streams. The fish migrate to salt water where they grow to adulthood. When sexually mature,

*Limburg, Peter, *Farming the Waters*, p. 13, Beaufort Books, New York, 1980.

they return to their point of release and can be captured. This is an inexpensive method since there is no cost to the farmer once the fish is released. Unfortunately, the rate of return is very low, between one and six percent.

Both bottom and off-bottom techniques are used for producing mollusks. With the bottom method, seed mollusks such as clams are usually left on the bottom to grow on their own, protected from predators by some kind of enclosure. A common off-bottom method uses ropes hung from floating rafts. Seed mussels are attached to the ropes away from bottom predators and silt. A raft sixty feet square can produce over 100,000 pounds of mussels per year.

Successful aquaculture requires considerable care and patience. A degree or two of difference in the water temperature may cause the crop not to gain weight, or it may interrupt the reproductive cycle. Factors such as resistance to disease and a short growth cycle make some species more suitable for farming than others.

What varieties of cultured fishes can you expect to see in the market? Farmed shellfish are abundant, especially mussels, oysters, and clams. A large proportion of mussels eaten in the United States are grown in Maine. Great strides have been made with crayfish, partially due to the demand for them in creole-cajun dishes. Freshwater trout, salmon, catfish, and carp are all successfully cultured. Sea trout and salmon are extensively farmed in the Pacific Northwest, while most catfish are farmed in Mississippi. Carp and tilapia have been raised in captivity since the third century B.C. in China. Although tilapia has been introduced in the United States, substantial demand for it has not yet developed. Sturgeon is also raised in captivity, but mainly for the purpose of extracting caviar. Striped mullet and black sea bass are cultured, but primarily for commercial use, so they are not as likely to be found in retail markets. Farm-raised striped bass shows great promise as an emerging industry, but legislation passed in many states to protect native stocks has hindered its retail sale.

Currently, less than ten percent of all United States fishery products are cultured, which is far less than in China, Japan, Korea, and Scandinavia. But success does not come overnight. The need and demand for cultured products is on the rise, and there are endless possibilities for advancement of the science. Many private researchers are studying disease resistance and breeding techniques. Major companies are investing funds in aquaculture research. The future looks promising and we are hopeful that within our lifetime, experimental projects with lobster and other species will become realities.

Credit for much of the above information belongs to the New England Fisheries Development Foundation, Susan M. Faria, Ed., *The Northeast Seafood Book: A Manual of Seafood Products, Marketing and Utilization*, Massachusetts Division of Marine Fisheries, Boston, 1984.

Appendix III
Suggestions for Fish Substitutions by Region

Here is a list of substitutions for the fishes that may not be available in your region of the United States. This list will not always agree with the suggestions in the recipe introductions, since those suggestions were alternatives that were chosen for those particular recipes. This is a more general list, with a geographical viewpoint. In many cases, it contains fishes that live great distances from each other but have similar tastes and textures.

Many of these substitutions are fishes within the same family that are grouped together in the book; closely related fishes can often be used in place of one another. Of course, tastes vary, and not everyone will concur with these suggestions. You should feel free to try your own alternatives. Some wonderful new discoveries will likely result.

The symbols after each fish denotes where it is most commonly found. Fishes from other regions that are good substitutes are listed under the name of each species.

N: Northern States
NE: Northeast coast
SE: Southeast coast, approximately Virginia to Florida
G: Gulf Coast
W: West Coast
Hawaii

Anchovies: (All oceans)
Bass, Freshwater (All regions)
  Freshwater perch: Northern states

Tilapia: Southeast (cultivated)
Bass, Sea (NE, SE)
  White sea bass: California
  Sea trout (weakfish): Southeast and Gulf Coast
  Grouper and jewfish: South Florida and the Caribbean
Bass, Striped (W, NE)
  Any sea bass: Atlantic coast
  Grouper: South Florida and the Caribbean
Bluefish (NE, SE, Gulf)
  Mackerel: East and West coasts
  King mackerel: Southeast and Gulf coast
  Jack mackerel: West coast
  Bonito, skipjack tuna, and wahoo: East, West, and Gulf coasts
*****Carp** (All regions—freshwater; Also cultivated)
  No substitute
Catfish (SE, G; also cultivated)
  Freshwater perch: Northern states
Clams (All oceans; also cultivated)
  While all types of clams can be interchanged in clam recipes, in New England, "steamers" are preferred for steamed clams.
Cod (NE)
  "Scrod" and haddock: Atlantic coast
  Rockfish and sable cod: Pacific coast (Except in finnan haddie and bacalao)
*****Conch** (SE)
  No substitute
Crab (All oceans)
  All kinds of hard-shell crabs can be substituted for one another.
*****Crayfish** (SE)
  No substitute

Cusk (NE)
Seatrout (weakfish): Gulf, West, and Southeast coasts
Members of the cod family—
  Haddock and cod: Northeast coast
  Pollock, whiting, and hake: Northeast and West coasts

Eel (NE)
No substitute; not morays, hagfish, or anything other than American or European eels.

Flounder (All oceans)
Almost any small "flatfish," sole and sandab: all oceans
Halibut when it is filleted: Northeast and West coasts

Grouper (SE, W)
Firm-fleshed fishes such as striped bass and halibut: Northeast and West coasts
California white sea bass and rockfish: West Coast
Drum: Atlantic and Gulf coasts
Cod: Northeast coast
Many snappers and any regional grouper can "fill in."

Grunt (SE, W)
Croaker: California
Seatrout (weakfish) and drum: Northeast, Southeast, and Gulf coasts
Corvina or totuava: California
Haddock: Northeast coast
Cod, "scrod," and whiting: Northeast coast
Sole: all oceans
Rockfish: West coast
Rockcod: California

Haddock (NE)
Cod: Atlantic coast
Rockfish and sable cod: West coast

Hake (NE, W)
Any member of the cod family—haddock, small cod (sometimes sold as "scrod,") and cod: Northeast coast
Pollock and whiting: Northeast and West coasts

*Halibut (NE, W)
No substitute

Herring (NE, SE, W)
Sardines or pilchards: canned, smoked or fresh

Lobster (NE)
Crayfish or spiny lobster: California. (Not the same taste, but can be substituted.)

Mackerel (NE, W, SE)
King mackerel: Southeast and Gulf coasts
Spanish mackerel: Atlantic and Gulf coasts
Jack mackerel: California

Mahi mahi (SE and Hawaii)
Only if broiling or barbecuing—
Swordfish: Atlantic and West coasts, or
Shark: all oceans, or
Halibut or salmon: Northeast or West coast
(All are great but not the same.)

*Marlin (All oceans)
No substitute

Monkfish (NE)
Only one real substitute, the giant sheepshead wrasse from California. Of course, one can use crab or lobster instead of monkfish.

Mullet
No substitute

Mullet, Red/Red Goatfish (SE, Hawaii)
Drum: Atlantic and Gulf coasts
Seatrout (weakfish): Northeast, Southeast, and Gulf coasts

*Mussels (all)
No substitute

Octopus (W)
No substitute, but squid in a

salad are just as good as their eight-armed relatives, although they will not taste the same.

*Oysters (NE, SE, G, NW; also cultivated)

No substitute

Perch, Freshwater (N)

Brim, bream, bluegill, crappie, largemouth or smallmouth bass, and farm-raised catfish: available in almost all regions of the United States.

Perch, Ocean (NE)

Pacific ocean perch and rockfish: California

Pike (N)

Pike, pickerel, walleye—these northern freshwater fishes are interchangeable.

Pike, Walleye (N)

See Perch, freshwater

Pollock (NE, W)

Cod and haddock: Northeast coast

Whiting: Northeast and West coasts

*Porgy (SE, G)

No substitute

Pout, Ocean (NE)

No substitute

Salmon (NE, W, and northern lakes; also cultivated)

Lake trout

Sardines (W)

No substitute

*Scallops (All oceans)

Mix and match bay, sea, and calico scallops, but no other substitutes

"Scrod" (NE)

This term fulfills a need in New England for the fresh white-fleshed fish of the day and is often used for any of several species of the cod family, especially when they are small. You can use the fishes listed under cod as substitutes, but the term belongs to Boston.

Sculpin (NE, W)

No substitute

Sea robin (NE, SE, Gulf)

No substitute

Seatrout/Weakfish (NE, SE, G)

Small drum: Southeast and Gulf coasts

Croaker: California

Shad (NE, SE)

No substitute for shad, but other fresh fish roe can be substituted for shad roe.

Shark (All oceans)

Mako shark (Southeast coast), great white shark (all coasts), and porbeagle shark (Northeast coast) are interchangeable with one another as well as swordfish; but do not mix these with dogfish or other species of sharks.

Shrimp (All oceans; also cultivated)

All species of shrimp (also known as prawns, depending on size and where you are)

*Skate (All oceans)

No substitute

Snapper, Red (SE, G)

"Scrod" and haddock: Atlantic coast

Red snapper on the West Coast belongs to the rockfish, rockcod family and cannot be substituted.

Sole (All oceans)

Flounder and sandab: All oceans

Halibut fillets: Northeast and West coasts

Squid (All oceans)

Octopus can sometimes be substituted, but it is not the same taste.

*Sturgeon (NE, W)

No substitute

Swordfish (NE, SE, W)
  Mako shark: Southeast coast
  Great white shark: All coasts
  Porbeagle shark: Northeast coast
Tautog (NE)
  Rockfish: Pacific coast
*****Tilapia** (South. Also cultivated.)
  No substitute
Tilefish (NE)
  Ocean whitefish: California
Trout, Freshwater (NE, W; also cultivated)
  Small salmon: West coast
Tuna (NE, SE, W)
  No substitute
Turbot (W)
  All of the other flatfishes, such as flounder: all oceans

Sole: Atlantic coast and Southwest coast
Whitefish, Freshwater (N)
  Trout: Northeast and West
Whiting (NE)
  Other members of the cod family, such as haddock and cod: Northeast coast
  Pollock: Northeast and West coast
*****Wolffish** (NE)
  No substitute.

---

*We cannot make *general* recommendations of other fishes to substitute for this species, but you will find suggestions for substitutions within specific recipes using this fish.

Index

Acknowledgments

This book is the result of the work of literally hundreds of people, and the authors are grateful to everyone who, in some way, contributed to its production. It would have been an impossible task without the continued enthusiasm and sound advice of the Aquarium staff. In particular, we extend our thanks to Lois Mann for compiling, editing, and coordinating all facets of the project; Dr. Leslie Kaufman, curator of exhibit research and development, whose scientific expertise guided the direction of the book; Michael Filisky, acting curator of education, for writing the chapter and section introductions; Acha Lord, Bob MacKenzie, and Steve Spina, Aquarists, for their help with the sidebar information; and John Prescott, executive director, for the very useful substitution list and for his encouragement throughout the project.

We are deeply indebted to all the professional consultants who willingly volunteered their expertise but especially to Malabar Hornblower, food consultant and author, for generously sharing her knowledge and for editing many of the recipes; and to Dr. Joyce A. Nettleton, nutritionist and author of the Appendix on fish nutrition. In addition, we greatly appreciate the good auspices of the Massachusetts Division of Marine Fisheries, whose *Northeast Seafood Book* was an important resource, and the patience and professionalism of our editor, Cary Hull.

We are grateful to all the Aquarium Council members for their support, but particular thanks are in order for the following: Frances Clark for organizing tester files and recipes; Peg Bassion, Rosemarie Van Otterloo, and Anne Gifford for researching information for sidebars; Dotty Corcoran for compiling the indices in her "spare" time; Constance Pond and Mickey Geller for amassing a truly wonderful collection of chef's recipes; Abby Ackerman, president of the council, for her leadership and enthusiasm and for guiding the design of the book; and Florence Gerstein, first president of the council, who originated the idea. And finally, a vote of thanks for all the wonderful recipes that were contributed; we wish we could have used them all. Little did we realize when we began how many people would help to create and influence the end result. Following is a list of some of those people. If we have overlooked anyone, we hope you will understand that it was not intentional.

Wendy Adams
Nancy Atkins
Victoria Baker
Caryl Barasch
Marygrace Barber
Al Barker
Carolyn S. Bell
Lisa Berezin
Mary Bland
Mrs. R.C. Boshco
Elizabeth Bourneuf
Dr. Paul Boyle
Connie Bransfield
Nadine S. Braunstein
Ann W. Brewer
Ellen H. Brewster

Jean Brooks
Sidney C. Brown
Helen C. Burns
Ellen Burr
Sandra Butzel
Ann Casey
Lizanne Chapin
Ron Della Chiesa
Meredith Clapp
Mrs. Wm. V. Clark
Barbara Clark
Joanne Coburn
Suzanne Conlin
Muffie Coolidge
Rebecca Cooper
Dotty Corcoran
Fiona Cortland
Jeremy Cutting
Helene Day
Nancy Devereaux
Kay Diamantas
Geoffrey Dutton
Cheryl Eber
Mrs. Leonard Elborn
Harron Ellenson
Judith A. Englander
Ellen P. Fallon
Peter G. Fallon
Karen Fawcett
Ellen Fenichel
Mary A. Fortuna
Kathy Fozio
Marsha W. Francis
Thomas A. Fulham
Serena Furman
Susan Gabaree
Mrs. J.L. Gardner
Naomi Gardner
Dirce S. Gastaldo
Patricia Day Gerrity
Anne Gifford
Gladys P. Gifford
Hannah Gilman
Tim Goff
Linda Gogain
Jeri Goldberg

Ann Goldstein
Sandra Golfarb
Judith Grassia
Helen Green
Peter Griffin
Gale R. Guild
Sandra Gustafson
Mary A. Haight
Barbara Hallowell
Robbie Hallowell
Shelly Humilburg
Tay Ann Harrington
Alice Harris
Ian Hayes
Cynthia Hayward
Kathy Hemstreet
Lindy Hess
Diane Hessan
Wendy Hilt
Susan Hirshberg
Barbara Hostetter
Margery Hobbs
Llewellen Howland
Pam Humphrey
Mrs. H. Waite Hurlburt
Patsy Ives
Jody Jennings
Joseph N. Jennings Jr.
Wendy Jennings
Perry Karfunkle
Connie Kaufman
Mrs. Kennett R. Kendall
Lily Kendall
Alison Kerr
Elizabeth C. King
Mary Kingsley
Peggy Kirk
Evan Kleiman
Joyce Knowles
Karen Kroner
Stephanie Kurzina
Jane Heald Lavine
Sandra Lawrence
Amy Lenoir
Janey Levine
Maureen Lumley

Jay Lupica
Margery Lyman
Beth Lyons
Sylvia B. Mackenzie
Eleanor Macusty
Mrs. Donald Maguire
Olivia Manice
John C. Masterson
Nancy McWilliams
Libby Meek
Joan C. Milliken
Ann Moses
Erica Mueller
Henry Mustin
Marie O'Neill
Biddy Owens
Hope Pantelioni
Mary Parker
Mary Parkhurst
Doris Parness
Susan Pasanen
John Peabody
Roger Philip
Dan Pierce
Renia Platt
James S. Plaut
Linda Pollard
Sandy Prescott
Lynn E. Pressey
Joyce Queen
Mimi Queen
Jeanne Rankin
Joan Rea
Joan Reese
Grace Riker
Barbara Rochatka Riley
Blake Roberts
Kim Rodgers-Bush
Bonnie Rosse
Alan R. Rowe
Joan Roy
Joanne Rusitzky
Pat Saniuk
Mary Ann Schultz
Andy Seplow
Patsy Sharaf

Randy Sheahan
Kathleen Sherbrooke
Carol K. Silver
Helen Spaulding
Susan Spooner
Diana Squibb
Ellen Stone
Vallie Swerdlow
Loyola Sylvan
John Tallon
Susan Lee Tamarkin
Phyllis Teiko
Helen Thomsen
Hanna Thyresson
Linda Tober
Nancy Tooke
Myra Vernon
Wesley A. Wagner
Linda Waitekunas
Cynthia Walker
Joanne Warshaver
Anne Weintraub
Elizabeth Werley
Sandra White
Julia Widdowson
Marion Wilson
Emmy Wolbach
Mary Anne Wood
Sally Worthen
JoAnne F. Young
Clarisse B. Zalcman
Dola Zarins
Sheila Zetlan
Christine Zuromskis